SECURITIES

S E R V

CW01401870

Dictionary of Financial and Securities Terms

Securities Institute Services

PROFESSIONALISM | *INTEGRITY* | *EXCELLENCE*

Dictionary of Financial and Securities Terms

Securities Institute Services

Second edition published in July 2002 in Great Britain by

Securities Institute (Services) Limited

Centurion House, 24 Monument Street

London EC3R 8AQ, England.

ISBN: 1 84307 023 5

Second edition, printed July 2002

First edition printed July 1999

Printed and bound in Great Britain by

Antony Rowe Limited, Chippenham, Wiltshire

Foreword

The Securities Institute is the major examining body for the securities and derivatives industry, and provides a wide range of industry qualifications. It is a substantial provider of training courses and of relevant publications. It promotes, for the public benefit, the advancement of knowledge in the area of securities and investments and consults and researches in matters of public interest concerning investment in securities.

Feedback from our Members and their clients, our students and our panel of securities practitioners, showed that there was a real need for a new dictionary of financial and securities terms. The financial services industry is dynamic and new products are continually being created. The industry is prone to the use of abbreviations and acronyms. There is a jungle of jargon which people who do not work in the industry find hard to penetrate.

I am pleased to introduce a second edition of the dictionary to meet a real need. It is aimed at students, financial professionals and the general public – anyone in fact, who wishes to acquire a clear understanding of a defined term of reference. The dictionary is intended to give a quick, clear and straightforward definition of frequently used terms in the financial and securities industry. Also included is a comprehensive listing of abbreviations and acronyms. New to this edition is a comprehensive list of UK and International websites which we hope the reader will find of use.

We have tried to make this dictionary as accurate as possible, but the Editor would welcome hearing from readers who wish to suggest alternative definitions or, indeed, new terms for inclusion.

We are publishing with the dictionary a free CD–ROM version for users to load on to their PC for easy reference at home or at work.

Geoffrey Turner
Chief Executive
August 2002

Securities Institute

Mission Statement:

"To set standards of professional excellence and integrity for individual practitioners, and provide the means of attaining them"

Established in 1992, the Securities Institute has become the most widely respected professional body for those who work in the securities and investment industry in the UK. Membership currently totals 16,000 and is rising.

Well known around the world for developing and promoting high standards of integrity, ethics and competence in financial services, the Institute speaks with unique authority in the financial services arena. It canvasses and expresses views on a wide range of issues including City regulation and investor confidence.

By bringing together thousands of practitioners from such a diverse and complex field into a single network, the Institute leads professionalism within the financial services industry. Alongside its serious business agenda however, it also provides opportunities for Members to meet socially.

List of Abbreviations

2BCD	Second Banking Coordination Directive
AA	Against Actual
ABI	Association of British Insurers
ACD	Authorised Corporate Director
ACT	Advanced Corporation Tax
ADL	Activities of Daily Living
ADP	Alternative Delivery Procedure
ADR	American Depositary Receipt
AER	Annual Equivalent Rate
AESOP	Employee Share Ownership Plan
AEX	Amsterdam Exchange
AGM	Annual General Meeting
AIM	Alternative Investment Market
AITC	Association of Investment Trust Companies
AMA	Advanced Measurement Approaches
AMEX	American Stock Exchange
AMPS	Auction Market Preferred Stock
AMS	Automatic Order Matching and Execution System for Hong Kong Stock Exchange
AON	All or None
APACS	Association for Payment Clearing Services
APCIMS	Association of Private Client Investment Managers and Stockbrokers
APR	Annual Percentage Rate
APSS	Inland Revenue Audit and Pension Schemes Services

ASB	Accounting Standards Board
ASSET	Automated System for the Stock Exchange of Thailand
ASX	Australian Stock Exchange
ATM	Automated Teller Machine
AUD	Australian Dollars
AUTIF	Association of Unit Trust and Investment Funds (see also IMA)
AVC	Additional Voluntary Contribution
BACS	Bank Automated Clearing System
BBA	British Bankers' Association
BDR	Bad Delivery Reversals
BE	Bond Exchange of South Africa
BIC	Bank Identifier Code
BIFFEX	Baltic International Freight Futures Exchange
BIS	Bank for International Settlements
BOJ	Bank of Japan
BOLT	Bombay Stock Exchange Online Trading
BVCA	British Venture Capital Association
BP	Basis Point
BRL	Brazilian Real (currency)
BTF	Basis Trading Facility
BWR	Bad Withdrawal Reversal
CAC	Compagnie des Agents de Change
CAD	Capital Adequacy Directive
CAO	Company Announcements Office
CAPM	Capital Asset Pricing Model
CAT	Charges, Access, Terms
CATS	Canadian Trading System
CA Type	Corporate Action Type
CBI	Confederation of British Industry
CBOE	Chicago Board Options Exchange
CBOT	Chicago Board of Trade
CCP	Central Counterparty

CCSD	CREST Claim Settlement Date
CCSS	CREST Courier and Sorting Service
CD	Certificate of Deposit
CDI	CREST Depository Interest
CDN	Canadian Dealing Network
CDP	Central Depository (Pte) Ltd
CDS	Canadian Depository for Securities
CFTC	Commodity Futures Trading Commission
CGO	Central Gilts Office
CHAPS	Clearing House Automated Payment System
CHESS	Clearing House Electronic Sub Register System
CHIPS	Clearing House Interbank Payment System
CISCO	City Group for Smaller Companies (now Quoted Companies Alliance or QCA)
CIF	Cost, Insurance, Freight
CLOB	Central Limit Order Book
CLS	Continuous Linked Settlement
CLT	Contingent Liability Transaction
CMA	Cash Memorandum Account
CME	Chicago Mercantile Exchange
CMO	Central Moneymarkets Office
COMEX	Commodities Exchange in New York
COMPS	Contracted Out Money Purchase Scheme
CORES	Computerised zdealing system of the Tokyo Stock Exchange
CP	Commercial Paper
CPA	Compulsory Purchase Annuity
CPU	Claims Processing Unit
CREST	UK Settlement System
CRESTCo	Owner of CREST
CSCE	Coffee, Sugar and Cocoa Exchange
CSD	Central Securities Depository
CTD	Cheapest to Deliver

CTF	CREST Transfer Form
CUSIP	Committee on Uniform Securities Identification Procedures
DAX	German Stock Exchange Index
DBR	Delivery by Value Return
DBV	Delivery by Value
DEL	Simple (one-to-one) Delivery
DEX	Data Exchange Manual
DIE	Designated Investment Exchange
DOL	Daily Official List
DRIP	See DRP
DRP	Dividend Reinvestment Plan
DTB	Deutsche Terminbörse
DTC	Depository Trust Company
DTCC	Depository Trust Clearing Corporation
DTI	Department of Trade and Industry
DVP	Delivery Versus Payment
EASDAQ	European Association of Securities Dealers Automated Quotation System
EBRD	European Bank for Reconstruction and Development
ECB	European Central Bank
ECHO	Exchange Clearing House
ECP	Euro Commercial Paper
ECSDA	European Central Securities Depository Association
EDC	Electronic Data Capture
EDSP	Exchange Delivery Settlement Price
EDVP	Enhanced Delivery versus Payment
EEA	European Economic Area
EGM	Extraordinary General Meeting
EI	Expert Investor
EIS	Enterprise Investment Scheme
EMI	European Monetary Institute
EMS	European Monetary System

EMU	Economic and Monetary Union
EMX	Electronic Message Exchange
EPA	Enduring Power of Attorney
EPM	Efficient Portfolio Management
EBRD	European Bank for Reconstruction and Development
ERM	Exchange Rate Mechanism
ERISA	Employee Retirement Income Security Act of 1974 (US)
ESA	Escrow Adjustment
ESCB	European System of Central Banks
ESO	European Settlements Office
ETD	Exchange-Traded Derivative
ETF	Exchange-Traded Funds
ETS	Energy Trading System
ETT	Electronic Transfer of Title
EU	European Union
EUCLID	Euroclear Electronic Communication System
EUREX	European Derivatives Exchange
FAS	Free Alongside
FAST	Fully Automated Securities Trading
FCSD	Finnish Central Securities Depository
FED	Federal Reserve Board (The)
FER	Foreign Exchange Requirement
FIB	Family Income Benefit
FMA	Fund Managers Association (see also IMA)
FOB	Free on Board
FOF	Futures and Options Fund
FOS	Financial Ombudsman Service
FOTRA	Free of Tax to Residents Abroad
FR	Financial Resources
FRA	Forward Rate Agreement
FRB	Federal Reserve Board
FRC	Financial Reporting Council
FRN	Floating Rate Note

FRR	Financial Resources Requirement
FRS	Financial Reporting Standard
FSA	Financial Services Authority
FSA 86	Financial Services Act (1986)
FSAVC	Free-Standing Additional Voluntary Contribution
FSCS	Financial Services Compensation Scheme
FSMA 2000	Financial Services and Markets Act 2000
FTSE	Financial Times Stock Exchange
FX	Foreign Exchange (Forex)
G30	Group of Thirty
GC	General Collateral
GCM	General Clearing Member
GD	Good for the Day
GDP	Gross Domestic Product
GDR	Global Depository Receipt
GEMM	Gilt Edged Market Maker
GFOF	Geared Futures and Options Fund
GNP	Gross National Product
GRY	Gross Redemption Yield
GSCC	Government Securities Clearing Corporation
GSTPA	Global Straight-Through Processing Association
GTC	Good till Cancelled
GUI	Graphical User Interface
HETI	Helsinki Exchanges Automated Trading and Information System
HEX	Helsinki Stock Exchange
HIC	Hold in Custody Repo
HMT	Her Majesty's Treasury
HR	Human Resources
IBRD	International Bank for Reconstruction and Development
ICAEW	Institute of Chartered Accountants in England and Wales
ICM	Individual Clearing Member
ICOM	International Currency Options Market

ICSA	Institute of Chartered Secretaries and Administrators
IDAS	Institutional Delivery and Affirmation System
IDB	Inter Dealer Broker
IDR	International Depository Receipt
IFA	Independent Financial Adviser
IIF	Institute of International Finance
IMA	Internal Measurement Approach
IMA	Investment Management Association
IMRO	Investment Management Regulatory Organisation
IOSCO	International Organisation of Securities Commissions
IPC	Investment Protection Committee
IPE	International Petroleum Exchange
IPMA	International Primary Markets Association
IPO	Initial Public Offer
IRG	Interest Rate Guarantee
IRM	Integrated Risk Management
IRR	Initial Rate of Return
IRS	Interest Rate Swap
ISA	Individual Savings Account
ISCC	International Securities Clearing Corporation
ISD	Investment Services Directive
ISDA	International Swaps and Derivatives Association
ISIN	International Securities Identification Number
ISMA	International Securities Markets Association
ISSA	International Securities Services Association
IT	Information Technology
JASDEC	Japan Securities Depository Centre
JATS	Jakarta Automated Trading System
JET	Johannesburg Electronic Trading
JMLSG	Joint Money Laundering Steering Group
JSCC	Japan Securities Clearing Corporation
JSE	Johannesburg Stock Exchange
KRIs	Key Risk Indicators

KSE	Korean Stock Exchange
KYC	Know Your Customer
LAN	Local Area Network
LAPR	Life Assurance Premium Relief
LCH	London Clearing House
LDA	Loss Distribution Approach
LER	Large Exposure Requirement
LGD	Loss, Given Default
LIBID	London Interbank Bid Rate
LIBOR	London Interbank Offered Rate
LIFFE	London International Financial Futures and Options Exchange
LIMEAN	London Interbank Mean Rate
LMA	Liquidity Memorandum Account
LME	London Metal Exchange
LSE	London Stock Exchange
MATIF	Marche a Terme International de France
MD	Modified Duration
MFR	Minimum Funding Requirement
MIT	Market-if-Touched
MLRO	Money Laundering Reporting Officer
MPC	Monetary Policy Committee
MOF	The Ministry of Finance (Japan)
MPL	Maximum Publication Level
MPS	Market Place Service
MQP	Mandatory Quote Period
MQS	Minimum Quote Size
MTM	Many-to-Many
MWR	Money Weighted Rate of Return
NAIRU	Non-Accelerated Inflation Rate of Unemployment
NAPF	National Association of Pension Funds
NASD	National Association of Securities Dealers

NASDAQ	National Association of Securities Dealers Automated Quotation System
NAV	Net Asset Value
NBV	Net Book Value
NC	Non-Central Settlement
NCBO	No Change of Beneficial Owner
NCSD	National Central Securities Depository
NCIS	National Criminal Intelligence Service
NCM	Non-Clearing Member
NDF	Non-Deliverable Forward
NFA	National Futures Association
NICs	National Insurance Contributions
NMS	Normal Market Size
NPV	(1) Net Present Value
	(2) No Par Value
NRE	Net Relevant Earnings
NRY	Net Redemption Yield
NSCC	National Securities Clearing Corporation
NYMEX	New York Mercantile Exchange
NYSE	New York Stock Exchange
OAT	Own Account Transfer
OECD	Organisation for Economic Cooperation and Development
OEICs	Open Ended Investment Companies
OFT	Office of Fair Trading
OMX	Swedish Equity Index
OPEC	Organisation of Petroleum Exporting Countries
OPRA	Occupational Pension Schemes Regulatory Authority
OR	Operational Risk
ORM	Operational Risk Management
OTC	Over-The-Counter
P&L	Profit and Loss
PAL	Provisional Allotment Letter

PAYE	Pay As You Earn
PD	Probability of Default
PE	Probability of Event
PEP	Personal Equity Plan
PHI	Permanent Health Insurance
PHLX	Philadelphia Stock Exchange
PIBS	Permanent Interest Bearing Shares
PLC	Public Limited Company
PMI	Private Medical Insurance
POTAM	Panel on Take-Overs and Mergers
PPP	Personal Pension Plan
PPS	Protected Payment System
PSNBR	Public Sector Net Borrowing Requirement
PSNCR	Public Sector Net Cash Requirement
PSR	Pre-Settlement Risk
QCA	Quoted Companies Alliance (formerly CISCO)
RAROC	Risk-Adjusted Return on Capital
RCH	Recognised Clearing House
RDC	Regulatory Decisions Committee (FSA Committee)
REG	Registrar Adjustment
RES	Residual Transaction
RIE	Recognised Investment Exchange
RITS	Reserve Bank Information Transfer System
RNS	Regulatory News Service
ROIE	Recognised Overseas Investment Exchange
RPB	Recognised Professional Body
RPI	Retail Price Index
RPIX	RPI excluding the impact of mortgage rates
RTGS	Real Time Gross Settlement
RUR	Register Update Request
RVP	Receipt Versus Payment
S&P	Standard and Poors
SAYE	Save As You Earn

SD	Standard Deviation
SDRN	Stock Deposit Reference Number
SDRT	Stamp Duty Reserve Tax
SEAQ	Stock Exchange Automated Quotations System
SEATS	Stock Exchange Automated Trading System
SEC	Securities and Exchange Commission
SEDOL	Stock Exchange Daily Official List
SEHK	Stock Exchange of Hong Kong
SERPS	State Earnings Related Pension Scheme
SETS	Stock Exchange Electronic Trading System
SFA	Securities and Futures Authority
SFE	Sydney Futures Exchange
SHSE	Shanghai Stock Exchange
SIB	Securities and Investments Board
SIBE	Sistema de Interconnexion Bursátil Español
SICOVAM	CSD for French corporate securities and OATs
SIMA	Securities Industry Management Association
SIMEX	Singapore International Monetary Exchange
SIS	SegaInterSettle
SLA	Stock Loan Agreement
SLR	Stock Loan Return
SPAN	Standard Portfolio Analysis of Risk
SPS	(Inland Revenue) Savings and Pension Schemes
SPSS	(Inland Revenue) Savings, Pensions, Shares Schemes
SR	Settlement Risk
SRO	Self Regulating Organisation
SSAP	Statement of Standard Accounting Practice
SSCCR	Shanghai Securities Central Clearing and Registration Corporation
SSI	Standard Settlement Instruction
SSRC	Shenzhen Securities Registration Company
STD	Stock Deposit Transaction
STF	Stock Transfer Form

STP	Straight-through Processing
STRATE	Share Transactions Totally Electronic
STW	Stock Withdrawal
SWIFT	Society for Worldwide Interbank Financial Telecommunication
SWX	Swiss Stock Exchange
SZSE	Shenzhen Stock Exchange
T	Trade Date
TACT	Tel Aviv Continuous Trading
TAPO	Traded Average Price Option
TARGET	Trans–European Automated Real–Time Gross Settlement System
TESSA	Tax Exempt Special Savings Account
TOREX	Toronto Stock Exchange dealing system
TRS	Trade Registration System
TSCD	Taiwan Securities Central Depository
TSE	Tokyo Stock Exchange
TU	Tariffable Unit
USM	Unlisted Securities Market
UCITS	Undertakings for Collective Investment in Transferable Securities
UITF	Urgent Issues Task Force
UKLA	United Kingdom Listing Authority
USE	Unmatched Stock Event
VaR	Value at Risk
VAT	Value Added Tax
VCT	Venture Capital Trust
XD	Ex Distribution
XDC	Cross Border Delivery Confirm
XDL	Cross Border Delivery
XDR	Cross Border Reversal
XR	Ex-Rights

Useful Websites

American Stock Exchange (AMEX)	www.amex.com
Athens Derivatives Exchange	www.adex.com
Australian Financial Markets Association	www.afma.com
Australian Stock Exchange	www.asx.com.au
Bank of England	www.bankofengland.co.uk
Bank for International Settlement	www.bis.org
Bolsa De Mercadorias and Futuros (BM&F)	www.bmf.com.br
Bolsa De Derivados De Porto (BDP)	www.bdp.pt
Bombay Commodity Exchange	www.booe.org
Bombay Stock Exchange	www.bseindia.com
Brussels Exchanges	www.bxs.be
Budapest Commodity Exchange (BCE)	www.bce-bat.com
Budapest Stock Exchange (BSE)	www.bse.hu
Buenos Aires Futures Market	www.matba.com.ar
Computer Based Learning Ltd	www.cbl-ltd.co.uk
Chicago Board Options Exchange	www.cboe.com
Chicago Board of Trade	www.cbot.com
Commodities Future Trading Commission	www.cftc.gov

Clearnet SA	www.clearnetsa.com
Clearstream	www.clearstream.com
Chicago Mercantile Exchange	www.cme.com
CRESTCo	www.crestco.co.uk
Depository Trust Company	www.dtc.org
European Central Securities Depositories Association	www.ecsda.com
EUREX	www.eurexchange.com
EUROCLEAR	www.euroclear.com
Futures and Options Association	www.foa.co.uk
Futures Industry Association	www.fiafii.org
Financial Services Agency Japan	www.fsa.go.jp
Financial Services Authority	www.fsa.gov.uk
Finnish Options Exchange (FOREX)	www.foex.fi
Finnish Securities and Derivatives Exchange (SOM)	www.som.fi
G30 Recommendations	http://risk.ifci.ch/
Guarantee Fund for Danish Futures and Options (FUTOP)	www.xcse.dk
Hanmon Commodity Exchange	www.hce.or.jp
Hannover Commodity Exchange	www.wtb-hannover.de
Hong Kong Exchanges and Clearing	www.hkex.com.hk
Intercontinental Exchange (ICE)	www.intx.com
Italian Derivatives Market (IDEM)	www.idem.it
International Securities Markets Association	www.isma.co.uk
International Securities Services Association	www.issanet.org
Istanbul Stock Exchange	www.ise.org
Johannesburg Stock Exchange (JSE)	www.jse.co.za
Kansas City Board of Trade (KCBT)	www.kcbt.com
London Clearing House	www.lch.co.uk

London International Financial Futures & Options Exchange	www.liffe.com
London Metal Exchange	www.lme.co.uk
London Stock Exchange	www.londonstockexchange.com
Korea Stock Exchange	www.kse.or.kr
Malaysian Derivatives Exchange	www.mdex.com.my
MEFF	www.meff.es
Minneapolis Grain Exchange (MGE)	www.mgex.com
Montreal Exchange (ME)	www.me.org
NASDAQ	www.nasdaq.com
National Stock Exchange of India	www.nseindia.com
New Zealand Futures & Options Exchange (NZFOE)	www.sfe.com.au
Norex Alliance	www.norex.com
New York Board of Trade (NYBOT)	www.nybot.com
New York Cotton Exchange (NYCE)	www.nyce.com
New York Mercantile Exchange (NYMEX)	www.nymex.com
New York Stock Exchange	www.nyse.com
OM London	www.stockholmborsen.se
OM Stockholmbörsen	www.stockholmborsen.se
Osaka Securities Exchange (OSE)	quote.ose.or.jp (NB: not www.)
Olso Stock Exchange	www.ose.no/english/
Philadelphia Stock Exchange (PHLX)	www.phlx.com
Rosario Futures Exchange	www.rofex.com.ar
Russian Exchange	www.re.ru
Sao Paulo Stock Exchange	www.bvrj.com.br
Securities Exchange Commission (US)	www.sec.gov
Shanghai Metal Exchange (SME)	www.shme.com
Singapore Commodity Exchange	www.sicom.com.sg
Singapore Exchange	www.ses.com.sg

South African Futures Exchange (SAFEX)	www.safex.co.za
Sydney Futures Exchange (SFE)	www.sfe.com.au
Tel Aviv Stock Exchange	www.tase.co.il
Tokyo Commodity Exchange (TCE)	www.tocom.or.jp
Tokyo Grain Exchange (TGE)	www.tge.or.jp
Toronto Futures Exchange (TFE)	www.tse.com
Tokyo International Financial Futures Exchange (TIFFE)	www.tiffe.or.jp
Tokyo Stock Exchange	www.tse.or.jp
virt-x	www.virtx.com
Winnipeg Commodity Exchange (WCE)	www.wce.ca

Numbers

17F-5

Legal requirements for worldwide correspondent banks which serve US mutual funds, pension funds and other regulated financial groups.

24x7, 24/7

A continuous trading environment. Operating a business 24 hours a day, seven days a week.

2BCD

Second Banking Co-ordination Directive.

30/360

Calculation of accrued interest on bonds assuming that the year comprises 12 months of 30 days each – used in the Eurobond market.

360/360

Same as 30/360.

FT 30

FTSE Ordinary Stock Index.

G30 (Group Of Thirty)

A private sector group set up to improve the workings of the international securities markets.

S2P

State Second Pension.

48 Hour Rule

The requirement that a company seeking a listing should submit any documents required in their final form to the Stock Exchange 48 hours prior to the hearing of the application to obtain a listing.

A

AA
See *Against Actual*.

AAA Rating
The highest credit rating for a bond or company – the risk of default (or non–payment) is negligible.

Abandon
Allow an option to expire worthless.

Abandonment
See Abandon.

ABI
See *Association of British Insurers*.

Abnormal Return
Part of a security's return which cannot be attributable to systematic influences (eg, market return).

Absolute Interest
The same person has both the legal ownership and the beneficial ownership of an asset.

Abstract
Short form of a report or document.

Abstracts
The Urgent Issues Task Force issues abstracts which companies are required to observe whilst preparing their accounts.

Acceptance
The act of accepting a rights issue or takeover offer. See *Bankers' Acceptance*.

Acceptor
Someone who accepts liability for a bill of exchange.

Account
A dealing period. See *Fixed Settlement*.

Accounting Risk
The risk of inaccurate financial reporting.

Accounting Standards
Issued by the Accounting Standards Board, Accounting Standards require specific principles and methods of accounting to be utilised by companies who publish their accounts in the UK. Originally called Statements of Standard Accounting Practice (SSAPs), from 1990 they have been referred to as Financial Reporting (FRS).

Accounting Standards Board (ASB)
Accounting Standards (see above) are issued by the Accounting Standards Board in the UK. See also *Financial Reporting Review Panel*, *Urgent Issues Task Force* and *Financial Reporting Council*.

Account Manager
A term used in the ISA Regulations to refer to a person (an individual or, more usually, a corporate body) approved by the Inland Revenue to manage ISAs. Often referred to as an ISA Manager.

Account Valuation
Regular valuation report sent to a client for whom the firm acts as investment manager and the portfolio comprises derivatives.

Accreting Swap
A swap where the notional principal increases during the life of the swap.

Accrual Basis
The number of days in both the interest period and the year that is used to determine the amount of interest. For example, most corporate and municipal debt instruments in the United States use as a basis a 360 day year comprising of 12 30–day months. Semi–annual interest payments consist of two payments of 180 days each. Other securities may accrue interest for the actual number of days in the interest period. Possible accrual bases include 30/360 day, actual/360 day and actual/actual.

Accrual Rate
The rate at which pension benefits build up each year with pensionable service in a defined benefit scheme. Accelerated accrual is an accrual rate of more than 1/60th of pensionable earnings for each year of service. Accrued benefits are the benefits from a pension scheme up to a particular point in time.

Accruals

1. Gradual increases by addition.
2. A basic tenet of accounting which is also referred to as Matching Concept. Income and payments are added to or removed from the profit and loss account for the year that they are earned or incurred rather than when the cash is received or paid.

   Example: cash is received in 2002 for a sale made in 2001; the sale is treated as income in 2001.
3. Monies owed by a company for which it has not yet received invoices. They appear in the company's balance sheet under creditors as estimated amounts accruing.

Accruals Accounting

Any expenses or income that have not been invoiced or paid when accounts are being drawn up are still included in the accounting figures.

Accrued Coupon

The amount of the next coupon payment on a security earned so far from the last coupon date until settlement date.

Accrued Income Scheme

The tax rules which specify how accrued interest on gilts and other bonds is to be taxed or relieved.

Accrued Interest

In general, when traded, interest on bonds is separated from the underlying principal or price of the bond. When a bargain is transacted, the purchaser not only buys the underlying bond, but also the right to the next coupon payment, including the interest due for the period before the bond was purchased. In order to compensate the seller for this interest built up until the bargain date, the purchaser pays over an extra amount equivalent to the accrued interest, ie, the amount of interest due from the last coupon date to the time of purchase. Gilts and domestic bonds calculate using a 365–day year, whilst eurobonds usually assume a 360–day year. With the advent of the EURO, there is a move towards these conventions across Europe. The amount of interest on a bond which has accrued since the most recent interest payment.

Accrued Rights Premium (ARP)

Premium paid by an employee to the state scheme for a pension member below state pensionable age to enable the state scheme, instead of the occupational scheme, to take over the provision to provide a Guaranteed Minimum Pension (GMP).

Accumulation and Maintenance Settlement

A trust where the trustees have discretion either to use the income for the maintenance, education or other benefit of the beneficiaries or to accumulate the income but the beneficiaries obtain an absolute interest in the trust property at a specific age.

Accumulation Shares

Shares or units where net income is automatically reinvested and is reflected either in the value of the units or in additional units being allocated. The unit holder benefits from not having to pay an initial charge on the reinvested income.

Accumulation Units
Units which do not pay income but roll the income into the value of the units.

ACD
See *Authorised Corporate Director.*

ACD's Box
See *Book/Box.*

ACID Test Ratio
Also called the quick ratio, this is an accounting ratio whose interpretation is akin to the Current Ratio. Normally it is current assets (except stocks) divided by creditors owed within one year. It tests a company's short term solvency.

Acknowledgement
See *Confirmation Note.*

ACT
Advance Corporation Tax.

ACT/360
A day/year count convention taking the number of calendar days in a period and a 'year' of 360 days.

ACT/365
(Or ACT/365 Fixed or ACT/365–F). A day/year count convention taking the number of calendar days in a period and a 'year' of 365 days. Under the ISDA definitions used for interest rate swap documentation, 'ACT/365' means the same as ACT/ACT.

ACT/365 Fixed
See *ACT/365.*

ACT/365–F
See *ACT/365*.

ACT/ACT
For an interest rate swap, a day/year count convention dividing the number of calendar days in the interest period that fall in a leap year of 366 and dividing the remainder by 365.

Acting in Concert
1. Under the Companies Act 1985 when two or more investors agree to acquire interests in shares of the same company.
2. In the Takeover Code, when two or more investors work together to acquire or consolidate control of a company.

Active Fund Management
Attempting to manage a portfolio so that it outperforms the market, either by choosing stocks expected to perform well, or by timing share purchases, ie, trying to purchase shares before the market rises and sell them before the market falls. This is also called market timing. Higher fees can be charged for active fund management than for passive fund management. See *Index Tracking Funds*.

Active Market
A stock market where trading in securities is extremely busy.

Active Risk
Risk arising from securities held in an actively managed portfolio in different proportions to their weighting in a benchmark index. Also known as *Tracking Error*.

Actively Managed Funds
See *Active Fund Management*.

Activities Of Daily Living (ADL)
Criteria used for defining when a person may claim under certain insurance policies, eg, long–term care. They include mobility, dressing, eating, continence, toileting and washing and bathing.

Actual/Actual
Calculation of accrued interest on a bond using the actual number of days of accrual and the actual number of days between interest payment dates – used in the UK gilts market and many other government bond markets.

Actual Price
The price of any commodity which can be immediately sold or delivered.

Actual Settlement Date Accounting (ASDA)
Global custodians will give good cash value only on settlement of the securities trade itself.

Actuarial Consultant
Firms who advise institutional portfolio management clients on the choice of portfolio manager and fund methodology to be employed in the running of a portfolio.

Added Years
Extra pension benefits based on additional periods of pensionable service within a final salary pension scheme. Added years are often purchased through AVC schemes.

Add–on
In capital adequacy calculations, the extra capital required to allow for the possibility of a deal moving into profit before a mark–to–market calculation is next made.

Additional Voluntary Contributions (AVCs)

Voluntary contributions made by a member of an occupational pension scheme over and above his or her normal contributions. They can buy either added years or be on a money purchase basis.

Administrator

A personal representative appointed by the probate registry either if there is no will or if there is a will but no executor appointed or willing to act.

ADJ

The transaction type for system controller adjustments, available only to the CREST System Controller.

Adjustable Peg

Management of a currency at a fixed exchange rate against another currency/currencies by adjustment as required of the fixed rate. See *Crawling Peg*.

ADP

See *Alternative Delivery Procedure*.

ADR

See *American Depository Receipt*.

Ad Valorem

In proportion to the value.

Advanced Measurement Approaches (AMA)

A group of methods used to calculate the capital charge for operational risk.

Advice Note

See *Confirmation Note*.

Advising
Giving advice to investors on specific investments with a view to it being acted upon.

Advisory ISA
Similar to a self select ISA, although the account manager offers advice as to what to buy and sell.

Advisory Service
A firm advises the client but the investment decision is made by the client.

AER
See *Annual Equivalent Rate.*

AESOP
See *Employee Share Ownership Plan.*

AEX
Amsterdam Exchanges now part of EURONEXT.

Aftermarket
See *Secondary Market.*

Affirmation
Affirmation refers to the counterparty's agreement with the terms of the trade as communicated.

After–Hours Trading
The facility whereby securities can be bought or sold at any time of the day after the relevant exchange is closed.

Agency Bargain

A trade that involves a client buying or selling stock through a broker acting as agent, with a broker dealer principal as the counterparty. Also known as an agent/principal bargain.

Agency Brokers

Brokers who do not deal as principals or act as market makers but act solely as agents.

Agency Cross

A trade between two customers of a broker executed through the broker's office acting as agent in the middle. The two customers act as principals. It will usually be carried out at the mid–market price for the stock in question. The broker will charge both customers commission.

Agency Trade

A trade that involves a client buying or selling stock through a broker, dealer, agent.

Agency Trading

Trading to make a profit by charging a commission to clients.

Agent

A legal person acting on behalf of a principal to a trade, eg, a broker buying or selling shares for a customer. See also *Principal*.

Agent/Agent Bargain

A trade that involves two London Stock Exchange member firms who are both acting in the capacity of agents for their own clients. One agent's client is selling stock which the other agent's client is buying.

Agent Bank

A commercial bank providing services for another party as per their instructions.

Aggregate Demand
The total demand for goods and services within an economy.

Aggregation
Procedure where customers' orders are added together or with those of the firm and are done as a single transaction. Customers must have been warned about the possibility and that it may sometimes work to their disadvantage. See *Allocation*.

AGM
See *Annual General Meeting*.

AIM
See *Alternative Investment Market*.

AITC
See *Association of Investment Trust Companies*.

Agreement Among (By) Underwriters
A legal document forming underwriting banks into a syndicate for a new issue and giving the lead manager the authority to act on behalf of the group. In the "among" form, a direct legal relationship links each underwriter to every other underwriter. In the "by" form, the legal relationship is established between the managers and the individual underwriter. However the agreement also serves to define relationships between underwriters.

Alleged
The description given to a transaction instruction which requires matching (eg, bargains, stock loans) but for which no matching instruction has been input. The unmatched instruction is said to be 'alleged' against the counterparty cited on the instruction.

Alleged Transaction
A transaction in CREST, the details of which the participant's counterparty has input to the system first.

All–in Price
See *Dirty Price*.

Allocation
The process of moving the trade from the executing broker to the clearing broker. Also the division of a single market trade across two or more investors/funds.

All or None (AON)
Instruction to buy or sell the entire order in a single transaction, ie, not to execute a partial transaction. AON restricts the size but not necessarily the time of the transaction.

Allotment
The amount of a new issue (ie, number of shares or bonds) given to a syndicate member by the lead manager.

Allotment Letter
A document issued to a shareholder as evidence of ownership of an underlying stock when a company has a rights issue or open offer entitling the shareholder to take up new shares. Some new issues commence trading in allotment letter form, usually for the first six–week period before the stock becomes fully registered.

Allowances
See *Subscription Limits*.

ALM
See *Association of Lloyd's Members*.

ALPHA
Return from a security or a portfolio in excess of a risk adjusted benchmark return. Also known as Jensen's alpha.

Alternative Delivery Procedure
The long and short sides of a transaction agree to deliver either a different specification of the product or to a different location to that stated in the contract, or both. Used on the International Petroleum Exchange (IPE), they are not covered by the London Clearing House guarantee.

Alternative Investment Market (AIM)
The second tier or junior market established by the London Stock Exchange in 1995 to provide trading facilities in the shares of smaller companies.

Alternative Investments
Investment in physical assets such as antiques, jewellery, works of art etc.

American Depository Receipt (ADR)
A negotiable receipt issued by a US bank or trust company certifying that shares of a non–US company are on deposit with it. The usual way for the shares of non–US companies to trade in the USA.

American Option
For an interest rate swap, a day/year count convention dividing the number of calendar days in the interest period that fall in a leap year by 366 and dividing the remainder by 365.

American Style Option
An option that can be exercised on any business day up to expiry. See *European Style Option*.

AMEX
American Stock Exchange.

AMS/3
Trading system for the Hong Kong Stock Exchange.

Amortisation
The gradual reduction over time of the principal of a bond or mortgage.

Amortising Swap
A swap where the notional principal decreases during the life of the swap.

AMPS
See *Auction Market Preferred Stock.*

AMS
See *Automatic Order Matching and Execution System.*

Amsterdam Stock Exchange
The Dutch stock exchange is thought to be the world's oldest stock exchange.

Announcement
In a new bond issue, the day on which a release is sent to prospective syndicate members describing the offering and inviting underwriters and selling group members to join the syndicate.

Annual Equivalent Rate (AER)
The notional annual rate if interest were compounded each time it is credited.

Annual General Meeting (AGM)

Meeting of shareholders which a company must call every year. Main purposes are to receive the accounts, vote on dividends and appoint directors.

Annual Management Charge

A charge usually in the order of 0.75 to 1.75% of the value of the fund levied for the management of a trust, ISA or other fund.

Annual Percentage Rate (APR)

The true cost of borrowing in terms of interest and fees, which must be shown on all advertisements for loans.

Annual Report and Accounts

The law requires all limited companies to prepare an annual report each year. It should include their financial statements and directors' and auditor's reports. It must also contain a five year summary of results. It must be sent to shareholders and to the Registrar of Companies. Once it has been received by the Registrar, it becomes a public document and anyone can look at it.

Annuity

A regular payment which may be level or subject to increases, normally made until the death of the person receiving it. Can be joint names, in which case, payments continue till death of the second person.

Annuity Certain

Annuity which makes payments for a specified period of time regardless of whether the annuitant is alive or dead during that period.

AON

See *All or None*.

APACS
See *Association for Payment Clearing Services*.

APCIMS
See *Association of Private Client Investment Managers and Stockbrokers*.

Appointed Representatives
Individuals or companies acting on behalf of an authorised person who take responsibility for everything done by the representative. The representative is exempt from obtaining his own authorisation. Also individuals or firms representing a single investment product provider. Can only advise on the investments offered by that particular product provider.

Appreciation
Increase in value. See *Depreciation, Revaluation*.

Appropriate Personal Pension Scheme (APPS)
A personal pension scheme (or Free Standing AVC) which can be used for contracting out of the State Earnings Related Pension Scheme (SERPS).

Approved Persons
Individuals undertaking controlled functions and who therefore require approval from the FSA. There are 27 categories.

Approved Profit Sharing Scheme

A profit sharing scheme which is a fund (a trust under the control of trustees) into which a company makes cash payments to enable the trustees to buy shares in the company. The shares are set aside for employees who are eligible to take part in the scheme. Provided the scheme meets certain requirements, as set out in the Taxes Act 1988, the scheme will be approved by the Inland Revenue and there are tax advantages for employees who receive the shares. Shares from the scheme can be transferred directly into an ISA within 90 days of appropriation to the employee.

APPS

See *Approved Personal Pension Scheme.*

APR

See *Annual Percentage Rate.*

APSS

Inland Revenue Audit and Pension Schemes Services.

APT

See *Automated Pit Trading System.*

Arbitrage

The simultaneous sale (or purchase) of a financial instrument and the taking of an equal and opposite position in a similar instrument to give a profit, ie, exploiting pricing anomalies across markets. True arbitrage should be risk free.

Arbitrage Channel

An area within which no arbitrage will take place, that exists both above and below the fair value of a future. This is because additional costs, such as exchange fees, bid/offer spreads and commissions, will exceed arbitrage profits within this channel. Thus, the width of the channel depends on the costs incurred by the participant in the market place.

Arbitrageur

A trader who takes advantage of profitable opportunities arising from price anomalies.

Arbitration

A way to solve disputes.

Arithmetic Mean Return

The average return (calculated by summing each period's return and dividing by the number of periods).

Arm's Length

A transaction between financially unrelated companies.

Around Par

If one side of a transaction is negative and the other positive in the same proportions.

ARP

See *Accrued Rights Premium*.

Arranging

Having some positive role in helping to promote an investment transaction.

Articles of Association

A document which sets out the rules by which shareholders and a company will be administered, eg, voting rights.

ASB

See *Accounting Standards Board*.

A Shares

Ordinary shares that do not carry voting rights. They tend to be cheaper than ordinary shares and few still exist.

Asian Option

See *Average Option*.

Ask Price

Price at which a market maker will sell stock. Also known as the *Offer Price*.

Asset

Something that has earning potential or value. See *Current Assets* and *Fixed Assets*.

Asset Allocation

Any general allocation of funds across sectors or markets. Deciding what proportions of a fund will be held in different classes of asset, eg, cash, bonds and shares.

Asset–backed Security

A debt market instrument raised against assets, eg, mortgages, car loans, credit card debt or other cash receivables. Includes mortgage–backed securities. Asset–backed securities are related to repackaged securities and collateralised debt obligations.

Asset/Liability Management

Active balance sheet management in order to maximise returns and minimise interest rate risk. Thus a bank might use an interest rate swap to convert a fixed–rate loan (asset) to match the interest basis of its floating–rate deposits (liabilities).

Asset Securitisation

The practice of pooling bonds or loans with credit risk and selling them as a package to outside investors.

Asset Swap

An interest rate swap or currency swap used to change the interest rate exposure and/or the currency exposure of an investment. Also used to describe the package of the swap plus the investment itself.

Assignee

The person to whom an asset is transferred.

Assignment

A transfer of ownership.

Assignor

The original beneficiary of an asset.

Association for Payment Clearing Services (APACS)

A group of major banks providing payment services.

Association of British Insurers (ABI)

A trade body of insurance companies through which they can air their views collectively on matters of common concern.

Association of Investment Trust Companies (AITC)

The trade body that exists to further the interests of the UK investment trust industry.

Association of Lloyd's Members (ALM)
A non–official association which informs and represents Lloyd's of London members.

Association of Private Client Investment Managers and Stockbrokers (APCIMS)
The trade association for private client securities firms and ancillary activities.

Association of Unit Trusts and Investment Funds
The trade association for the collective investment industry, now subsumed into the Investment Management Association.

Assured
The person who has contracted with the life office, for cover against specified contingencies.

Assured Payment
A payment which is made by way of the assumption of an assured payment obligation by a payment bank. CREST offers an assured payment mechanism.

ASX
Australian Stock Exchange.

At Best Order
Any order to buy or sell at the best prevailing price in the market at the time the order is executed.

At–Call
See *Call Money.*

At–The–Money
An option where the strike price is the same as the current spot or forward market rate.

Auction
The method by which the Bank of England issues gilts. In an auction the investors specify the amount they wish to purchase and the price they are prepared to pay. Successful applicants then pay the price that they offered.

Auction Market Preferred Stock (AMPS)
Preference shares issued by a company which have a variable dividend and which are set at a market rate at regular periods by an auction between investors.

Audit
The independent verification of the financial statements of a company by an independent firm of accountants.

Audit Trail
A historical record of all price quotations and transactions. Checks can be made to ensure that the buying and selling of securities has been carried out in an accurate manner.

Auditor's Report
Companies above a certain size must have their financial statements audited, ie, checked for truth, probity and accuracy by a registered auditor who prepares a report which is attached to the financial statements. This states the auditor's opinion as to whether the company's accounts provide a true and fair view of its results and financial position.

Authentication

The technical process of ensuring that all messages and files sent across a communications network are from the purported source and have not been modified in transit.

Authentication Agent

A bank putting a signature on each physical bond to certify its genuineness prior to the distribution of the definitive bonds on the market.

Authorised Corporate Director (ACD)

A corporate body and an authorised person given powers and duties under FSA regulations to operate an OEIC.

Authorised Fund

A term used in the ISA Regulations to refer to an authorised unit trust or an OEIC.

Authorised Investments

Investments in which trustees may invest under the Trustee Investments Act 1961.

Authorised Person

A firm authorised by the FSA to conduct investment business in the UK.

Authorised Unit Trust

A unit trust scheme authorised by the FSA. A UK unit trust must be authorised before it can be offered to the general public in the UK.

AUTIF

See *Association of Unit Trusts and Investment Funds*.

Automated Input Facility

An index arbitrage trading system or any other electronic trading system which fully automates the decision to submit orders to the Exchange with the capability of submitting at least 20 simultaneous orders.

Automated Pit Trading (APT) System

The automated trading system used by LIFFE, usually for after hours trading.

Automatic Accrual

An agreement under which a deceased partner's share passes automatically to the surviving partners. The partners agree to insure their lives for their shares in the value of the business.

Automatic Exercise

This is when a clearing house exercises all *in–the–money* options at expiry without requiring instructions (in the form of an *exercise notice*) from the holder. Most automatic exercise routines will not exercise options which are only just in–the–money.

Automatic Order Matching and Execution System (AMS)

Dealing system of the Stock Exchange of Hong Kong.

Automatic Partials Processing

An end of settlement day process, whereby transactions which are ready to settle, but cannot because of insufficient stock or cash, are split into two parts by CREST. One part will settle immediately because sufficient stock or cash is available. The other part remains within the settlement queue; see *Settlement Queue*.

Automatic Reinvestment

The use of income or realised capital gains for the purchase of additional shares or units of a fund.

Auto Unfreeze

The automatic CREST process by which, at a point during the day,
transactions with zero cash priority ("frozen" transactions) are allowed
to settle, securities and headroom permitting. Some transaction types
are unaffected by the process, eg, claims.

AVCs

See *Additional Voluntary Contributions*.

Average Option

Also known as Asian Option. An option whose value depends on the
average value of the underlying over the option's life.

Average Rate Option

Also known as Asian Option. A cash–settled option that pays the
difference between the average rate of the underlying over the life of the
option and a pre–determined strike rate.

Average Strike Option

An option that pays the difference between the average rate of the
underlying over the life of the option and the rate at expiry.

B

Back Office
The settlement, processing and accounting departments of a bank or broking firm. Now more usually referred to as Operations.

Back Testing
A means of stress testing a VaR model using actual historical data.

Back–to–Back Delivery
A market transaction requiring two transactions in CREST to deliver stock and/or cash consideration from one CREST member to another, passing through the account of a third party (eg, a broker).

Back–to–Back Loans
A method of hedging foreign exchange risk if, for example, a fund's base currency is sterling and the investments are based on a foreign currency.

Back–to–Back Plan
A combination of a life assurance policy and an annuity.

Backwardation

A situation where the offer price of one market maker is lower than the bid price of others.

BACS

See *Bank Automated Clearing System.*

Bad Delivery

The situation in which a company registrar rejects a request (which has settled in CREST) to transfer shares or stock ownership so the transfer is not registered.

Bad Delivery Reversal (BDR)

A transaction type which can only be input by the CREST System Controller. It is used to reverse a transfer in CREST that was previously rejected by the appropriate registrar.

Bad Withdrawal Reversal (BWR)

A transaction type which is created automatically by the CREST system. It is used to reverse a settled stock withdrawal that was previously rejected by the appropriate registrar.

Balance

1. Amount to be put in one of the columns of an account to make the total details and credits equal.
2. The rest of an amount owed.
3. The quantity of any stock held in a CREST member account is sub–divided into three balance types:
   - one or more "deposit link" balances (if the member is using the deposit link function);
   - one or more "escrow" balances (if the member has transferred securities into escrow); and
   - a single "available" balance, a pool of securities free for use in settling any outstanding transaction.

Securities can only be moved into the first two balance types using specific transactions – Stock Deposits and Transfers To Escrow – and is then held unavailable for any other use.

Balance Certificate
Certificate issued if the number of shares being sold is less than the number of shares shown on the certificate.

Balance of Payments
The accounts of a country's trade with other countries. If imports are greater than exports there is a deficit; and if exports are greater than imports there is a surplus.

Balance Sheet
A financial statement showing, at a point in time, the assets and liabilities of a company and how the assets have been financed by shareholders.

Balloon Maturity
A debt that requires a lump–sum payment at maturity.

Ballot
A method used to allocate shares in a new issue, if there are more applications than available shares.

Bancassurance
The amalgamation of assurance and banking business within a financial environment, ie, bank or building society.

Bank Automated Clearing System
A debit and credit system used to make direct transfers to/from clients' accounts.

Bank – Commercial
Organisation that is licensed to take deposits and can make loans.

Bank for International Settlements (BIS)
The bank for central banks. Based in Basel, it produced the Basel Capital Accord in 1988.

Bank – Merchant
Organisation that specialises in advising on takeovers and corporate finance activities.

Bankers' Acceptance
A bill of exchange that has been endorsed and accepted by a bank for guarantee of payment of the face value of the bill at maturity date.

Banking Book
The part of a bank's business which involves its lending department and long term investments.

Banking Code
Code of practice produced by the banks and building societies, governing relationships with customers.

Bank of England
The UK's central bank which undertakes overall monetary policy and determines interest rates.

Bank of England Register
Gilts purchased through a stockbroker are normally registered on the Bank of England Register and interest is payable subject to deduction of tax.

Barber v Gre (1990)

The case before the European Court which ruled that from 17 May 1990, men and women in occupational pension schemes have rights to the same retirement age and not to be discriminated against generally. The date from which this was to be effected was confirmed in the Maastricht Protocol 1993.

Bare Trust

A trust where the trustee holds the trust property for a single beneficiary. His duty is to carry out the beneficiary's instructions and to transfer the property to the beneficiary when requested.

Bargain

A Stock Exchange or unit trust buy/sell transaction.

Barrier Option

(Also known as *Trigger Level, Trigger Option, Exploding Option* and *Extinguishing Option*). An option which is either cancelled or activated if the underlying price reaches a pre–determined barrier or trigger level. See *Knock–out Option* and *Knock–in Option*.

Base Currency

The foreign exchange deal currency against which another currency is measured.

Basel Capital Accord

Capital rules issued by the Basel Committee on Banking Supervision in1988. They set minimum rules for capital allocation which are enforced by national regulatory authorities. They are in the process of being updated (Basel II).

Basel II

See *Basel Capital Accord*.

Base Price
Base Bid and Base Offer Prices will be the first Best Bid and Best Offer Prices on the order book offer the completion of any uncrossing auction. Used for price monitoring.

Base Rate
The rate of interest used as a basis by UK banks to make loans to their customers or pay interest on deposits.

Base Requirement
Part of a firm's funding requirement to allow for the possibility of a downturn in business and a reduction in revenue for the firm. It is calculated on the basis of three months' worth of expenses.

Basic Pension
State pension payable to all those with an adequate *National Insurance Contributions* payments record.

Basis
The difference between the price of a futures contract and the underlying cash market asset.

Basis (Gross)
The difference between the relevant cash instrument price and the futures price. Often used in the context of hedging the cash instrument.

Basis (Value or Net)
The difference between the gross basis and the carry.

Basis Point (BP)
A measure which is mainly used in the statement of interest rates. One basis point is one hundredth of 1%.25 basis points is equal to 0.25%.

Basis Risk
The risk that the price or rate of one instrument or position might not move exactly in line with the price or rate of another instrument or position which is being used to hedge it.

Basis Swap
An interest rate swap where the interest payments that are exchanged between each party are based on different indices.

Basis Trading
The simultaneous entry into a cash position for a particular product and an equal and opposite futures position on the same underlying. A basis trader tries to profit from a change in the relationship between the cash price and the future, ie, from a change in the basis.

Basis Trading Facility (BTF)
Allows for the simultaneous execution of cash and futures trades (basis trades) without entering the futures pit. It is a system operated on the LIFFE market for certain bond futures.

Basket
A group of currencies, each weighted differently, against which another currency is measured or managed.

BBA
British Bankers' Association.

BDR
See *Bad Delivery Reversal*.

Bear
A person who sells shares in the hope of buying them back at a lower price. The term describes someone who thinks a price will fall.

Bear Call Spread
The buying and selling of two calls that have the same expiry date where the option bought is at a higher exercise price than the one sold.

Bear Market
A market in which prices are falling.

Bear Put Spread
The buying and selling of two puts that have the same expiry date where the option bought is at a higher exercise price than the one sold.

Bear Spread
A vertical spread, achieved by purchasing a high strike call (put) and selling a low strike call (put), both options being on the same underlying and having the same delivery month.

Bearer Document
Document which states that the person in physical possession (the bearer) is the owner.

Bearer Securities
Securities for which there is no register of beneficial ownership. For certificated bearer securities, the certificate itself is proof of ownership. Dividends (for shares) and interest (bonds) are collected by clipping the coupons from the certificate and sending them to the paying agent.

Bearer Shares
Shares which transfer by hand without the need for registration of the change of ownership.

Bearer Stock
An instrument for which there is no register of the owner held by the company.

Benchmark

A bond whose terms set a standard for the market. The benchmark usually has the greatest liquidity, the highest turnover and is usually the most frequently quoted.

Benchmark Bond

Used as a comparison by which the attractiveness or worth of other bonds may be judged.

Benchmarking

The comparison of a firm's data with competitors and other firms in the industry.

Beneficial Owner

The underlying owner of a security who has paid for the stock and is entitled to the benefits of ownership.

Beneficiary

The person entitled to the benefit derived from a trust property, eg, the income or the capital.

Benefit Distribution

Corporate actions in which cash and/or stock distributions are made by companies to their shareholders. Benefits are usually distributed in proportion to the investor's holding. Examples include Dividends and Scrip Dividends, Rights Issues and Capitalisations (Bonus Issues). See *Corporate Action*.

Bermudan Option

An option which the holder can choose to exercise on any of a series of pre-determined dates between the purchase of the option and expiry. See *American Option*.

BES

See *Business Expansion Scheme*.

Best Advice

Duty on financial advisers to recommend products that are the most suitable for the client.

Best Bid

The highest priced buy order on the order book for a specified order book security.

Best–Efforts Basis

The term used when a custodian or broker receives an instruction that it cannot guarantee to execute because of deadline, local market practices, or factors beyond the custodian's or broker's control.

Best Execution

Dealing for a client at the best available price for the size and kind of transaction concerned.

Best Offer

The lowest priced sell order on the order book for a specified order book security.

Best Price

The top buy order will be at the best bid price (highest priced order) and the top sell order will be at the best offer price (lowest priced order).

Beta

A measure of how much a stock will move in relation to an index. It is a measure of its volatility and therefore its risk.

Better Than Best
Obligation on Independent Financial Advisers (IFAs) when they recommend the product of a connected person.

Bid
The rate at which the market or a particular trader is willing to buy.

Bid/Ask Spread
See *Bid/Offer Spread*.

Bid Basis
A fund is said to be on a bid basis if it is priced on the basis of the minimum bid price required by regulations laid down by the Financial Services Authority.

Bid/Offer Spread
The standard differential between the price of buying and selling securities. It is usually quoted as a monetary amount for shares and a percentage term for unit trusts.

Bid Price
The price at which units are sold back to the managers by investors. The difference between the bid and offer prices is known as the bid and offer spread. It is generally about 6% on an equity unit trust. Bid price is also the price at which a market maker will buy a share from an investor. See *Ask Price, Middle (Mid) Price*.

BIFFEX
The Baltic International Freight Futures Exchange.

Big Bang

The changes in the rules of the Stock Exchange which occurred on 27th October 1986, so called because the abolition of fixed commissions, precipitating a complete alteration in the structure of the stock market, took place on one day and not over a period of time.

Big Figure

The exchange rate without the last two decimal places. See *Points*.

Bilateral Arrangement (of Collateral)

Both parties post collateral for the value of their total obligation to the other.

Bilateral Netting

Offsetting trades between the same two counterparties in the same security so that there is only one transfer of cash and securities. See also *Netting*.

Bilateral Payment

A payment type, indicating arrangements where a payment bank settles its payment obligations on a net basis with each of its counterparty banks separately.

Bill of Exchange

An unconditional order in writing, addressed by one person to another, signed by the person giving it, requiring the person to whom it is addressed, to pay on demand or at a fixed period in the future, a sum of money, to the order of a specified person, or to the bearer.

BIS

Bank for International Settlements.

Black Monday
Monday 19 October 1987 when the world stock market prices crashed.

Black Scholes
A theoretical option pricing model widely used in the market. Named after Fischer Black and Myron Scholes who first propounded the model.

Blanket Bond Insurance
A certificate of debt, generally long–term, under the terms of which an issuer contracts, inter alia, to pay the holder a fixed principal amount on a stated future date and, usually, a series of interest payments during its life.

Block Trading
The trading of a trade of large parts of a portfolio. Often referred to as *Upstairs Trading* in the USA.

Blue Book (The)
See *City Code on Takeover and Mergers (The)*.

Blue Chip
Originally an American expression, to denote the shares of companies which are well established, usually large and highly regarded.

BMV–SENTRA
Equity dealing system for the Mexican Stock Exchange.

Board Lot
A standard dealing quantity of shares. Also called a *Round Lot*. Dealing is normally in multiples of the board lot. See *Odd Lot*.

Bobl

German government security issued with a 5 year maturity. It is a contraction of Bundesobligationen.

BOJ

Bank of Japan which also runs BOJ–NET, a Yen payment system.

Bolsa Mexicana de Valores (BMV or Bolsa)

Mexican Stock Exchange.

BOLT

Trading system of the Bombay Stock Exchange (Bombay Stock Exchange Online Trading).

Bona Fide

In good faith, without fraud or deceit.

Bond

1) An alternative name for fixed interest securities. A marketable debt instrument issued by a company or a government.
2) Normally a single premium life assurance policy, either guaranteed or unit–linked. Normally a non–qualifying policy.

Bond Basis

An interest rate quoted on an ACT/365, 30/360 or ACT/ACT basis. See *Money–market Basis*.

Bond Borrowing

Authorised organisations borrow bonds from institutional investors or other organisations with long positions in exchange for a fee. See *Bond Lending*.

Bond Fund

A fund that holds a portfolio that consists primarily of bonds.

Bond House

A securities firm that creates, distributes and markets bonds.

Bond Lending

Authorised organisations and institutional investors make their long positions available to organisations who have short positions or short–term settlement fails. The lender receives a fee for this service See *Bond Borrowing*.

Bond Market Association

Trade association of the US domestic bond market. Previously called the *Public Securities Association (PSA)*, it produced the original master repo agreement which became the basis of the PSA/ISMA master repo agreement, used in international repo markets.

Bond Washing

Selling a bond cum dividend and then repurchasing it ex dividend in order to convert the coupon element of the bond's price into a capital gain, rather than receiving the coupon as income. It does not affect the investor's tax liability, because the gain on sale due to the interest accrual in the bond's price is taxed as income in the UK.

Bonus

Profit allocated to a with profits policy. Once allocated it cannot be withdrawn.

Bonus Issue

A free issue of shares to a company's existing shareholders. No money changes hands and the share price falls pro rata. It is a cosmetic exercise to make the shares more marketable. Also known as a *Capitalisation* or *Scrip Issue*.

Book/Box

The stock of units owned by managers acting as principals. Incoming unit holders buy their units from managers. If the managers act only as agents for the trustee in the issue of units, then units are transferred directly into the unit holder's name (ie, not from the managers) and all the dealings with the fund by investors are effected at maximum spread.

Bookbuilding

A way to implement an Offer for Subscription or Offer for Sale. It is a compromise method of issue combining elements of a Fixed Price Offer and a Tender. Before the issue of shares, the issuing house conducts a bookbuilding exercise. It obtains the commitment of a number of investors to purchase shares at a specified price. Once the demand for shares is established, the issuing manager sets the fixed price for the issue in line with the demand levels that have been established. Bookbuilding is often used to implement large offers if the issue price is hard to determine in advance and if it is difficult to obtain underwriting for it.

Book Cost

The original cost of an investment generally used to compare against the current market value.

Book Entry

The term to describe the electronic recording of an asset which is either in an immobilised or dematerialised form.

Book Entry Transfer

A method whereby the transfer of ownership of securities is effected electronically by debits and credits to accounts without the need for the movement of physical certificates or documents.

Book Runner
An organisation responsible for a bond from its initial launch through to issue and maintaining a secondary market.

Book Transfer
A type of payment where the clearing house debits the participant's cash account and credits the funds internally to the beneficiary's participant cash account. See *Wire Transfer*.

Book Value
The value at which a loan is shown in the balance sheet of the company that has borrowed the money. This is not necessarily the market value of the loan.

Books Closed Day
Last date for registration of shares or bonds for the payment of the next dividend or interest payment, or for processing a Corporate Action. It is also called *Record Day*.

Bootstrapping
The term used to describe a method for deriving the spot (zero–coupon) curve from the coupon or par yield curve.

Borrower
1. Stock lending: the counterparty supplies cash or stock as collateral for borrowing a specified security.
2. Repo: the counterparty that is taking stock, ie, lending cash.

Borrower's Option
See *Interest Rate Guarantee*.

Borrowing
A futures trade on the LME which involves buying near dated contracts and selling long dated contracts. Sometimes known as 'buying the spread' it is the equivalent of an Intramarket Spread trade. Also known as a *Carry*.

Bottom Up Management
A method of active portfolio management where securities are selected on their own merits without consideration of the asset class or security sector.

Bottom Up Measurement
A method of measurement of operational risk that builds up a detailed profile of risk occurring in each process, aggregating them to provide overall measures of exposure for the department or the firm as a whole.

Bought Deal
A way to issue Eurobonds. The issuer buys the entire issue on predetermined terms and price and then places the bonds with its own clients. See also *Fixed Price Re–offer*.

Box
Name given to the system through which Unit Trust managers store units, that have been redeemed by unit holders for subsequent onward sale.

Box Management
Managers dealing in units in a Unit Trust with investors.

Break
A term used for any out–of–balance condition. A money break means that debits and credits are not equal. A trade break means that some information such as that from a contra broker is missing to complete that trade.

Breakeven Point

The underlying price at which a strategy is neither profitable nor unprofitable.

Bretton Woods

The US venue of a conference in 1944 which established a system of fixed exchange rates, the International Monetary Fund (IMF) and the World Bank.

Bridge

An electronic link between CEDEL and Euroclear, the two Eurobond clearing houses.

Bridging Pension

A scheme may provide a temporary extra pension equal to state benefits between scheme retirement age and state retirement age.

British Government Stocks

See *Gilts*.

British Standards Institution (BSI)

The UK national standards body which is a member of the International Organisation for Standardisation (ISO). Recognises the Technical Standards Committee as the focal point for input to the UK and ISO standards setting process on behalf of practitioners in the UK Securities industry.

British Venture Capital Association (BVCA)

The trade association that represents all principal sources of private and venture capital in the UK.

Broken Date
A value date outside the normal run of money market value dates (1, 2, 3, 6, 12 months). A maturity date other than the standard ones normally quoted.

Broken Period
A period other than the standard ones normally quoted.

Broker
Bank or other institution which acts as an intermediary, bringing together buyers and sellers or borrowers and lenders.

Broker/Dealer
Any member firm of the LSE except the specialists which are Gilt Edged Market Makers (GEMMs) and Inter–dealer Brokers (IDBs).

Broker Dealer Agent
A member firm of the LSE which is authorised by the Exchange to trade on behalf of clients. Sometimes called an *Agent*.

Broker Dealer Principal
A member firm of the LSE which is authorised by the Exchange to trade as a wholesaler, buying and selling stock on their own behalf. A Market Maker is a specific type of broker dealer principal.

Brokerage
1. Commission charges paid on securities transactions.
2. A stock broking firm (US) .

Broking
The activity of representing a client as agent and charging commission for doing so.

BSI
See *British Standards Institution.*

BTAN
French government bond issued with a maturity of either 2 or 5 years.

BTF
See *Basis Trading Facility.*

BT Syntegra
CREST network providers, the systems integration business of British Telecom plc.

Building Society
Owned by its depositors and borrowers. Sometimes called mutuals, they were founded in order to accept deposits and recycle them as house loans.

Building Society Act
Act of Parliament governing Building Societies; they do not, therefore, require authorisation under the Financial Services Act unless they are undertaking investment business.

Bull
Someone who expects a share/unit price will rise.

Bull Call Spread
The buying and selling of two calls with the same expiry date if the option bought is at a lower price than the one sold.

Bull Market
A market in which prices are rising.

Bull Put Spread
The buying and selling of two puts with the same expiry date if the option bought is at a lower price than the one sold.

Bulldog Bond
A bond denominated in sterling, issued on behalf of a non–resident borrower and listed on the LSE.

Bullet Bond
A bond for which there is one single repayment on maturity by the borrower with no amortisation clauses.

Bullet Loan
A debt issue where capital is redeemed on the final day of the bond's life, rather than in instalments over its life. The only payments over the bond's life are the coupon.

Bund
German government bond issued with maturity between 8 and 30 years (Bundesanleihen).

Bundesanleihen
See *Bund*.

Bundesoligationen
See *BOBL*.

Business Day
Any day other than weekends or bank holidays under the Banking and Financial Dealings Act 1971.

Business Expansion Scheme (BES)
An investment scheme that ended 31 December 1993 for new investment. Tax relief was available on subscriptions to shares in qualifying companies. Proceeds were tax–free after five years.

Business Risk
The risk of loss due to an adverse external environment such as high inflation affecting labour costs, an over–competitive market reducing margins, or legal, tax or regulatory changes in the markets.

Buy and Sell Agreement
An agreement between partners or shareholder directors for a deceased person's estate to sell their share of the business/company and the survivors to buy it.

Buyer's Guide
Document that must be provided to all prospective purchasers of long term insurance products which explains the difference between an IFA and a Company Representative and identifies the status of the person supplying the document.

Buying Broker
The broker or dealer who represents the purchaser of the securities in market trades and settlements.

Buying In
Process whereby, on failure by the seller to deliver securities, the purchaser buys from an alternative source and any additional costs are passed on to the defaulting seller.

BVCA
See *British Venture Capital Association*.

BWR
See *Bad Withdrawal Reversal*.

C

C&F

Cost and freight included in price, but not insurance. See *CIF*.

CAC

Compagnie des Agents de Change the dealing system of the Paris Böurse (Stock Exchange).

CAC 40

Index of the Paris Stock Exchange comprising the top 40 listed shares.

CAD

Capital Adequacy Directive; an EU directive providing rules for all ISD firms.

CA Types

See *Corporate Action Types*.

CBOE

See *Chicago Board Options Exchange.*

CBOT
See *Chicago Board of Trade.*

CME
See *Chicago Mercantile Exchange.*

Cabinet Trade
An alternative to the simple abandonment of a long options position. A worthless position is sold for a notional consideration in order to crystallise losses for taxation and accounting purposes.

Cable
Dealers' word for the US$/GB£ exchange rate.

Caja de Valores
Depository/custodian for Argentinian shares.

Calendar Spread
Options trading strategy. One option is bought and another sold; the two contracts have the same exercise prices but different expiry dates.

Call
The early redemption of Bonds at the bond issuer's option.

Callable Bond
A bond which provides the borrower with an option to redeem the issue before the original maturity date. In most cases certain terms are set before the issue, such as the date after which the bond is callable and the price at which the issuer may redeem the bond.

Callable Service
Unsolicited call allowed about the provision of services in conservative investments, eg, non–geared packaged products and readily realisable securities.

Call Chairman
The exchange official responsible for overseeing the opening and closing procedures on the LIFFE Commodity market.

Call Deposits
Deposits which can be called (or withdrawn) at the option of the lender (and in some cases the borrower) after a specified period. The period is short, usually one or two days, and interest is paid at prevailing short–term rates.

Call Money
A loan or deposit that has no fixed maturity date.

Call Option
A deal giving one party the right, without the obligation, to buy an agreed amount of a particular instrument or commodity, at an agreed rate, on or before an agreed future date. The other party has the obligation to sell if so requested by the first party. See *Put Option*.

Call Payments
Payments made by allotment letter holders when taking up a share offer, eg, in a rights issue or privatisation. Call payments must be made by the acceptance date specified in the allotment letter.

Call Spread
The purchase of a call option coupled with the sale of another call option at a different strike, expecting a limited rise or fall in the value of the underlying.

Calling the Mark
Calling for margin to be reinstated after a Mark–to–Market revaluation of a repo transaction.

Cancellation Price
This is the lowest price at which the ACD may repurchase shares and the price which he receives for a share when he cancels shares off his Book/Box. Also applies to Unit Trust Managers.

Cancellation Rights
Under the Financial Services (Non–Life Cancellation) Rules 1997, there are certain circumstances when an investor has the right to cancel a purchase of shares, but cancellation rights only apply if the investment was made through an IFA, or after receiving advice from a company representative of the fund manager. They are not available for execution–only transactions or if terms of business with the IFA exclude cancellation rights.

Cancellation Rules
The rules which allow purchasers of certain products a period of time (Cooling Off Period) during which they can change their minds and cancel the agreement.

Cap
An option which fixes a maximum interest rate payable for a series of interest periods. Also a line of credit agreed between a CREST or CGO participant and their Settlement Bank. See *Ceiling*.

Capital Account (Balance of Payments)
Surplus or deficit between the UK and overseas on the movement of both short term and long term flows of investment money.

Capital Adequacy
Requirement for firms conducting investment business to have sufficient funds.

Capital Adequacy Directive (CAD)
European Union Directive implemented in the UK in January 1996. It establishes minimum funding requirements for all Intended Settlement Date (ISD) businesses.

Capital Adequacy Ratio
The minimum level which supervisors require a bank to maintain for the size of its own funds (available capital and reserves) as a proportion of its risk–weighted assets (the amount of money which it has put at risk in the course of its business).

Capital Asset Pricing Model (CAPM)
Economic theory describing the relationship between security returns and risk.

Capital Bonds (National Savings)
National Savings product designed for lump sum investments. Return is maximised if held for five years and is liable to income tax.

Capital Employed
The total of fixed assets plus current assets less current liabilities. It also means the shareholders' funds plus borrowing.

Capital Gains Tax (CGT)
Capital gains tax is payable by the individual taxpayer at rate equivalent to the taxpayer's highest rate of income tax on gains (over £7,700 for 2002/03) arising from the sale of securities or other chargeable assets. Most trusts will be exempt on the first £3,550 of gains.

Capital Market Line
The line defined by every portfolio formed by the combination of the risk free asset and the equity market portfolio.

Capital Markets
The means by which large amounts of money (capital) are raised by companies, governments and other organisations for long term use and the subsequent trade of the instruments issued in recognition of such capital. New money is raised in the Primary market by issuing shares or bonds to investors who can then trade them on the relevant Secondary market.

Capital Protected Annuity
Annuity where the total payments will not be less than the cost of the annuity.

Capital Repayment
A corporate action in which the company partly repays the capital in issue by paying the holders a proportion of the paid–up capital of the security.

Capitalisation
The value of a company in terms of issued share capital. It is the number of shares x price quotation.

Capitalisation Issue
A corporate action (also known as a bonus issue) in which a company issues fully paid shares to existing shareholders as a result of a rearrangement of a company's capital structure. The issue does not result in any new funds for the company.

Carries
See *Carrying*.

Carry
The cost of holding an inventory or portfolio of securities after deducting the funding costs from the interest received.

Carrying
Borrowing or lending on the LME. Also known as intramarket spread. See also *Borrowing, Lending and Intramarket Spread*.

CASCADE
Name of the settlement system used by Clearstream for German equity settlement.

Cash
Money in coins or notes.

Cash Against Documents
Settlement arrangement so that neither buyer nor seller is at risk from default, ie, not having the cash or the securities. CREST provides such a structure. See *CREST* and *Delivery versus Payment*.

Cash and Carry Arbitrage
An arbitrage trade. A futures contract is sold and the underlying asset is purchased in the cash market. Such a trade will be effected if the trader believes that the future is trading relatively expensive to its fair value.

Cash Driven Repo
Repo transaction initiated by someone wanting to invest cash against security collateral.

Cash Equivalent
Short term bonds, notes and repurchase agreements, usually government backed.

Cash Flow Statement

Financial statement showing the major cash flows of a company for a year.

Cash Funding

Process whereby the buyer ensures that there will be sufficient cash to pay for the purchase. Also called positioning.

Cash Market

The market in an underlying instrument, on which a derivative instrument is based.

Cash Memorandum Account (CMA)

A Cash Memorandum Account is the record of a CREST member's cash obligations arising from their settlement activity in any given day. Separate CMAs are maintained for each of the currencies settling through CREST.

Cash Posting

An individual credit or debt entry on a CMA.

Cash Queue

A cash queue (also known as a credit queue) is a list of settlement instructions for bought trades and other outward deliveries of cash for which the member requires the use of the credit made available by his payment bank.

A record within CREST of the cash available in a CREST member's bank account.

Cash Sale

A stock exchange transaction which calls for delivery of the securities that same day. In 'regular way' trades, the seller delivers securities on the fifth business day.

Cash Settlement

1. Derivatives: settlement of futures and options contracts for cash instead of physical transfer of goods. Utilised generally for index–based products, eg, FTSE 100 futures and options.
2. Securities: settlement one business day after the day of trade.

CAT

Charges Access Terms – government sponsored scheme to identify ISAs meeting certain criteria for the level of charges, ease of access and reasonable terms.

Category A Firms

Classification of firms for financial rules purposes. Comprises firms that underwrite or trade as principal.

Category B Firms

Classification of firms for financial rules purposes. Comprises agency brokers, which hold client money.

Category C Firms

Classification of firms for financial rules purposes. Comprises firms which manage client assets on a discretionary basis or undertake agency business but do not hold client assets or trade as principal.

Category D Firms

Classification of firms for financial rules purposes. Comprises firms which only receive and transmit orders.

Category 1 Persons

One category of person to whom a firm can market unregulated collective investment schemes. These are people who are already investors in an existing unregulated scheme or who have been, within the last 30 months. A firm can promote that scheme and one 'substantially similar' to it. This expression describes a scheme that invests in the same type of underlying assets as the one in which the customer has already invested.

Category 2 Persons

One category of person to whom a firm can market unregulated collective investment schemes. These are people for whom the firm has established that the scheme is suitable and who is either an existing customer or has signed an agreement becoming one. This allows the firm to promote unregulated schemes to existing customers who it believes would benefit.

CAVALI

Depository and clearing organisation for the Lima Stock Exchange.

CBLC

Brazilian Clearing and Depository Corporation – Clearing organisation and CSD for BOVESPA.

CB

Convertible Bond. See *Convertible*.

CBOE

Chicago Board Options Exchange.

CBOT

See *Chicago Board of Trade*.

CCJ
County Court Judgement.

CCASS
Clearing system for the Stock Exchange of Hong Kong (Central Clearing and Settlement System).

CCSS
See *CREST Courier and Sorting Service.*

CCT
Italian government FRN issued with maturities of 5, 7 and 10 years.

CD
See *Certificate of Deposit.*

CDI
See *CREST Delivery Interest.*

CDP
Central Depository (Pte) Ltd is the clearing and depository house for the Singapore securities market.

CDS
Canadian Depository for Securities.

CEDCOM
Communication system operated by Clearstream.

CEDEL
Founded in September 1970 by participants in the Eurobond market. Cedel has now merged with Deutsche Börse Clearing to form Clearstream.

Ceiling

A package of interest rate options whereby, at each of a series of future fixing dates, if an agreed reference rate such as LIBOR is higher than the strike rate, the option buyer receives the difference between them, calculated on an agreed notional principal amount for the period until the next fixing date. See *Cap*.

Central

The default payment type for UK and Irish registered securities, indicating that payment obligations between payment banks are settled on a multilaterally–netted basis, eg, each bank makes or receives a single payment in settlement of all that day's payment business in CREST.

Central Bank

The bank that provides financial and banking services to the government of a country and its commercial banking system and which implements the government's monetary policy.

Central Counterparty

A participant type in CREST. Used by the London Clearing House (LCH) in its capacity as the CCP to settle transactions agreed on SETS.

Central Depository System

CSD for the Malaysian market.

Central Gilts Office (CGO)

Book entry transfer system for gilts run by the Bank of England.

Centrally–Generated Transactions

A terms used to encompass all transaction types which are created automatically by CREST rather than input by users.
Centrally–generated transactions include:

- claims;
- stock loan returns and revaluations;
- DBV returns; and
- stamp duty payment transactions.

Central Moneymarkets Office (CMO)

CMO is the system operated by CRESTCo for settling various money market instruments (treasury bills and certificates of deposit).

Central Payments

See *Assured Payments*.

Central Securities Depository (CSD)

The principal function of a CSD is to immobilise or dematerialise securities, assuring that the bulk of securities transactions are processed in book–entry form. CSDs may also have the capability for trade clearance, safe custody and settlement/post settlement processing of securities and information. (Refer also to *International CSDs, National CSDs, Euroclear and CEDEL.*)

Certificate

A document issued by the issuer of a security stating either that a named person is the registered owner or that the bearer is the owner.

Certificated Holdings

Holdings of securities which are evidenced by paper certificates instead of an entry in a dematerialised account.

Certificated Securities

Securities represented in the form of a paper certificate.

Certificated Shape

The total quantity of securities in a CREST transaction involving paper–based investors may be represented by several certificates, each for a number of securities less than the total. The quantity on each certificate is sometimes known as a shape.

Certificate of Deposit

A negotiable instrument issued by a bank in return for a fixed deposit of up to five years.

Certification

The process of authorising a stock transfer form to be deposited and registered without the cover of a share certificate.

Certified High Net Worth Companies

The company must have more than 20 shareholders or share capital/net assets above £500,000. For a partnership the net assets test is at £5m and a trust with assets under management of £10m would also qualify. Usually, the financial promotions rules do not apply to promotions made to these types of organisations.

CFTC

The Commodity Futures Trading Commission (United States).

CGO

See *Central Gilts Office*.

CGO Reference Prices

Daily prices of gilt–edged and other securities held in CGO which are used by CGO in various processes, including revaluing stock loan transactions, calculating total consideration in a repo transaction, and DBV assembly.

CHAPS
See *Clearing House Automated Payment System.*

Chargeable Accounting Period (CAP)
Usually the same period of time as the company's accounting year. A company calculates its profits for its CAP and then pays corporation tax on them. Large companies pay quarterly with two instalments before the year end and two after. Small companies pay nine months after the end of the CAP.

A CAP cannot be for longer than one year. If a company changes its accounting year, it will have a fifteen month accounting period, eg, from 1st April one year to 30th June the next year. For tax purposes, it will be obliged to break this down into two CAPs, one of twelve months and one of three months.

Chargeable Disposal
Disposal of an asset for capital gains tax purposes. Includes the sale or gift of an asset; or when an asset becomes worthless, eg, shares after a company becomes insolvent.

Chargeable Estate
The monetary value of a person estate on death and on which inheritance tax is calculated.

Chargeable Event
In the case of an insurance policy or contract, where the investor initiates action designed to gain value from the policy before it has run full term or matured (eg, surrender of policy).

Charges
These arise if a bond is issued with security over certain assets. Should the borrower default on the bond, the charged assets can be sold and the proceeds used to repay the debt to the lender.

Charterparty
A legal document on the Baltic Exchange of an agreement to charter a ship. It records terms and conditions for the voyage being undertaken.

Charts, Chartism
A system of analysis which believes that there are trends and patterns in share prices. By plotting a graph, or chart, showing a share price over a period of time. Trends and patterns can be identified and decisions made as to when to buy and sell. An example of technical analysis.

Cheapest to Deliver
The cash security that provides the lowest cost (largest profit) to the arbitrage trader; the cheapest to deliver instrument is used to price the futures contract.

Cheap to the Curve
A bond whose yield is above the point on the yield curve where, given its maturity, the yield would be expected to lie, is said to be trading 'cheap to the curve'.

Cherry Picking
Consummating profitable deals and ignoring on unprofitable ones with a particular counterparty.

CHESS
See *Clearing House Electronic Sub Register System*.

Chicago Board of Trade (CBOT)
One of the two futures exchanges in Chicago, USA and one of the largest in the world.

Child Benefit
State benefit paid in respect of all children.

Children's Bonus Bonds
National Savings product which enables parents to save money for children in a tax efficient way.

Chinese Walls
Artificial barriers to the flow of information set up in large firms to prevent the movement of sensitive information between departments.

CHIPS
See *Clearing House Interbank Payments System*.

Choice Price
The touch bid and offer prices for a stock are identical. See also *Backwardation*.

Churning
Excessive trading which means the broker generates to derive a profit from commissions, while disregarding the best interests of the customer.

CIF
Cost, insurance, freight. Used in international trade to identify what is included in a price for a specified destination.

Circles
A series of transactions in CREST that are mutually dependent on each other's settlement.

Circles Processing
Whilst most CREST transactions will settle normally, gridlock is sometimes caused by mutually dependent transactions. CREST resolves the problem by simultaneously settling them, whilst ensuring that no member has insufficient stock or credit.

Circuit Breaker

An arrangement which, at times of high price volatility, halts trading on a stock exchange for a short period.

CISCO

City Group for Smaller Companies.

City Code of Takeovers and Mergers (The)

Principles and rules written by the panel to regulate conduct during a takeover, also known as the *Blue Book*. The code comprises of 10 general rules and around 38 detailed rules.

City Panel

Panel on Takeovers and Mergers: A non–statutory body which enforces the Takeover Code and Substantial Acquisition Rules.

CLA

The transaction type for claims, standard transactions which are generated automatically prematched by the Claim Processing Unit (CPU), with a priority of zero, settling as standard deliveries.

Claims Processing Unit (CPU)

The part of CREST which identifies transactions settling through the system where parties entitled to receive a benefit distribution (eg, a dividend) failed to appear on the legal register in time to receive the benefit directly.

Class

All calls and puts, of the same type, on one underlying instrument.

Class A Shares

These shares normally do not carry any voting rights.

Classic Repo

Generic sale and repurchase transaction.

Claw Back

1) The recovery by the Inland Revenue of Life Assurance Premium Relief (LAPR) given under a life assurance policy.
2) The right of an issuer to take back stock – usually in privatisations indemutalisations – from institutions to which it was initially issued and reallocate it to private investors, if there is a high demand from the latter.

CLC

Clearing organisation and CSD for the Rio de Janerio Stock Exchange.

Clean Payment

A payment of cash for which there is no directly associated countervalue.

Clean Price

The price of a bond before any adjustment has been made. See *Dirty Price*.

Clean–up of Interest

Transferring repo interest before the repo termination date.

Clearance

Checks and procedures undertaken immediately after execution of a trade prior to settlement.

Clearance Broker

A broker who will handle the settlement of securities related transactions for himself or another broker. Sometimes, small brokerage firms may not clear for themselves and therefore employ the services of an outside clearing broker.

Clearing

The centralised process whereby transacted business is recorded and positions are maintained.

Clearing Agent

An institution which is in the business of settling transactions for a large number of counterparties.

Clearing House

An organisation which guarantees the performance and settlement of futures and options contracts, eg, the London Clearing House in London or the Options Clearing Corporation in Chicago.

Clearing House Automated Payment System (CHAPS)

System in the UK for making cash payments in sterling. The recipient receives same day funds.

Clearing House Electronic Sub Register System (CHESS)

Organisation for holding shares in dematerialised form in Australia.

Clearing House Funds

Also known as next–day funds, the method by which the largest number of trades in the US market settled prior to 22 February 1996. The proceeds of a trade settled in clearing house funds are available for disbursement on the day following the actual settlement date.

Clearing House Interbank Payments System (CHIPS)

A US real–time final payments system for business–to–business transactions. CHIPS clears and settles transactions for large value payment transactions worldwide.

Clearing Member

A member of an exchange who undertakes to settle the derivatives business which is registered in its name at the clearing organisation.

Clearing Organisation
The clearing organisation acts as the guarantor of the performance and settlement of contracts that are traded on an exchange or OTC.

Clearing System
A system for transferring bonds and cash between buyers and sellers. Transfers of bonds are usually made by book entry transfer. The system may be a department of an investment exchange or it may be a separate entity. See *Clearing House*.

Clearnet
The sole clearing organisation and central counterparty for markets operated by EURONEXT.

Clearstream
CSD and clearing house for Eurobonds and German securities – based in Luxembourg and Frankfurt. Created by a merger of Cedel Bank and Deutsche Börse Clearing.

Click
Marketed by OM London Exchange, it is a computer based trading platform.

Client
All people with whom an authorised person does business. Comprises market counterparties and customers.

Client Agreement Letter
A legal agreement between client and broker, setting out terms and conditions for the broking arrangement.

Client Money

Money belonging to clients which an investment business is holding. It could either be free money or settlement money and in either case it must be kept in a bank account separate from the firm's own money.

Client Money Calculation

The daily calculation that a firm must do to check that it has the required amount in its client money bank accounts.

Client Money Reconciliation

Every 25 business days, the firm must reconcile its internal client bank account records, with those maintained by the bank.

Client Money Requirement

The sum of individual customers credit balances and the total margined transaction requirement.

Clients Assets

Securities or other assets held by an agent on behalf of customers, and not constituting part of their balance sheet assets.

Clients' Ledgers

The Clients' Securities Ledger and the Clients' Cash Ledger which record, respectively, clients' securities and cash positions with the broking firm.

Client Transaction Account

An account opened by a firm with an exchange, clearing house or intermediate broker. Used for recording margined transactions undertaken by the firm for its client.

CLOB

Dealing system of the Singapore Stock Exchange.

Close (Out)
A purchase if the initial transaction was a sale and vice versa in order to extinguish commitments to the markets.

Close Company
A company where five or fewer people and their associates (eg, families) control over 50% of the votes.

Closed End Fund
A collective investment scheme which has a fixed capital, or a share capital which can be changed only after the completion of certain formalities.

Closed Competition
A form of competition where there is a perception that there must be a winner and a loser

Closing
The procedure whereby obligations under an existing position in a derivative are cancelled by undertaking a transaction which is the reverse of the original one.

Closing Date
The last date by which a new issue should be taken up and paid for.

Closing Day
In a new bond issue, the day when securities are delivered against payment by syndicate members participating in the offering.

Closing Order
Used if an order must be executed during any official closing period in the market concerned.

Closing Purchase

A position purchased to cancel a sold position already established. See also *Offset*.

Closing Sale

A position sold to cancel a purchased position already established. See also *Offset*.

Closing The Books

A Registrar closing his register for the payment of a dividend etc.

Closing Trade

A trade to reduce an investor's position. A closing buy reduces a short position and a closing sale reduces a long position.

CMA

See *Cash Memorandum Account*.

CME

Chicago Mercantile Exchange.

CMO

See *Central Moneymarkets Office*.

Code of Practice for Approved Persons

Code that supplements the Statements of Principle providing detail on the standards required.

Cold Call

See *Unsolicited Call*.

Collar
(Or cylinder or tunnel or fence or corridor). The sale of a put (or call) option and purchase of a call (or put) at different strikes – typically both out–of–the–money – or the purchase of a cap combined with the sale of a floor. See *Range Forward*.

Collateral
A borrower will pledge collateral (securities, property etc) in order to demonstrate the ability to meet obligations to repay monies loaned.

Collateralised Mortgage Obligations
Bonds backed by a pool of mortgages owned by the issuer. They usually reimburse capital at each coupon payment as per reimbursement of the underlying mortgages.

Collective Investment Schemes
A generic term encompassing authorised unit trusts, common investment funds, OEICs and investment trusts. Also called a *Mutual Fund*.

Collective Investment Schemes Regulations
Industry name for The Financial Services (Regulated Schemes) Regulations 1991 published by FSA.

Co–Manager
A bank or bond house that assists a lead manager in assessing and distributing new bond issues. A co–manager will receive a larger allotment of bonds than the underwriters to an issue.

Combination
An options trade which involves both calls and puts on the same underlying asset.

Combined Code
The code that embodies best corporate governance practice for all public limited companies (plcs) quoted on the London Stock Exchange (LSE). Also known as the *Code of Best Practice*.

Commercial Bank
A bank specialising in the provision of retail banking services to the corporate and individual banking sectors.

Commercial Bills
IOUs issued by companies and usually guaranteed ('accepted') by a bank. Also known as trade bills, they do not pay interest and are, therefore, issued at a discount to nominal value. They have varying maturities. If they are eligible bills, it means that the Bank of England is prepared to purchase them in the money markets.

Commercial Paper (CP)
A short–term debt instrument issued by a company. Often issued as part of a longer term programme. It is an example of a money market instrument.

COMMEX
Commodities Exchange for New York.

Commission
A fee paid to an agent for services rendered, and often expressed as a percentage of the value of the deal.

Commodities Exchange Act
US legislation governing the commodities and futures markets.

Commodity
Any item that can be bought and sold. Taken to refer to Exchange–traded items including sugar, wheat, soya beans, coffee and tin.

Commodity Futures
Contracts to supply quantities of the underlying commodity at a future date.

Commodity Price Risk
This is the risk of an adverse movement in the price of a commodity.

Common Stock
The US term for securities which represent ownership in a corporation. The two most important common stockholder rights are the voting right and dividend right. Common stockholder's claims on corporate assets are subordinate to those of bondholders preferred stockholders and general creditors. See *Equity Shares*.

Company
A business entity, ownership of which is divided into units called shares, which are owned by persons called shareholders who have limited liability. The business is managed by persons called directors.

Company Representative
Name given to employee of a financial services provider who is only allowed to recommend that company's products.

Compensation Scheme
See *Investors Compensation Scheme*.

Competent Authority (The)
The FSA acting in its capacity as the Listing Authority.

Competition Commission
Statutory body responsible for investigating mergers and takeovers in the UK to ascertain that they are not against the public interest. This is normally considered in terms of the impact of the merger on competition in the relevant sector. Formerly called the Monopolies and Mergers Commission, it investigates a merger at the instigation of the Secretary of State for Trade and Industry and will recommend whether the merger should be cleared or blocked. See also *Office of Fair Trading*.

Complaints Bureau
An FSA service provided for customers who have made a written complaint to a member firm and are still dissatisfied.

Complaints Procedure
The FSA procedure whereby customer complaints about late payments and other inefficiencies by brokers can be made. To start with, the complaint would be made to a firm, and if the customer is still not happy to the FSA itself.

Complex Delivery
See *Many–to–Many (MTM)*.

Compliance Officer
Person appointed within an authorised firm to be responsible for ensuring compliance with the rules.

Compliance Risk
The risk to earnings or capital from violations, or non–conformance with laws, rules, regulations, prescribed practices or ethical standards.

Compound Interest
Interest calculated each period on the amount outstanding at the beginning of that period including any interest previously earned.

Compulsory Purchase Annuity (CPA)
An annuity that has to be bought at retirement for a member of an occupational pension scheme retiring from service.

Concert Party
Investors buying securities in agreement between themselves to suit some wider purpose (eg, to evade the disclosure rules of the Takeover Panel).

Conduct of Business Rules
Rules made by the FSA under the Financial Services and Markets Act 2000, deal mainly with the relationship in firm and client.

Confidence Level
An assessment of the probability that an event will occur.

Confirm
An agreement for each individual Over the Counter (OTC) transaction which has specific terms.

Confirmation
An acknowledgement of a securities transaction between two counterparties.

Confirmation Note
Other descriptions would include *Advice Note* or *Acknowledgement*. Confirmation to a client of the details of a derivatives transaction undertaken for the client.

Confirmation Process
The process of agreeing the details of a transaction with a counterparty.

Conflicts of Interest
Circumstances that arise where a firm has an investment which could encourage it not to treat its clients favourably. The more areas in which a firm is involved the greater the number of potential conflicts.

CONNECT™
Screen based trading system used by LIFFE. It outlines the details of a trade just undertaken; usually sent with 'due despatch' ie, at the end of the next business day.

Consideration
The value of a contract for buying or selling financial instruments before commission and charges have been applied.

Consistency
A basic concept of accounting. A company must prepare its accounts on a consistent basis year on year in order to facilitate comparisons.

Consolidated Stock
Various issues of UK government bonds, the most common of which is 2.5% Consolidated Stock. Also known as *Consols*.

Consolidation
A corporate action in which a company proportionally increases the nominal value of each share whilst decreasing the number of shares in issue. A consolidation is effectively the opposite of a subdivision.

Consolidation of Control
Defined in the *Takeover Code* as an investor owning between 30% and 50% inclusive of the voting rights in a company and adding on more shares. The investor will be required to make a mandatory offer for all the other shares in the company.

Consols
See *Consolidated Stock*.

Consumer Panel
Panel representing users of financial products, which the FSA has set up to consult on proposals for new rules.

Consumer Price Index
A measurement of retail price inflation.

Consumer's Hedge
See *Long Hedge*.

Contango
Where the spot price is lower than longer term prices. See *Backwardation*.

Contingent Liability Transaction (CLT)
Derivatives transactions where the customer will or may be liable to make further payments when the transaction fails to be completed, or upon earlier closing out of the position eg, buying or selling futures or writing options.

Continuation Option
Option offered by an insurance company for a pension scheme member leaving a scheme to take out a life assurance policy (or PHI or PMI policy) without evidence of health.

Continuing Obligations
Rules for listed companies, particularly on disclosure of information on an ongoing basis – detailed in the FSA Handbook.

Continuous Auction
See *Instant Auction*.

Continuous Linked Settlement (CLS)

A proposal to reduce settlement risk in FX transactions.

Continuous Net Settlement

Extends multilateral netting to handle failed trades brought forward –
See *Multilateral Netting*.

Contract

The standard trading unit for a future or an option, also known as a
'lot'. The contract size for UK equity options is 1,000 underlying shares.

Contract for Differences

Contract designed to make a profit or avoid a loss by reference to
movements in the price of an item. The underlying item cannot change
hands.

Contract Note

A document sent to the investor on a purchase or sale being made,
detailing the price at which the shares were bought, sold or redeemed
together with other charges, any conditions of sale and statutory notes.

Contract Size

The amount of the underlying asset which one futures contract
represents.
Example: the contract size for a zinc contract is 25 tonnes. This means
that underlying one zinc future is 25 tonnes of zinc which the investor
has the obligation to buy (long future) or sell (short future).

Contract Specification

The legal documentation that details a futures or options contract such
as trading times, delivery procedures, quantities of underlying
items/products per one contract etc. The use of contract specifications
leads to standardised products and thus maintains liquidity.

Contracted Out Money Purchase Scheme (COMPS)
A money purchase scheme which is contracted out of SERPS by providing protected rights.

Contracted Out Rebate
The amount by which employers' and employees' NICs are reduced for employees who are contracted out through an occupational scheme.

Contractual Capacity
The legal ability to make a contract.

Contractual Income Collection
The policy by which global custodians agree to credit income on or after a pre–determined number of days after the official pay–date irrespective of the actual date of receipt.

Contractual Settlement Date Accounting (CSDA)
Global custodians will, in certain conditions and in pre–determined countries, give clients good cash value for securities trades irrespective of the settlement of the securities themselves. See *Actual Settlement Date Accounting*.

Control
1. Legal: usually owning more than 50% of the voting rights of a company or having the right to appoint directors to the company's board with a majority of voting rights.
2. Takeover Code: owning 30% of a company gives effective control. If an investor obtains control of a company covered by the Code, they must make a mandatory offer to buy out all the other shareholders.
3. FSA Handbook: see *Controlling Shareholder*.

Controlled Functions
Activities for which individuals require approval from the FSA. There are 27 categories.

Controlling Director
A director who controls or owns 20% or more of the ordinary shares of his or her employing company. The shares of associates (eg, family members) are taken into account. Special restrictions apply to such directors who are members of occupational pension schemes.

Controlling Shareholder
An investor who holds 30% or more of a listed company's shares. This will not be allowed unless it can be demonstrated that any conflict of interest with other shareholders will be suitably managed.

Conventional Gilts
Any gilts except index–linked ones.

Convergence
The movement of the cash asset price toward the futures price as the expiration date of the futures contract approaches.

Conversion
A type of corporate action involving, for example, the transformation of a debt security into shares or other forms of debt.

Conversion Factor
Income shares and accumulation shares are linked by a conversion factor so from day to day the two types of share will always move in line. Each time the income units are quoted xd the conversion factor is adjusted, so there will be a proportionate difference between the two types of share. The conversion factor tells you that each accumulation unit is the equivalent of that number of income shares. The factor is calculated to 5 significant figures.

Conversion Notice
Notice given by a shareholder in an OEIC to the ACD to convert from a holding of one type of share to another. Charges may be made for such conversions.

Conversion Period
The period during which a bondholder may convert the bond into shares.

Conversion Premium
A measure of the effective cost of acquiring the underlying shares by either converting the bond or buying the shares in the market.

Conversion Price
The price, specified in the issue prospectus, at which the nominal amount of the bond may be converted into the shares.

Conversion Rate
The number of shares that result from the conversion of one bond.

Conversion Ratio
The number of shares into which a given amount (eg, £100 or $1,000) of the nominal value of a convertible can be converted.

Convertible
A convertible is a debt instrument, paying a fixed coupon, which offers the holder the right (but not the obligation) to covert into the underlying shares of a company (usually, but not always, the issuing company).

Convertible Bond
A bond that can be converted at the choice of the bondholder into the shares of the issuer. The bondholder receives redemption proceeds on maturity of a bond which has not been converted.

Convertible Currency
One that can be freely exchanged for other currencies.

Convertible Debt
The lender has the option to convert the debt into ordinary shares in the company rather than receiving repayment in cash.

Convertible Gilt
UK government bond, the holder of which has the option to convert the bond into another issue of government bonds rather than receive repayment in cash.

Convertible Loan Stock
A fixed interest loan stock where the investor has the right to convert it or part of it into an agreed number of shares at a fixed time.

Convertible Securities
Securities issued in one form with provisions allowing them to be converted into securities in another form, eg, debt instruments that can be converted into common or preferred shares, subject to specific circumstances.

Convertible Term Assurance
Type of term assurance which carries an option to convert to whole life or endowment.

Convertible Unsecured Loan Stock (CULS)
A convertible bond which is not backed by any specific asset.

Convexity
A second order measure of the exposure of fixed income products to interest rate risk by calculating how much duration changes with respect to interest rates.

Conveyancing

The legal transfer of ownership of land or property, normally carried out by a solicitor or licensed conveyancer.

Cooling-Off Period

The period in which investors have the chance to change their mind and withdraw from a life assurance policy or some other financial service – 14 days.

COREDEAL

Electronic market established for trading in international bonds.

Core Service

Dealing, arranging or managing certain financial instruments. Derived from the Investment Services Directive (ISD).

CORES

Computer dealing system of the Tokyo Stock Exchange.

Corporate Action

A term given to an action taken by a company which distributes cash, stock or a combination to shareholders or stock holders, usually in proportion to the investor's holding (eg, benefit distribution) or which changes the nature or description of a company's stock (ie, stock event). Corporate actions include dividends, rights issues, redemptions, consolidations, placings, etc.

Corporate Action (CA) Type

These are:

CAP – Capitalisations   CHD – Cash Dividends
CPP – Call Payments/Partly Paid   CRP – Capital Repayments
CSL – Consolidations   CVN – Conversions
DRW – Drawings   ENF – Enfranchisements
ESD – Enhanced Scrip Dividends   ITP – Interest Payments
OOE – Open Offer Entitlements   OOO – Other types of Open Offer
PPU – Pari Passu   RII – Rights Issues
SCD – Scrip Dividends   SDV – Subdivisions
SOA – Schemes of Arrangements   SUB – Subscriptions
RDM – Redemptions   TKO – Takeovers

Corporate Debt Securities

Bonds or commercial paper issued by private corporations.

Corporate Finance

General title which covers activities such as raising cash through new issues of securities and mergers/acquisitions.

Corporate Governance

The mechanism that seeks to ensure that directors run companies in the best long term interests of their shareholders. Also see *Combined Code*.

Corporate Investor

A company that holds shares in another company.

Corporation Tax

Taxation paid by companies on their assessable profits.

Corporation Tax Rates

The rate at which companies pay corporation tax. It may vary depending on the size of the company, a small company may pay a lower rate than a large one.

Correlation
The extent to which two sets of data move in line with each other.

Correlation Coefficient
Measure of the closeness of the relationship between two variables.

Correlation Simulation
A VaR measure that calculates the volatility of each risk factor from historical data and estimates its effect on the portfolio to give an overall composite VaR that includes all risk factors.

Correspondent
A financial organisation that regularly performs services for another in a place or market to which the other does not have direct access. Banks may, for example, use correspondent banks to hold their foreign currency accounts.

Corridor
See *Collar*.

Cost–Based Provisioning
A means of accounting for the financial impact of operational risk that assumes that all operational losses result in increased cost and then uses an overall estimate to represent this cost.

Cost of Carry
The net running cost of holding a position (which may be negative) – for example the cost of borrowing cash to buy a bond, less the coupon earned on the bond while holding it. See *Position*.

Council of Mortgage Lenders
Voluntary association of mortgage lenders, which regulates the activities of its members and produces the Code of Mortgage Lending.

Counter Currency
See *Variable Currency*.

Counterparty
One of the parties to a transaction – either the buyer or the seller.

Counterparty Credit Risk
The risk of loss from one party to a contract failing to fulfil its obligations.

Counterparty Risk
See *Counterparty Credit Risk*.

Counterparty Risk Requirement (CRR)
Part of the financial resources for both *ISD* and *non–ISD firms*, requiring that timely provision is made in case of bad debts/non–deliveries.

Countervalue
The cash amount to be received in return for a specified delivery of securities.

Coupon
1. The annual interest rate paid on a bond. The coupon rate is expressed as a percentage of the nominal (par) value.
2. The physical coupon detached from a bearer certificate in order to claim a dividend or interest payments.

Coupon Clipping
The process by which coupons are detached from the certificates prior to collection of the interest payment.

Coupon Payment Period
The time that has elapsed between two consecutive interest payments on a bond.

Coupon Stripping
Selling on each of the coupons separately as zero coupon bonds in their own right.

Coupon Swap
An interest rate swap in which one leg is fixed–rate and the other is floating rate. See *Basis Swap*.

Covariance
Measure of the co–movement between two variables (eg, security prices). It is particularly important in modern portfolio theory which examines the relationships of individual shares within a portfolio of shares (or other securities).

Cover
To remove the risk of an exposure by reversing the position or hedging (dealing in an instrument with a similar but opposite risk profile).

Covered Interest Arbitrage
Creating a loan or deposit in one currency by combining a loan or deposit in another currency with a forward foreign exchange swap.

Covered Option
An option bought or sold offsetting an existing underlying position. See also *Naked Option*.

Covered Sale (Write)

The situation where an option writer has existing holdings to cover a position, eg, where the writer of a call owns the underlying stock or where the writer of a put is either short of stock or has sufficient cash (or near cash) to cover an assignment.

Covered Warrant

A call option on the shares of a company issued by a bank. The bank hedges its position in the underlying stock, generally by holding shares of the company in question.

Covered Writing

The sale of call options where the seller owns the stock which would be required to cover the delivery, if called.

CP

See *Commercial Paper*.

CPU

See *Claims Processing Unit*.

Crawling Peg

Management of a currency at a fixed exchange rate against another currency/currencies with regular adjustments to that fixed rate. See *Adjustable Peg*.

Credit Control

The regulation of credit of banks and other financial institutions in the pursuit of monetary policy.

Credit Creation

Ability of private sector banks to expand the money supply by creating credit.

Credit Default Swap

A bilateral financial contract in which one counterparty (the protection buyer) pays a periodic or one–off fee (typically expressed in basis points on the notional amount), in return for a contingent payment by the other counterparty (the protection seller) following a credit event of a reference entity.

Credit Derivatives

These are contracts designed to transfer the credit risk on loans or other assets from one party to another. There are four main types of contract: credit default swaps, total return swaps, credit–linked notes and credit spread options.

Credit Event

An event such as bankruptcy, insolvency, receivership, material adverse restructuring of debt, or failure to meet payment obligations when due.

Credit Exposure

The amount that can potentially be lost if a debtor defaults on their obligations.

Credit Limits

The maximum limits for lending set by financial institutions to prevent too much lending to, or investment in, a company or individual in a particular firm.

Credit Rating

For example, AAA issued by companies such as Standard & Poors, and Moodys to rate the level of security of a bond or note issue.

Credit Risk

The risk that a counterparty will be unable to perform his side of an agreed contract.

Credit Risk Premium

The difference between the interest rate a firm pays when it borrows and the interest rate on a default–free security, such as a government bond.

Creditor

Person to whom money is owed.

CREPON

A CREST member which acts as a pooled nominee, allowing members, such as market makers, to retain anonymity by holding stock in CREST but not appearing in the register.

CREST

The organisation in the UK that holds UK and Irish company shares in dematerialised form and clears and settles trades in UK and Irish company shares.

CRESTCo

The owner of CREST, a consortium of firms who have provided the necessary capital to fund the development of the system.

CREST Claim Settlement Date

The intended settlement date for any claim transaction raised by CREST. It is equal to the pay date for the distribution (if there is one) or else the ex–date.

CREST Courier and Sorting Service (CCSS)

The organisation responsible for the controlled transportation of documents, supporting the administration for settling deliveries in certificated securities.

CREST Delivery Interest
An English law security which represents an underlying international security that is held in an overseas depository by CREST International Nominees.

CREST Depository Interest
An English law security which represents an underlying international security that is held in an overseas depositary by CREST International Nominees.

CREST Member
A person or organisation participating in CREST (typically a broker, institutional investor, custodian, market maker, money broker, or inter–dealer broker) who holds stock in accounts with the system and whose name is on the register as the owner of securities.

CREST Member Accounts
One or more separate designations (identities) set up by a CREST member for holding stock. The member account facility enables members to segregate holdings of different kinds, eg, individual client holdings, although the member's name is on the register for each member account, designated by that code.

CREST Operator
The organisation at the centre of CREST responsible for system security, for settlement and for maintaining records of its members' stock holdings and reconciling them with the records of legal title held by company registrars. It also provides various functions to facilitate settlement of transactions between its members.

CREST Participant
A person or organisation that has a formal relationship with CREST, eg, members, registrars, receiving agents, payment banks, regulators, the Inland Revenue, and information providers.

CREST Personal Member
Private clients who are sponsored members of CREST.

CREST Sponsored Member
A participant within CREST who holds stock in stock accounts in CREST and whose name appears on the share register. Unlike a member, a sponsored member is not their own user. The link to CREST is provided by another user who sponsors the sponsored member.

CREST Stock Account
Each member account contains a stock account reflecting each individual line of stock held.

CREST Transfer Form
Stock transfer form for settlement through CREST of certificated sales.

CREST User
A participant within CREST who has an electronic link to CREST.

Criminal Justice Act 1993
Act which contains legislation on Insider Dealing and Money Laundering.

Critical Illness Policy
A policy which pays out on the diagnosis of a critical illness as defined by the policy. Where the policy is part of an endowment or whole–life plan, the payment may be made on earlier maturity or death.

Cross
See *Cross Rate.*

Cross Border Custody
Cross border custody occurs where the securities are actually held in custody in a country different from the domicile of the owner of the securities. It is not necessarily a result of cross border trading or settlement.

Cross Border Delivery (XDL)
The transaction type for delivering securities between a CREST member and a participant in another CSD.

Cross Border Delivery Confirm (XDC)
The transaction type for confirming delivery of stock overseas, based on CREST's receiving a SWIFT message. This transaction type is not visible to CREST members.

Cross Border Reversal (XDR)
The transaction type for returning securities to a CREST member if it is not possible to complete their delivery to a participant in another CSD.

Cross Border Settlement
Cross border settlement occurs where the settlement takes place in a country different from the domicile of one or both trading parties.

Cross Border Trade
A cross border trade occurs where the trading parties are in different countries.

Cross Currency Interest Rate Swap
An interest rate swap where the interest payments are in two different currencies and the exchange rate, for the final settlement, is agreed at the outset of the transaction.

Cross Default

The right of a lender to accelerate the repayment of a debt if the borrower defaults on the repayment of another debt.

Cross Rate

An exchange rate between two currencies that does not involve a standard reference currency such as the USD.

Crossing

When a firm has both the buy and the sell sides of an order. There are rules about derivative exchanges governing the crossing of trades. Also known as *Matching* and *Self Trading*.

CSCE

Coffee, Sugar and Cocoa Exchange, New York.

CSD

Central securities depository; an institution that provides central facilities for book–entry holdings and transfers of securities.

CTD

See *Cheapest to Deliver*.

CTF

CREST Transfer Form. The paper transfer form that authorises a company registrar to register shares into a CREST membership.

CULS

A bond that can be converted into shares of the issuing company on terms specified at the time of issue. Also called a Convertible Bond or Convertible Unsecured Loan Stock.

Cum

Latin for "with". Refers to the right to receive a benefit or entitlement on securities that have been purchased.

Cum Distribution

Unit trusts are assumed to be cum distribution (ie, the buyer is entitled to the next income distribution and the seller is not) unless they are expressly stated to be ex–distribution.

Cum Dividend/Cum Interest

The purchaser of the bond or share is entitled to receive the next interest or dividend payment. The alternative is ex–dividend or ex–interest, where the seller retains the right to receive the next interest or dividend payment.

Cum Period

During a benefit distribution, the period before ex–date when a buyer of stock is normally contractually entitled to a benefit, whether or not he is on the register as at record date.

Cum Rights Price

Share price before a rights issue takes place – the price with the entitlement to the rights issue.

Cum Scrip Price

Share price before a scrip issue takes place – the price with the entitlement to the scrip issue.

Cumulative Preference Share

If a company fails to pay a preference dividend the entitlement to the dividend accumulates and the arrears of the preference dividend must be paid before any ordinary dividend.

Cumulative Probability Distribution
The probability that any one of a series of numbers will be no greater than a particular number.

Currency Exposure
Currency exposure exists if assets are held or income earned, in one currency while liabilities are denominated in another currency. The position is exposed to changes in the relative values of the two currencies such that the cost of the liabilities may be increased or the value of the assets or earning decreased.

Currency Futures
Contracts calling for delivery of a specific amount of a foreign currency at a specified future date in return for a given amount of, say, US Dollars.

Currency Swap
An exchange of a series of cashflows in one currency for a series of cashflows in another currency, at agreed intervals over an agreed period. See *Interest Rate Swap*.

Current Account (Balance Of Payments)
A statement of imports and exports of visibles and invisibles.

Current Assets
Obligations of a company that are payable within 12 months of the balance sheet date; examples are bank overdrafts, short term loans and accounts payable.

Current Exposure
The current obligation outstanding.

Current Liabilities

The obligations of a company that are payable within 12 months of the balance sheet date, for example, bank overdrafts, short–term loans and accounts payable.

Current Maturity

The remaining life of a bond from today to the redemption date.

Current Ratio

This is an accounting ratio, which is normally defined as current assets divided by creditors falling due within one year. It is designed to assess short term company solvency. Put simply, if it exceeds one, then the value of current assets is larger than the value of the short term creditors, indicating that the company is able to pay its short term debts as they fall due.

Current Yield

A measure of the annual income on a bond as a percentage of the price of the bond.

CUSIP

The system created by the Committee on Uniform Securities Identification Procedures to assign unique identifying numbers to securities in the US and Canadian markets.

Custodian

Organisation which holds clients assets in safe custody, ensures that they are not released without proper authorisation and ensures that timely and accurate collection of dividends and other benefits.

Custody

The storing and safekeeping of securities together with maintaining accurate records of ownership. The term also implies management of those securities such as the collection of dividends.

Custody Risk

The risk of loss on securities in safekeeping, (custody) as a result of the custodian's insolvency, negligence, misuse of assets, fraud, poor administration or inadequate record keeping.

Customer Agreement

A written contract detailing the basis on which services are to be provided to the customer by the firm.

Customer Borrowing

Funds lent to private customers by member firms.

Customer – Intermediate

A customer who is assumed to understand the workings of the investment world and therefore receives less protection from the Conduct of Business Rules than a private customer.

Customer Order Priority

FSA Rule requiring a firm to deal with a customer and their own account orders fairly and in due turn.

Customer – Private

A customer who is assumed to be financially unsophisticated and therefore receives more protection from the Conduct of Business Rules.

Cycle

The expiry dates applicable to a class of options. There are three cycles in London: Jan/Apr/Jul/Oct; Feb/May/Aug/Nov; Mar/Jun/Sep/Dec.

Cylinder

See *Collar*.

D

Daily Cash Sweep
The action of investing a client's cash balance that would otherwise lie idle overnight, in an interest bearing deposit or investment vehicle. Generally performed on an overnight basis.

Daily Official List (DOL)
A daily publication of the London Stock Exchange which lists the trading prices of securities traded in the main market.

Data Exchange Manual (DEX)
The document that gives full details of CREST messages and interface specifications for the file transfer interface.

Data Protection Act 1998
Legislation governing how data may be held and rights of access to it.

Dated Stock
An interest bearing security that has a stated date for redemption or repayment.

DAX

Index of the German Stock Exchange.

Day Count Fraction

The proportion of a year by which an interest rate is multiplied in order to calculate the amount accrued or payable.

Daylight Exposure

The deliverer of securities or payer of countervalue is exposed to the risk that the counterparty may default on his obligations at some stage during that business day.

Daylight Limit

The maximum size of position a dealer is allowed to take during the day.

DBR

The transaction type for a delivery for a delivery by value return.

DBV

See *Delivery by Value*.

Dealer

Individual or firm that acts as principal in all transactions, buying for his own account.

Dealing

Entering into transactions in investments either for others or on one's own account.

Dealing Ahead

Practice where a firm deals for itself, knowing that it is going to publish a recommendation or piece of research about a security. The firm is restricted from doing so subject to five exceptions of which the most important is that it is able to disclose in the research that it may have dealt. Also known as Front Running.

Debenture

A secured fixed interest loan; these are usually dated to be redeemed 10–40 years hence. Interest on this form of loan has to be paid by a company whether it makes a profit or not.

Debenture Stock

Bonds issued with a fixed charge.

Debt/Equity Ratio

A measurement of gearing defined as:

$$\frac{\text{Borrowings + Preference shares}}{\text{Ordinary shareholders funds}} \times 100\%$$

For example, the debt equity ratio for XYZ Ltd is:

$$\frac{\text{(loan stock) + (preference shares)}}{\text{(shareholders funds)} - \text{(preference shares)}} \times 100\%$$

$$\frac{\$60m + \$10m}{\$120m - \$10m} \times 100\%$$

$$= 63.6\%$$

Debt Management Office

Department of the Treasury responsible for new issues of gilts.

Debt Securities

Securities created by the issuer as evidence of a loan made to it, such as, bonds, certificates of deposit (CDs), commercial paper.

Debtors

Amounts owed by the customers of a company and other third parties. Debtors are shown as part of current assets in a company's balance sheet.

Decision Notice

Notice sent by the Regulatory Decisions Committee of the FSA advising a firm or approved person of a disciplinary decision taken against them.

Declaration Day

The expiry date of an option contract. Used by the LME. See *Expiry Date*.

Decreasing Term Assurance

Type of term assurance where the amount of cover decreases over the life of the policy. Often used in conjunction with repayment mortgages.

Deep Discount Bond

Stock issued at a low price compared with par value and redemption price. The rate of interest and the running yield are low, indeed may be zero, with most or all of the benefit to the investor coming from the capital gain between the issue and redemption prices. The benefit of deep discount bonds to the issuing company is the low interest commitment; to the high rate taxpayer they provide (relatively low tax) capital gain instead of (more highly taxed) income. See *Zero Coupon Bond*.

Default

A breach of the terms of a bond issue, eg, inability to pay interest when due.

Default Risk
The risk that the issuer of a bond will be unable to meet the payments of interest or the repayment of the capital.

Deferred Annuity
Annuity which does not start immediately.

Deferred Liabilities
Obligations that are repayable after more than one year. The main categories are the longer term borrowings of the company or the bonds issued by the company.

Deferred Share
A class of share where the holder is entitled to a dividend only if the ordinary shareholders have been paid a specified minimum dividend.

Defined Benefit Scheme
A pension scheme in which the rules define the benefits to be paid. Normally such schemes pay benefits based on a member's final pensionable earnings and number of years' service and are often known as final salary schemes.

Defined Contribution Scheme
A scheme where the contributions made by employer and employee are agreed and benefits are normally based on the accumulated funds and the annuity purchased with them. An alternative term is money purchase scheme.

Definitive Bond
Any bond issued in final form. It is used particularly in reference to permanent bonds for which Temporary Bonds or Interim Certificates were issued.

DEL
The basic CREST transaction type for a simple (one–to–one) delivery, involving a transfer of stock, stock and cash, or cash between two CREST members.

Deliver Out Repo
Conventional classic repo; the buyer takes delivery of the collateral.

Deliverable Basket
The list of securities which meets the delivery standards of futures contracts.

Deliveries by Value (DBV)
A CREST transaction, created by matching instructions, in which a package of securities up to a nominated value is transferred as overnight collateral between a borrower and lender. The transaction is for same–day settlement with collateral being returned the next morning.

Delivery
The satisfying of an assignment in either a put or call option by delivery of stock. Alternatively, the settlement of a futures contract during delivery month.

Delivery Repo
The lender of cash takes delivery of the collateral.

Delivery by Value Return (DBR)
A set of special transactions created automatically by CREST at the settlement of a delivery by value (DBV), with a settlement date of the following day.

Delivery versus Payment (DVP)
The simultaneous and irrevocable transfer of ownership of an asset in exchange for the equivalent assured countervalue in same day funds.

Delta
The amount by which an options price will move for a given movement in the underlying asset. Also known as the hedge ratio.

Delta Hedge
See *Delta Neutral*.

Delta Neutral
Also known as Delta Hedged, it describes when the net delta of a portfolio of options and futures is zero. A position such as this means that there is no exposure to directional movements in the underlying portfolio. This does not, however, mean that there is no risk attached to such a position. Option deltas change for a variety of reasons, and so the portfolio must be constantly readjusted in order to maintain a delta neutral position.

Demand Deposit Account
An account that gives its owner the right to withdraw funds from a commercial bank on demand.

Demand Repo
A repo trade that has no fixed maturity term and is renewed daily at one or both counterparties' agreement.

Dematerialisation
Replacement of paper share certificates by electronic storage, eg, CREST.

Dematerialised
The term used to describe stock which is held in electronic accounts, rather than issue paper certificates.

Dematerialised Shares
Shares which are recorded in a central computer system and for which no certificates exist. Transfer is by book entry transfer.

Demutualisation
Process by which a mutual organisation such as a building society or insurance company converts into a limited liability company.

Depositary (Depository)
An organisation such as a bank or insurance company designated as an authorised person in whom property of a UK OEIC is entrusted. Broadly similar to a trustee of a unit trust.

Depositary Interest
Investors' interest in shares of a company which have been issued to and held by a Custodian or Depositary. Shareholders' interests are uncertificated and ownership is evidenced by an entry on a Register maintained by the Custodian or Registrar.

Depositary Receipts
Bearer instruments created to confirm that an underlying instrument has been lodged with the depositary. American Depositary Receipts are created to provide an instrument giving non–US holders rights over non–US securities, which can be traded in the manner familiar to the American markets. The holder of the receipt is entitled to all the benefits of ownership of the underlying security and can convert back at will.

Deposit Linking
A facility which enables a CREST member (typically a broker) to link a standard intra–CREST delivery (typically to a market maker) to particular physical transfers into the CREST system.

Deposit Protection Fund

Fund set up under the Banking Act 1975 to pay compensation in respect of deposits held by a bank which goes into liquidation. Now part of the general Investors' Compensation Scheme.

Deposit Set

A group of documents, including transfer form and stock (ie, either certificate or certified transfer form), used for settling a sold bargain involving certificated holdings.

Depository Trust Clearing Corporation

The major Clearing Agent/Central Depository for US domestic equities.

Depository Trust Corporation (DTC)

A depository for USA company shares.

Depreciation

Amounts charged to the profit and loss account to reflect the wearing out of a fixed asset over its useful life.

Example: a company buys a photocopier for £100,000 with an expected useful life of five years. It will charge the £100,000 cost to the profit and loss account over a five year period. The simplest way to do this is to charge £20,000 expense per year. This is called straight line depreciation. The purpose of depreciation is to comply with the accruals concept. Since the benefit of the photocopier is received over a five year period, the cost of acquiring the photocopier is charged against profits over a five year period.

Derivative

An instrument encompassing options, futures or contracts for differences, whose price is derived from, and dependent upon, the price of an underlying asset.

Designated Client Bank Account
Client bank account which contains the money of one or more customers and the account title includes the word 'designated'. Each customer's money is segregated from the money belonging to others.

Designated Investment Business
Specified categories of investment business under FSMA 2000. The Conduct of Business rules do not apply to those activities which are not so defined, ie:
a)   Deposit taking – banking.
b)   General insurance – insurance on car, home or similar.
c)   Pure protection products – life policy for a maximum of 10 years and having no surrender value. If it is a single premium policy, it may have a surrender value, but not exceeding the amount of the premium.

Designated Investment Exchange (DIE)
Overseas exchange recognised by the Financial Services Authority as having sufficiently similar standards (efficiency, transparency, liquidity, etc) to those of Recognised Investment Exchanges.

Designated Nominee Account
Individual beneficial owners' securities are registered in the name of the nominee company and will have a designation added. This designation identifies the beneficial owner eg, ABC Nominees Ltd (AO1 account).

Designated Professional Body (DPB)
Status granted by the FSA to organisations such as the Law Society and Institutes of Accountants. Their members are authorised through this membership to conduct a limited amount of investment business.

Designated Time Net Settlement (DNS)
The settlement of payment obligations at an agreed time or times on a net basis.

Detective Controls
Operational controls that detect errors once they have occurred.

Deutsche Börse
The German Stock Exchange.

Deutsche Börse Clearing
Now merged with Cedal Bank to form Clearstream.

Devaluation
A decrease in the value of a currency against other currencies. See *Depreciation*.

DEX
See *Data Exchange Manual*.

Diagonal Spread
An option spread where one option is bought and another sold. The sold option has a different strike price and expiry date from the bought. The spread will be constructed with either all calls or all puts on the same underlying asset.

Difference Account
Sets out details of a derivatives transaction, (difference = profit or loss).

Dilution
An increase in the number of shares issued by a company which will reduce the earnings per share and the percentage interest of existing investors.

Dilution Levy

An ACD may be permitted to require payment of a dilution levy because of reduction in value of OEIC property as a result of costs incurred in dealing in investments and any spread between buying and selling prices.

Direct Credit Risk

The simple risk of loan default where money is lent to a customer.

Direct Loss

The direct financial penalty that a firm incurs as a result of a risk being realised.

Direct Market Participant

A broker, broker/dealer or any direct member of an exchange.

Direct Market Risk Factors

The factors that have a direct bearing on an instrument's price, such as the financial performance of a company and the health of its balance sheet.

Direct Offer Advertisement

An advertisement which invites investors to enter into an investment agreement, and specifies how such a response is to be made.

Direct Offer Financial Promotion

Form of promotion where customers can commit themselves without subsequent discussion. Would include tear off forms with magazine adverts or anything similar.

Direct Placement

Selling a new issue by placing it with one or several institutional investors rather than offering it for sale publicly.

Direct Quote

Arises in the foreign currency markets if the variable currency is the US dollar and the other currency is fixed as one unit.

Example: sterling is quoted directly against the dollar. This means that the quote is always expressed in terms of £1 and the number of dollars it takes to buy £1 or the number of dollars £1 will buy. Most currencies are quoted indirectly against the dollar, rather than directly.

Direct Securities Lending

Securities lending takes place between the institution holding the securities and the borrower.

Direction

A mandatory warning issued by the FSA Investigation Department when a breach of rules has either occurred or might occur.

Directors

Those individuals appointed to run a company by the shareholders. Directors have legal responsibilities for the proper running of the company. Formerly administered by the Stock Exchange, it is now the responsibility of the FSA, as Listing Authority.

Directors' Model Code

The Model Code for Securities transactions by directors of listed companies. This will stipulate that a company director may not deal in company shares at certain times.

Directors Report

Legally required part of a company's annual report. The directors must summarise the company's performance over the year, its future prospects and certain other required disclosures.

Dirty Price

The price in a bond transaction which includes accrued interest. Now prices are quoted "clean" with accrued interest added–on.

Disallowed Expenditure

Expenses such as entertainment expenditure and depreciation, charged by a company in arriving at its accounting profit before tax. They are not allowable as a deduction when calculating its taxable profits on which its corporation tax charge is based. Although a company is not allowed to charge depreciation, it is permitted to charge in its place capital allowances which is effectively the same thing.

Disclaimer

A notice or statement intending to limit or avoid potential legal liability.

Discount

1   The difference between the market price of a financial instrument and its par value.
2. The amount by which an option or a future trades below its fair value. See *Backwardation*.

Discount Factor

The number by which a future cashflow must be multiplied in order to calculate its present value.

Discount Instrument

Does not pay a coupon and is therefore always worth less than its face value except when interest rates are negative.

Discount Rate

The percentage rate used to calculate the present value of a future cash flow.

Discount Securities
Non–interest bearing short term securities that are issued at discount and redeemed at maturity for full face value.

Discretionary Customers
Customers who entrust their funds to a firm which is then empowered to invest them without price consultation with the customer. Full customer documentation is required.

Discretionary Fund Management
The investing of clients' money by a member firm on a discretionary basis, ie, customers' specific approval is not needed. Instead, customer leaves specific decisions to manager's discretion.

Discretionary Manager
Portfolio manager who has the power to make investments without the customer's prior approval.

Discretionary Securities Lending
The custodian initiates all lending activities without referral to the beneficial owner.

Discretionary Trust
A trust where the trustees have discretion as to the distribution of the income and capital of the trust.

Disqualification Notice
Notice issued by FSA on an individual prohibiting him from working for anyone conducting investment business.

Distributable Profits
The profits of a company available for payment to the shareholders as a dividend comprises realised profits.

Distribution

A payment made to unit holders out of the unit trust fund's income from its investments. Distributions received in an ISA may be paid out or reinvested within the account.

Distribution Analysis

A statistical means of using historical data to predict future events.

Distribution/Dividend Warrant

A statement issued with an accompanying cheque when a dividend or interest payment is made on securities.

Distributor Fund

An offshore fund which distributes at least 85% of its income.

Diversification

Investment technique of spreading available money over a range of investments to reduce risk.

Dividend

A distribution of profits to the shareholders of a company.

Dividend Cover

Net earnings per share divided by net dividend per share. An accounting ratio whose purpose is to identify how much of a company's profits is being distributed to shareholders and how much is being retained to finance future expansion of the business. A company with a low dividend cover is paying out most of its earnings as dividends. A company with high dividend cover is paying out a smaller percentage of its earnings.

Dividend/Distribution

A payment made to shareholders/unit holders out of the underlying companies' earnings. Dividends/distributions received in a PEP/ISA may be paid out or reinvested within the plan.

Dividend per Share

Annual dividend based on the most recently announced dividend.

Dividend Yield

The dividend yield is the relationship between the dividend per share and the share price. The yield in general relates to a measurement of the return from an investment to its current market price, and is expressed as a percentage. The different types of yield simply use different measurements of the return.

A dividend yield is defined as:

$$\frac{\text{Dividend per share}}{\text{Current market price per share}} \times 100\%$$

For example, the dividend yield for ordinary shares for XYZ Ltd is as follows:

Dividend per share:

$$\frac{\text{Ordinary dividend}}{\text{Number of shares}}$$

$$= \frac{\$4.0m}{12m}$$

$$= \$0.33 \text{ per share}$$

The dividend yield is therefore:

$$\frac{\$0.33 \text{ (Dividend per share)}}{\$11.0 \text{ (Current market price per share)}} \times 100\%$$

$= \underline{3.0\%}$

DNS
See *Designated Time Net Settlement.*

DOL
See *Daily Official List.*

Dollar Repo
Collateral returned at maturity need not be exactly the same as that originally transferred but must be equivalent.

Dollar Roll
Similar to a repo, it is used solely for mortgage–back securities in the US market.

Domestic Bond
A bond issued in the domestic market by a domestic issuer in the domestic currency.

Domicile
The country or territory which is a person's long term permanent home.

Don't Know (DK)
Applies to a securities transaction pending settlement where fundamental data is missing which prevents the receiving party from accepting delivery.

Double-Dated Stocks
Bonds whose issuer has the option to redeem the stock on or between two specific dates.

Double Option Agreement
An agreement between partners or shareholder directors whereby a deceased person's estate has the option to sell his share and the surviving partners have the option to buy his share. It has the same effect as a buy and sell agreement but the business assets will qualify for Inheritance Tax business property relief.

Double Taxation Treaty
An agreement between two countries intended to avoid or limit the double taxation of income. Under the terms of the treaty an investor with tax liabilities in both countries can either apply for a reduction of taxed imposed by one country (generally the country in which the dividends are received) or can credit taxes paid in that country against tax liabilities in the other usually the country where the payment originated.

Double Tax Relief
Relief given for the double taxation which would otherwise occur on income and other profits arising in one country, and which are taxed in that country, and which belong to the resident of another country and would also be taxed in that other country. Relief is given either under the terms of a double tax agreement or through unilateral provisions.

Dow Jones Average
Main share index of share prices used in the USA. Dow Jones compiles daily indices of the share prices quoted on NYSE.

Dow Jones Index
Index of 30 shares from New York Stock Exchange and NASDAQ.

Down–and–In Option

A knock–in option where the trigger is lower than the underlying rate at the start. See *Up–and–In Option, Up–and–Out Option, Down–and–Out Option.*

Down–and–Out Option

A knock–out option where the trigger is lower than the underlying rate at the start. See *Up–and–In Option, Down–and–In Option, Up–and–Out Option.*

Downside

The negative aspect of incurring risk.

Down tick

The last trade in a share is at a price lower than the one before.

Drawee

The person on whom a bill of exchange is drawn.

Drawer

The person who initiates a bill of exchange, which is sent to the drawee for him to acknowledge the debt.

Drawing

A corporate action in which a company redeems (ie, buys back) specific holdings, according to the terms of issue of the security.

Dread Disease

See *Critical Illness Policy.*

Drop Lock FRN

An FRN which converts into another FRN or fixed rate bond once a trigger rate has been reached.

Drop Number

A digit at the end of an identifying reference (eg, bargain reference) which signifies that the transaction is logically associated with an earlier transaction that has the same reference less the identifying digit.

DTB

Deutsche Terminbörse – the German derivatives exchange. It merged with the Swiss derivatives exchange SOFEX to form EUREX.

Dual Capacity

The ability of a firm to act either as principal with the customers when trading or as agent on their behalf. See also *Agent*, *Principal* and *Broker Dealer*.

Dual Currency

A bond denominated in one currency with a coupon and/or maturity value payable in another currency at a predetermined exchange rate.

Dual Input Transaction

CREST transactions that require input and matching of instructions by two parties, ie, simple deliveries (DEL), stock loans (SLO), deliveries by value (DBV) and many–to–many deliveries (MTM). Also know as a matchable transaction.

Dual Pricing

Method of quoting prices on unit trusts where the manager quotes a lower price at which it will buy and a higher price at which it will sell. Charges are included in the difference between the two prices.

Dual Rate

Different exchange rates for a currency, used for different types of transaction.

Due Diligence

The appraisal of a business before it floats on the Stock Exchange, or changes ownership in a corporate finance deal carried out by accountants.

Duration

Measure of the remaining life of bond adjusting for the impact of the coupon.

Duration Weighting

The process of using the modified duration value for bonds to calculate the exact nominal holdings in a spread position.

DVP

See *Delivery versus Payment*.

E

Early Leaver
A person who leaves a pension scheme before normal retirement without being provided with immediate retirement benefits.

Earnings
This is a company's net profit after tax, less minority interests and dividends. In other words it is the profit available for equity holders.

Earnings–Based Measurement
A means of accounting for the financial impact of operational risk by assessing the volatility of earnings after credit and market risk factors have been discounted and attributing this volatility to operational risk factors.

Earnings Cap
A limit to the pensionable earnings on which pension contributions attract tax relief under exempt approved schemes.

Earnings per Share (EPS)

EPS shows the amount of profit earned by the company for each ordinary share. The standard definition is:

$$\frac{\text{Profit after tax and preference dividends}}{\text{Number of ordinary shares in issue}}$$

EPS is therefore the profit available to the ordinary shareholder after the deduction of all costs, taxes and preference dividends, and represents the maximum amount which could be paid out as a dividend from this year's profits.

Earnings Threshold

The maximum level of personal pension contributions for which no earnings evidence is required.

Earnings Yield

The ratio of earnings to the share price. Generally, the lower the earnings yield, the higher company's share price and the more highly rated the company.

EASDAQ

European Association of Securities Dealers Automated Quotation System. Now part of NASDAQ.

EBS

See *Electronic Broking Service*.

ECA Regulations

The Open Ended Investment Companies (Investment Companies with Variable Capital) Regulations, 1996. They are known as ECA Regulations because they were enacted under the European Communities Act 1972.

ECB
European Central Bank.

ECHO
The Exchange Clearing House: a multi–lateral foreign exchange netting system.

ECOFIN
Council of finance ministers of the European Union

Economic & Monetary Union (EMU)
The system that links together the economies and currencies of the participating Euro countries. In January 1999, exchange rates were linked, the Euro became a currency in its own right and the European Central Bank became responsible for centralised monetary policy. See *Euro*.

Economic Cycle
The course an economy conventionally takes as economic growth fluctuates over time. Also known as the business cycle.

Economic Exposure
Exposure to currency movements excluding transaction and translation exposure.

Economic Growth
The growth of GDP or GNP expressed in real terms usually over the course of a calendar year. Often used as a barometer of an economy's health.

Economic Pricing Models
Models that are used to account for the financial impact of operational risk by linking the consequences of operational risk with fluctuations in the firm's share price.

Economies of Scale
The resulting reduction in a firm's unit costs at output as the firm's productive capacity and output increases.

ECP
See *Commercial Paper*.

ECSDA
European Central Securities Depository Association, of which CREST is the UK member.

ECU
European Unit of Account. A so–called 'basket currency' made up of the EU currencies. The forerunner of the euro used by the European Commission for accounting purposes and also for financial transactions such as bond issues and loans.

EDC
See *Electronic Data Capture*.

EDSP
Exchange Delivery Settlement Price is the exchange designated settlement price for delivery (or cash settlement) of the underlying instrument.

Effective Date
The date on which the interest period to which a FRA or swap relates, is to start.

Effective Rate
Also known as Annual Equivalent Rate. The rate which, earned as simple interest over 1 year, gives the same return as compound interest paid more frequently than once annually.

Efficient Frontier
A line connecting the mean–variance efficient portfolios (the best portfolios available from a set of assets).

Efficient Markets Hypothesis
A theory which states that market prices react instantly to all new information, so that no investor can consistently outperform the market portfolio.

Efficient Portfolio
A portfolio which achieves a given return at the lowest risk or which achieves the highest return for a given level of risk.

EFP
See *Exchange of Futures for Physical.*

EGM
Extraordinary General Meeting of a company's shareholders.

Elective Event
Corporate action which requires a choice from the security owner.

ELECTRA
Trading system for the Danish Stock Exchange.

Electronic Broking Service (EBS)
An automated broking system for dealing in currency. EBS was formed in 1993.

Electronic Data Capture
Input into CREST of the details of a stock deposit. See *Stock Deposit.*

Electronic Order Book
The electronic order matching system used as the system for dealing in the shares which comprise the FTSE 100 index.

Electronic Transfer of Title
The process whereby securities transferred in CREST are deemed to be registered at the point they settle. For UK securities and CREST Depository Interests, the legal register of owners comprises a record of investors who hold certificates (the issuer register) and a record of investors who hold shares in dematerialised accounts in CREST (the operator record maintained by CREST). As shares move between accounts in CREST the operator record is updated so that delivery coincides with the change in the record of legal title.

Eligible Bill
A bill of exchange which the Bank of England will take as security when acting as 'lender of last resort' to the banking system.

Eligible Market
A securities market in which a unit trust can invest. Either a market within the EU on which transferable securities are traded or any other market agreed between the unit trust manager and the trustee because it meets certain criteria, eg, adequate liquidity.

Embedded Option
An option which is included as part of a financial product.

Emerging Markets
A term which refers to newer securities markets. Generally these may be relatively illiquid, under–regulated, with poor settlement systems etc. but have attracted high levels of cross–border investment because of their perceived long–term attractions.

Emerging Markets Clearing Corporation
A clearing house for emerging markets securities used by market dealers and brokers.

Emerging Markets Traders Association
An association of investment banks involved in emerging markets trading activities.

EMI
See *European Monetary Institute*.

Employee Share Ownership Plan (AESOP)
A plan established under the Finance Act 2000 by a company providing for 'free' shares to be appropriated to employees without payment or 'partnership' shares to be acquired on behalf of employees out of sums deducted from their salary. A plan which provides for partnership shares may also provide for 'matching' shares to be appropriated to employees, without payment, in proportion to the partnership shares acquired by the employee.

EMU
See *Economic & Monetary Union*.

EMX
Electronic Message Exchange – a service launched by the Association of Unit Trusts and Investment Funds (AUTIF) to allow brokers and financial advisors to communicate electronically with unit trust/OEIC management groups.

End–end
A foreign exchange swap or money–market deal starting on the last working day of a month, lasting for some months and maturing on the last working day of a month.

Endowment Mortgage
Form of mortgage where the lender is only paid the interest on the loan and a separate endowment policy is taken out to provide sufficient funds to repay the loan on maturity.

Endowment Policy
A life policy which pays out on maturity or earlier in the case of death. Saving linked in with a life policy must be held for at least 10 years to get full benefit.

Enforcement Inspectors
FSA employees working within the Monitoring Department. Powers include entering any member firm's office without notice, interviewing any member of staff, and copying any document or computer record.

Enfranchisement
A corporate action in which a company extends voting rights to a non–voting or restricted voting class of shares.

Enhanced Delivery versus Payment (EDVP)
Singapore based settlement system.

Enterprise Investment Scheme (EIS)
Replaced the BES for new shares issued after 31 December 1993 in qualifying companies. Investors can claim income tax relief at 20% on qualifying investments up to £100,000 in any tax year, and also claim 'roll–over' relief for capital gains, giving a maximum effective relief of 60%.

Entitlement
See *Open Offer.*

EONIA
Euro overnight interest rate reference index. It is calculated as the average of the range of overnight interest rates during the day.

Equalisation
The amount of a distribution from a unit trust on newly purchased units which is treated as a return of capital and not income.

Equilibrium
A condition that describes a market in perfect balance, where demand is equal to supply.

Equities Fund
A fund that invests primarily in equity shares

Equity
The share capital of a company. See *Shareholders' Funds*.

Equity Index Swap
An obligation between two parties to exchange cash flows based on the percentage change in one or more stock indices, for a specific period with previously agreed reset dates. The swap is cash settled and based on notional principal amounts. One side of an equity swap can involve a LIBOR reference rate.

Equity Price Risk
The risk of adverse movements in share prices affecting a portfolio.

Equity Repo
A transaction in which two parties agree that one will sell equity securities to the other and (at the same time and as part of the same transaction) commit to repurchase equivalent securities on a specified future date, or at call, at a specified price.

Equity Shares

Shares in a company that are entitled to the balance of profits and assets after all prior charges. Also called ordinary shares or common stock.

Equity/Stock Options

These are contracts based on individual equities or shares. On exercise of the option the specified amount of shares is exchanged between the buyer and the seller through the clearing organisation. See *Traded Option.*

Equivalent Rate

The interest rate equivalent to the nominal rate quoted, after compounding at a different frequency of interest payment.

Equivalent Securities

A term used in repo to denote that the securities returned must be of identical issue (and tranche, where relevant) and nominal value to those reported.

ERISA Funds

US domestic funds permitted under the Employee Retirement Income Security Act 1974 to diversify into non–US securities.

ERM

See *Exchange Rate Mechanism.*

ERNIE (Electronic Random Number Indicator Equipment)

Colloquial name for the computer which selects the winners of premium bonds prizes.

ESCB

European System of Central Banks.

Escrow Account

An account controlled by a third party into which a buyer places funds or other assets (eg, shares) to meet a commitment, pending specified actions by the seller. In CREST, when a corporate action involves acceptance of an offer, the affected dematerialised stock is transferred by the accepting holder into a special escrow account within the Receiving Agent's membership. The stock remains in the name of the holder, but is under the control of the receiving (escrow) agent. An escrow account can also be used to place stock under the control of a bank, to give effect to an equitable mortgage.

Escrow Adjustment

This is stock only transaction used by members of CREST to move stock between escrow balances within a member account. It is used in takeovers where elections are allowed and enables a member to withdraw his election or amend the alternative outturn elected. This transaction requires acceptance by the receiving agent before settlement.

Escrow Agent

A CREST member to whom another CREST member has given sole control over securities which it has transferred to an escrow balance.

ESO

European Settlements Office. Now defunct, this unit was run by the Bank of England to hold ECU denominated instruments, which are now held in CMO, Euroclear or Cedel.

ESOS

Executive share option schemes.

ETD

This is the common term used to describe Exchange–Traded Derivatives which are standardised products. It differentiates products which are listed on an exchange as opposed to those offered Over–The–Counter (OTC).

ETS

Energy Trading System; the screen trading system used by the International Petroleum Exchange.

ETT

See *Electronic Transfer of Title.*

EUCLID

The Euroclear electronic communication system.

EUREX

German–Swiss derivatives exchange created by the merger of the German (DTB) and Swiss (SOFFEX) exchanges.

EURIBOR

A rate used for Euro interest rate fixings based upon dealings in the markets of Euro zone.

The benchmark money market interest rate for the euro published by the European Central Bank.

Euro

The name of the currency in the countries within the Economic and Monetary Union which from 1 January 2002 become legal tender. The countries which joined at the outset were: Austria, Belgium, Finland, France, Germany, Greece, Ireland, Italy, Luxembourg, Netherlands, Portugal and Spain.

EURO LIBOR

A rate used for Euro interest rate fixings based upon dealings in the London market.

Eurobond

A negotiable debt security issued outside the country of its currency and intended for international distribution.

Euroclear
Founded in 1968, Euroclear provides clearing, settlement and custody for a wide range of internationally traded eurobonds, domestic bonds and equities. Euroclear is one of two International Central Securities Depositories; the other being Cedel.

Eurocommercial
Unsecured corporate debt with a short maturity structured to appeal to large financial institutions active in the Euro Market.

Eurocommercial Paper
Commercial paper denominated in a currency other than that of the country in which the issuer is based.

Eurocurrency
A currency held on deposit in a country other than its country of origin.

Eurodollar
A US–denominated deposit located in a bank outside the United States.

Euromarket
An international market with no central location where organisations invest in international securities such as eurobonds, international/ foreign bonds, warrants, convertibles etc. The unofficial headquarters is generally recognised to be London.

EURONEXT
Stock Exchange formed by the merger of the Paris, Brussels and Amsterdam exchanges.

European Central Bank
Organisation responsible for setting the single rate of interest applicable to all of the countries participating in the Euro.

European Council
Made up of EU heads of State plus the President of the European Commission.

European Depositary Receipts
Used to deal in UK, US and Japanese stocks, traded in bearer form on European markets.

European Economic Area (EEA)
Area comprising the 15 full member states of the European Union plus Iceland, Liechtenstein and Norway.

European Institution
A European authorised institution that is authorised in its home state to carry out any listed activity as a credit institution. Such activities include acceptance of deposits, lending, financial leasing, money transmission, issuing and administering means of payment and similar financial services.

European Monetary Institute (EMI)
Agreement between most members of the common market on how to organise their currencies. Superseded by Economic and Monetary Union.

European Style Option
An option that can only be exercised on the expiry date in contrast with an American Style Option.

European Union (EU)
Political union of the following: Austria, Belgium, Denmark, Finland, France, Germany, Greece, Holland, Ireland, Italy, Luxemburg, Portugal, Spain, Sweden, United Kingdom.

Evidential Provisions

Provisions in FSA's handbook which do not impose obligations or carry sanctions in their own right, but which help to demonstrate observance or breach of binding requirements. Compliance with an evidential provision will help establish compliance with the rules and breach will be prima–facie evidence of a breach of the rule.

Ex

Indication that the seller retains the right to any benefits and entitlements; consequently the buyer does not receives them. See *Cum*.

Exchange Rate Agreement (ERA)

A contract for differences based on the movement in a forward–forward foreign exchange swap price.

Ex–Date

The date specified by the local stock exchange used to determine whether the buyer or seller of the security is entitled to the benefit. The seller of a security during the ex period will normally be entitled to the benefit.

Ex–Distribution Price

A price which entitles a seller of units to the next income payment. A fund with an ex–dividend price is denoted in the financial press by xd. Where xd is not quoted on the contract note it is assumed it is cum–div and the buyer will receive the distribution. (Such notation will not appear on accumulation unit contracts.)

Ex–Dividend/Ex–Coupon (XD)

The seller of the bond or share retains the right to receive the next interest or dividend payment. The alternative is cum dividend or cum interest, where the purchaser has the right to receive the next interest or dividend payment.

Ex–Period

During a benefit distribution, the period between the ex–date and payment date during which the seller will normally be entitled to the benefit, unless specifically agreed otherwise in the terms of the trade.

Ex–Rights (XR)

The period during which the purchase of a company's shares does not entitle the new shareholder to participate in a rights issue announced by the issuing company. Shares are usually traded ex–rights (xr) on or within a few days of the company making the rights issue announcement.

Ex–Rights Price

Share price after a rights issue. Shares sold without the entitlement to the rights.

Ex–Scrip Price

Share price after a scrip issue.

Ex–Warrants

Trading a security so that the buyer will not be entitled to warrants that will be distributed to holders.

Exception–Based Processing

Transaction processing where straightforward items are processed automatically, allowing staff to concentrate on the items which are incorrect or not straightforward.

Exceptional Item

Part of the *profit and loss account* of a company. Any material item not derived from events or transactions within a company's ordinary activities needs to be disclosed separately so that the company's accounts give a true and fair view. Contrast with an *Extraordinary Item*.

Exchange
A market place where any form of trading takes place.

Exchange Delivery Settlement Price (EDSP)
The price determined by the exchange for physical delivery of the underlying instrument or cash settlement.

Exchange of Futures for Physical (EFP)
Common in the energy markets. A physical deal priced on the futures markets.

Exchange–Owned Clearing Organisation
Exchange– (or member–) owned clearing organisations are structured so that the clearing members guarantee each other. A members' default fund and additional funding like insurance provide mutual cover, with no independent guarantee.

Exchange Price Feeds
The link from exchanges to information providers which gives information on dealings.

Exchange Rate
The rate at which one currency trades against another.

Exchange Rate Mechanism (ERM)
A system of adjustable exchange rates used by certain European countries whereby currencies operated within defined exchange rate bands. Superseded by Economic and Monetary Union.

Exchange Risk
Additional risk incurred by holding assets in foreign currencies.

Exchange–Traded
Contracts traded on a futures exchange, as opposed to OTC deals.
Some option contracts are similarly exchange–traded rather than OTC.

Exchange–Traded Funds (ETF)
Passively managed basket of stocks that mirrors a particular index and
that can be traded like ordinary shares. They trade intraday on stock
exchanges, like securities, at market determined prices. In essence, ETFs
are index funds that trade like stocks.

Execute and Eliminate Order
Type of order input into SETS. The amount that can be matched
immediately against displayed orders is completed, with the remainder
being rejected.

Execution
The action of completing a trade in the markets.

Execution and Clearing Agreement
An agreement signed between the buyer/seller and the clearing broker.
This agreement sets out the terms by which the clearing broker will
conduct business with the buyer/seller.

Execution-Only
Instructions to buy or sell, given directly by the investor to the broker,
without receiving any advice.

Execution–Only Customers
Customers who do not want the firm's advice but wish to be able to
execute transactions by instructing the firm.

Execution–Only or Give–Up Agreement
Tri–partite agreements which are signed by the executing broker, the clearing broker and the client. This agreement sets out the terms by which the clearing broker will accept business on behalf of the client.

Executive Director
Director with an operational responsibility for managing the company's business.

Executive Pension Plan (EPP)
An individual money purchase arrangement, normally for senior executives and directors. EPPs are usually provided by insurance companies.

Executor
A personal representative appointed by a will.

Exempt Approved Scheme
An Inland Revenue approved scheme (not a personal pension) which provides the tax relief set out in Taxes Act 1988.

Exempt Legacies and Transfers
Bequests made during an individual's life or at death (ie, by means of a will) which, because of the nature of the gift or the recipient, are automatically exempt from inheritance tax.
Examples: transfers between spouses, gifts to charities and to political parties. Charities and political parties must be recognised by the Inland Revenue.

Exempt Trusts/Funds
Unit trusts and investment funds only open for investments from Charities and Pension Funds. These tax–exempt bodies are not liable to either UK income or Capital Gains Tax (CGT).

Exercise

The process by which the holder of an option may take up their right to buy or sell the underlying asset.

Exercise an Option

Take up the right to buy or sell the stock which is the subject of the option.

Exercise Notice

Sent by the holder of an option to indicate they wish to exercise their rights under the option.

Exercise Price

The fixed price, per share or unit, at which an option conveys the right to call (purchase) or put (sell) the underlying shares or units.

Exercise Style

Defines the date(s) when an option holder has the right to exercise their option. See *American Style Option* and *European Style Option*.

Exit Charges

With effect from 1st November 1994, under revised FSA regulations, unit trust managers have been given the option to levy a charge on redemption of units in place of, or in combination with, their initial charge. This new charge is referred to as an exit charge. Because it is levied on the bid value and initial charges on creation value, a 4.762% exit charge equates to a 5% initial charge.

Exotic Options

New generation of option derivatives, including look–backs, barriers, baskets, ladders, etc. They have different terms to standardised traded options.

Expected Return

Weighted average of possible returns.

Expiry

The date on which an option or future becomes void, ie the last day on which an option may be traded or exercised.

Expiry Date

The last date on which option holders can exercise their right. After this date an option is deemed to lapse or be abandoned.

Exploding Option

See *Barrier Option.*

External Detective Controls

Controls that detect errors and losses once they have been realised, ie, they detect the consequence.

External Environmental Causes

Environmental causes of operational risk arising from external influences such as economics, law, tax policies and natural events (eg, fire and flood).

Extinguishing Option

See *Barrier Option.*

Extraordinary General Meeting (EGM)

A meeting of shareholders which is held by a company on an ad hoc basis for a particular purpose. A period of notice (usually 21 days) must be given.

Extraordinary Item

Part of the profit and loss account of a company. Any material item which is abnormal, is not expected to recur and is derived from events or transactions outside of the ordinary activities of a company. Because the definition of ordinary activities is wide, it is rare that a company will show an extraordinary item in its accounts in any one year. Contrast with an Exceptional Item.

F

Face Value
The value of a bond, note, mortgage or other security that appears the face of the issue, unless the value is otherwise specified by the issuing company. Face value is ordinarily the amount the issuing company promises to pay at maturity. Face value is also referred to as *Par Value* or *Nominal Value*.

Factfind
The questionnaire created by most financial advisers and sellers of insurance products or packaged products to find out the details about a prospective client. Information from it provides the basis for structuring suitable advice.

Factoring
A process whereby one company takes over the responsibility of debt collection from another.

Failed Trade

Any securities transaction that does not settle on contractual settlement date because one of the settlement parties does not meet the settlement conditions. A failed trade may have negative consequences for the party at fault, including buy–ins, sell–outs and penalties. *See Buying–in* and *Selling–out.*

Fair Value

A mathematically calculated value for an option or future that accommodates a trader's parameters for interest rates, dividends etc. Different tax regimes or interest rate environments may give rise to different fair values for different investors in the same instrument.

False Market

See *Misleading Statement.*

Family Income Benefit (FIB)

Term assurance which pays money to the life assured's dependants for a set period, rather than paying a lump sum.

FAS

Free Alongside. Used in the freight market. The price includes delivery alongside the vessel in a specified port, but the freight and insurance cost are for the buyer's account.

Fast Market

If markets are hectic and turbulent so that prices are rapidly changing, prices quoted on electronic trading systems may not be up to date.

Federal Reserve Book Entry System

CSD for US government securities.

Federal Reserve System

The central banking system of the USA. It comprises a number of regional supervised by the Federal Reserve Board banks which regulates banking activities.

Fed Repo

Repo trade between the US Federal Reserve and US Treasury primary dealers in order to supply liquidity to the market.

Feeder Fund

A relevant pension scheme dedicated to a single regulated collective investment scheme or to a single eligible investment trust.

Fiduciary

An individual, corporation or association holding assets for another party, often with the legal authority and duty to make decisions regarding financial matters on behalf of the other party.

Figure

When the last two digits in a foreign exchange price are zero.

Fill or Kill order

Type of order input into SETS or the options market. It is either completed in full against displayed orders or rejected in full.

FIMBRA

Former SRO responsible for regulating members which comprise mainly Independent Financial Advisers (IFAs). See also *Personal Investment Authority*.

Final Dividend

The dividend paid by a company as the final payment for a particular financial year.

Financial Gearing
Measured either by Gearing Ratio or by Interest Cover. See *Gearing*.

Final Remuneration
The maximum earnings that can be used for the purpose of calculating maximum approvable pension benefits. It may include the value of benefits–in–kind as well as salary.

Final Salary Scheme
Pension scheme where the benefit is based on the member's pensionable earnings for a period ending at or before normal retirement date or leaving service.

Final Settlement
The completion of a transaction when the delivery of all components of a trade is performed.

Financial Futures/Options Contracts
Financial futures is a term used to describe futures contracts based on financial instruments like currencies, debt instruments and financial indices. An agreement to buy or sell a fixed quantity of a specified interest rate or currency product for delivery at a fixed date in the future at a fixed price.

Financial Instruments
See *Instrument*.

Financial Measurement
The calculation of a sterling or dollar figure that represents the amount of risk exposure.

Financial Ombudsman Service
Facility established to hear complaints by customers and make awards where appropriate. Can award a maximum of £100,000.

Financial Promotion
Generic name given to all types of promotion of financial activities. Includes advertising through any medium and conversations with prospective customers.

Financial Reporting Council
Provides the strategic direction behind the development of Accounting Standards in the UK. It owns two subsidiary companies, the Accounting Standards Board and the Financial Reporting Review Panel, which issue and enforce Accounting Standards in the UK.

Financial Reporting Review Panel
A subsidiary of the Financial Reporting Council, it ensures that companies in the UK follow *Accounting Standards*. See also *Accounting Standards Board* and *Financial Reporting Council*.

Financial Reporting Standard
See *Accounting Standards*.

Financial Resources (FR)
The elements which must be maintained by firms at all times. It comprises own funds subject to two adjustments.

Financial Resources Requirement (FRR)
The amount of financial resources that a firm must maintain at all times. Comprises a primary requirement and a secondary requirement.

Financial Risk
The quantifiable likelihood of loss or less–than–expected returns.

Financial Services Act 1986 (FSA 86 or FSA 1986)
This act provided the framework for regulation of the financial services industry in the UK and a regime for the protection of investors. It has been superseded by the Financial Services and Markets Act 2000 .

Financial Services Compensation Scheme

Scheme designed to provide an element of protection in the event of default by an investment business. The maximum claim depends on the nature of the business.

Financial Services Authority (FSA)

The agency created by the Financial Services and Markets Act 2000 to be the sole financial regulator in the UK.

Financial Services and Markets Act (FSMA 2000)

The legislation that created the unified regulatory role of the Financial Services Authority and replaced various pieces of law. Became effective at midnight on 30 November 2001.

Financial Services and Markets Tribunal

Body which hears appeals from authorised persons or approved persons who have been disciplined. It is run by the Lord Chancellor's department and is independent of the FSA.

Financial Statements

Document which shows the financial situation of a company. Comprises a balance sheet, profit and loss account, cash flow statement, related notes and other statements required by regulation.

Financial Year

The UK government's official financial year runs from 1 April to 31 March and is denoted by the year in which it starts. Thus the financial year 2001 starts on 1 April 2001 and ends on 31 March 2002.

Firm Price

A guaranteed price.

First Order

A general sensitivity measure of how much the value instrument or portfolio is affected by (ie, is sensitive to) changes in a risk factor.

First Notice Day

The first day that the holders of short positions can give notification to the exchange/clearing house that they wish to effect delivery.

Fiscal Agent

A commercial bank appointed by the borrower to undertake certain duties related to the new issue, such as assisting the payment of interest and principal, redeeming bonds or coupons, handling taxes, replacement of lost or damaged securities, destruction of coupons and bonds once payments have been made.

Fiscal Policy

Form of economic policy implemented by governments in attempt to influence levels of economic activity. Concentrates on levels of taxation, government borrowing and spending.

Fiscal Year

The relevant period for assessing total income and capital gains for liability to tax. Runs from 6 April in one year to 5 April in the following year.

Fit and Proper

Under FSMA 2000 everyone conducting investment business must be a 'fit and proper person'. The Act does not define the term, a function which is left FSA.

Fitch IBCA

A credit rating agency.

Five Year Summary
Summary of the last five years results of a listed company. The Stock Exchange requires this to be prepared by the company and included in its annual report.

Fixed Assets
The assets of a company acquired for long–term use within the company, for example, buildings, plant and equipment.

Fixed Charge
Mortgage on a specific asset, usually land and buildings. See *Mortgage*.

Fixed–Coupon Repo
Collateral returned must have the same coupon as that originally transferred.

Fixed Deposit
A non–negotiable deposit for a specific term.

Fixed Exchange Rate
System whereby the rate of a country's currency is established at a particular level in relation to other currencies and is not allowed to move from that level, except within very small margins.

Fixed Income
Interest on a security which is calculated as a constant specified percentage of the principal amount and paid at the end of specified interest periods, usually annually or semi–annually, until maturity.

Fixed Interest Securities
Also known as bonds. Securities which carry rights to a fixed rate of interest and eventual repayment of the capital sum.

Fixed Leg

In a coupon swap, the flow of a fixed rate interest payment from one party to the other.

Fixed Price Offer

A method of implementing an Offer for Subscription or Sale. A company issuing shares will invite applications for shares at a predetermined price under a fixed price offer. The advantage is that it eliminates uncertainty as to the price that will be set for the issue. The disadvantage is that it can be difficult to identify an appropriate price at which to sell the issue. See also *Tender Offer* and *Bookbuilding*.

Fixed Price Re–offer

A means of issuing eurobonds. The lead manager of the issue distributes the bonds to the management group which then the places bonds with clients. They must not place the bonds at a price below the fixed price agreed in advance until the syndicate is broken. It is broken by the lead manager when most of the issue has been placed at the fixed price. The purpose of the rule is to ensure that when managers bid to participate in the management group, they bid at prices which are realistic. See also *Bought Deal*.

Fixed–Rate

A borrowing or investment where the interest or coupon paid is fixed throughout the arrangement.

Fixed Rate Borrowing

A fixed rate borrowing establishing the interest rate that will be paid throughout the life of the loan.

Fixed Rate Payer

In a coupon swap, the party that pays the fixed rate.

Fixed Rate Receiver
In a coupon swap, the party that receives the fixed rate.

Fixed Settlement
All trades within a specified period, called a dealing period or account, are settled on one fixed day, a specified number of days after the end of the account. Also called *Account Settlement*.

Fixing
The calculation of the coupon rate for a FRN covering the next coupon payment period.

Flat Position
In the options and futures markets, a position which has been fully closed out and no liability to make or take delivery exists.

Flat Repo
Repo undertaken with no margin.

Flat Yield
Also known as income yield. Income return on owning a bond. Calculated by dividing the coupon by the market price and multiplying by 100.

Flex (Contract)
A derivatives contract traded on an exchange. The contract specification allows some terms (including maturity, strike price and exercise style) of the contract to be negotiated between buyer and seller, unlike a normal standardised derivative contract, where only the price is negotiated.

Flex Options
Newly introduced contracts which are a cross between OTCs and exchange traded products. The advantage of flex options is that participants can choose various parts of the contract specification such as the expiry date and exercise price.

Flex Repo
The lender of cash can draw down the cash supplied in accordance with a schedule agreed at the inception of the trade.

Flight to Quality
The movement of capital to a safe haven during periods of market turmoil to avoid capital loss.

Floating Charge
Charge over a class of assets, such as the stock in trade of the business.

Floating Exchange Rate
System whereby the rate of a country's currency against others is determined by market forces without any intervention from the government.

Floating Leg
In a coupon swap, the flow of a floating rate interest payment from one party to the other.

Floating Rate
A borrowing or investment where the interest or coupon paid changes throughout the arrangement in line with some reference rate such as LIBOR.

Floating Rate CD (FRCD)
Certificate of deposit on which the rate of interest is refixed in line with market conditions at regular intervals.

Floating Rate Note (FRN)
Eurobonds with a rate of interest that varies from coupon period to coupon period. The rate is usually established as a margin over LIBOR.

Floating Rate Payer
Same as fixed rate receiver in a coupon swap.

Floating Rate Receiver
Same as fixed rate payer in a coupon swap.

Floor
An option which fixes the minimum interest rate receivable on a deposit/loan for a series of interest payments.

Floor Brokerage
The process of delegating the execution to another counterparty.

Flotation
The process of bringing a company's shares to the market for the first time.

FOB
Free on Board. Used in the freight market to indicate that the price includes delivery to the port and the loading into a vessel.

FOF
See *Futures and Options Fund*.

Foreign Bond
Like a Eurobond, it is a debt security issued by non-resident borrowers but is underwritten by a syndicate of banks composed primarily of institutions from one country. It is denominated in that country's currency and sold principally in that country.

Foreign Exchange (Forex)
A term commonly used to encompass the buying and selling of foreign currencies. 'Forex' is used as an abbreviation for foreign exchange.

Foreign Exchange Requirement (FER)
Part of a firm's funding requirement to allow for the possibility of adverse fluctuations in exchange rates which would cause the firm to lose money.

Foreign Income Dividends (FID)
Income paid from overseas earnings on which tax is treated as paid but on which there is no tax credit, therefore no tax may be reclaimed.

Forex
See *Foreign Exchange*.

Forward
A deal for settlement later than the normal settlement date for that particular commodity or instrument.

Forward Contract
A contract between two counterparties where one person agrees to buy from the other person, who agrees to sell, a certain amount of a financial instrument or a commodity at a stated price but for delivery at an agreed future date.

Forward Currency Transaction
The rate of exchange is agreed now but delivery occurs in the future on an agreed date. The difference between the forward rate and the spot rate is the mathematical result of the difference in interest rates of the two countries concerned.

Forward Delivery
Transactions which involve a delivery date in the future.

Forward Exchange Agreement (FXA)
A contract for difference designed to create the same result as a foreign exchange cash forward–forward deal.

Forward Exchange Rate
An exchange rate set today, embodied in a forward contract, that will apply to a foreign exchange transaction at some pre–specified point in the future.

Forward Forward
An agreement at a future date, to purchase an instrument which will mature at a period some time in the future.

Forward Market
Dealings that are made for delivery and settlement on a date other than the spot.

Forward Outright
The rate at which a foreign exchange contract is struck today for settlement at a specified future date. A compilation of the Spot exchange rate plus or minus the forward points.

Forward Points
The interest rate differential between two currencies. Quoted as forward foreign exchange points or pips, and added to or taken from the spot exchange rate.

Forward Pricing
System for pricing units in a unit trust, where buyers and sellers trade on the basis of prices to be set at the next price fixing for units, ie. after an instruction from an investor has been received. See *Historic Pricing*.

Forward Rate Agreement (FRA)
An agreement to pay or receive, on an agreed future date, the difference between a fixed interest rate agreed at the outset and a reference interest rate actually prevailing on a given future date for a given period.

Forwards

These are very similar to futures contracts but they are not normally traded on an exchange. They are not marked to market daily but settled only on the delivery date.

FOTRA

Free of Tax to Residents Abroad. Investors who are neither resident nor ordinarily resident in the UK can register to receive coupon payments on a UK government stock free of withholding tax in the UK.

FRA

See *Forward Rate Agreement*.

FRABBA

Standard BBA documentation for dealing a FRA.

Franked Income

Dividends from UK companies are paid after the company has paid corporation tax. This income is referred to as 'franked'.

Free Asset Ratio (FAR)

The surplus assets of a life assurance company over its liabilities in relation to its total assets. The FAR shows the company's capacity for future growth and to make future bonus payments to with–profits policyholders.

Free Delivery/Free Payment

A settlement situation. One side of the trade is delivered in the absence of the other, ie, the free delivery of securities in a bonus issue or the free payment of dividends.

Free Issue

See *Bonus Issue*.

Free of Payment
The movement of assets for which there is no associated (cash) countervalue. The movement of assets which is not dependent on the simultaneous payment of the cash countervalue.

Free of Tax To Residents Abroad (FOTRA)
See *FOTRA*.

Free-Standing Additional Voluntary Contributions (FSAVC)
An AVC arrangement which is not directly linked to the employer's main scheme. See *AVCs*.

Friendly Societies
Organisations that are set up for the mutual benefit of their members and are non–profit making. Although the term covers building societies, co–operatives and trade unions, some friendly societies are focused on retail financial services and offer 10 year endowment policies. There are tax benefits to the policies but only modest sums can be invested.

Friendly Society Exempt Policy
A savings policy issued by a friendly society where the fund is free of UK tax on investment income and capital gains.

FRN
See *Floating Rate Note*.

Front End Loading
Some investment products such as life assurance policies and unit trusts have a higher charge in the first year or when units are purchased. This is referred to as front end loading.

Front Office
The term used for the Trading or Dealing room.

Front Running
See *Dealing Ahead.*

FSA
See *Financial Services Authority.*

FSA 86 or FSA 1986
See *Financial Services Act 1986.*

FSA Handbook
FSA's requirements including rules and principles are all set out in its handbook.

FSMA 2000
See *Financial Services and Markets Act* .

FTSE 30
See *FTSE Ordinary Share Index.*

FTSE 100 Index
Weighted arithmetic index of the prices of the UK's leading 100 shares. It is a real time index calculated by FTSE International.

FTSE All Share Index
The Financial Times Actuaries measure of the leading 850 companies listed on the UK Stock Market.

FTSE Eurotop 100
The index containing the top 100 shares in Europe.

FTSE Indices
Family of UK indices for the London Stock Exchange.

FTSE International
A joint venture between the Financial Times and the London Stock Exchange which produces indices such as the FTSE 100 and the FT–Actuaries All Share Index.

FTSE Mid 250 Index
Index of the prices of the 250 shares below the top 100. Calculated in the same way as the FTSE 100.

FTSE Ordinary Share Index
The index containing the top 30 shares in the UK, also known as the FTSE 30.

Full Listing
See *Official Listing.*

Full Replication
A method of running an index–tracking fund in which all the shares comprising an index are held in their respective market weightings.

Fully Automated Securities Trading (FAST)
Dealing system in Taiwan.

Fully Diluted Earnings Per Share
A calculation performed by companies to advise shareholders of potential deterioration of earnings per share in the future because of new shares being issued by the company on the exercise of convertible debt warrants or options already in issue. The calculation reworks the earnings per share figure for the current year on the basis that the dilution had already occurred, as if the exercise of the convertibles had already taken place.

Fully Paid Shares
Shares on which no further 'call' is due. Once a call has been paid to the company for new shares offered to existing shareholders, they can be traded in the form of allotment letters until definitive certificates become available. Dealing is on a cash settlement basis. See *Record Date, Allotment Letter*.

Fund
Used to describe a collective investment scheme, into which investors' monies is pooled and managed as a single entity with a common investment aim.

Fund Managers Association (FMA)
The trade association that represents the interests of UK based institutional fund managers. Now merged with AUTIF to form Investment Managers Association (IMA).

Fundamental Accounting Concepts/Principles
The assumptions which companies must follow when preparing their accounts. Fundamental Accounting Principles are Going Concern, Accruals, Consistency, Prudence and No Netting Off. The first four are also known as fundamental accounting concepts.

Fundamental Analysis
Detailed analysis of a company and the industry in which it operates political and external factors to identify whether the shares are over–valued or undervalued.

Fundamental Equilibrium Exchange Rate (FEER)
The exchange rate needed to achieve a sustainable balance in the country's external current account. See *Purchasing Power Parity*

Funded Debt
Short–term debt converted into long–term debt.

Funded Pension Scheme
A pension established either as a personal or company scheme to provide pensions in retirement. The company and/or the employee, pay contributions to be invested in the fund during the employee's working life.

Fund Manager
An organisation that invests money on behalf of someone else.

Fund of Funds
Authorised unit trust which invests in the units of other unit trusts.

Fungible
Able to be co–mingled, identical securities in a bookkeeping system in which no specific securities are assigned by serial number to any one holder's account. See *Non–Fungible.*

Fungible Bonds
An interchangeable pool of securities of the same security code from which deliveries are made without reference to any particular identifiable certificate. See *Non–Fungible.*

Fungibility
In addition to its general meeting fungibility is also applied to a futures contract with identical administration in more than one financial centre. Trades in various geographical locations can be off–set (eg, bought on the IPE and sold on SGX–DT). See *Fungible.*

FUTOP
Danish Clearing Centre.

Future

A futures contract is a legally binding arrangement by which one party commits to buying a standard quantity and quality of an asset from another party on a specified date in the future, but at a price agreed today. The counterparty is obliged to sell the asset at the agreed price and agreed date. Because the price is agreed at the outset the seller (buyer) is protected from a fall (rise) in the price of the underlying in the intervening time period.

Futures and Options Fund (FOF)

A unit trust scheme dedicated to approved and other derivatives (where most or all the transactions are fully covered by cash, securities or other derivatives), whether with or without transferable securities.

Futures Contract

A deal, traded on a recognised exchange, to buy or sell some financial instrument or commodity for settlement on a future date.

Future Value

The equivalent value at a future date of a set sum of money and stream of cash flows.

FX Rate Risk

The risk of adverse movements in exchange rates.

G

G30 Recommendations
Nine recommendations made in 1989 by the G30 to improve the
Clearing and Settlement Systems in the world's securities markets and
thus reduce risk and increase efficiency.

Gamma
A second order measure of the exposure of derivatives to a risk factor
such as the change in value of the underlying instrument.

Gap
Mismatch between differing maturities of deposits and loans.

Gap Analysis
The difference in exposures to interest rates in different periods.

Gateway
A computer with a tamper–resistant hardware encryption unit, supplied
by the network supplier to a CREST user, which enables
communication through the network gateway to CREST.

GD
See *Good for the Day*.

GDP
See *Gross Domestic Product*.

GDR
Global Depository Receipt. See *American Depository Receipt*.

Geared Futures and Options Fund (GFOF)
A unit trust dedicated to approved and other derivatives where most or all of the extent of investment is limited by the amount of property available to be put up as initial outlay, whether with or without transferable securities.

Gearing
The proportion of the assets that have been funded from borrowing and the proportion funded by the shareholders. A common measurement is the debt/equity ratio defined as:

$$\frac{\text{Borrowing}}{\text{Shareholders' Funds}} \times 100\%$$

See *Leverage*.

Gearing Ratio
An accounting ratio also known as the debt/equity ratio. It measures the level of debt finance a company has raised relative to its level of shareholders' funds. It is usually defined as a debt divided by shareholders' funds, expressed as a percentage. The higher the percentage from the calculation , the more highly geared a company is. It is possible to calculate the net gearing ratio, where cash balances are deducted from debt in the calculation. See also *Interest Cover* and *Gearing*.

Geisha Bond
A Yen bond issued both inside and out of Japan, unlike a Euro Yen bond or a domestic Yen bond.

General Clearing Member
A client member of a clearing house able to clear for the firm, its clients and other investment businesses. Contrast with Individual Clearing Members, who can clear for the firm and its clients but not for other individuals' businesses.

General Client Bank Account
All clients' money is pooled in one account although the firm's own accounting records will record how much belongs to each customer.

General Collateral (GC)
Securities, which are not "special", used as collateral against cash borrowing. A repo buyer will accept GC at any time that a specific stock is not quoted as required in the transaction. In the gilts market GC includes *Delivery by Value (DBVs)*.

General Insurance
Product insurance such as motor, fire or home.

General Principles
11 fundamental principles written by FSA to apply to all investment businesses.

General Risk
The risk arising from the market position held by the bank when measuring position risk for capital adequacy purposes. See *Specific Risk*.

Generic
A generic swap is one for a standard period, against a standard fixing benchmark such as LIBOR.

GFOF
See *Geared Futures and Options Fund*.

Gilt-Edged Market Makers (GEMMs)
A firm that is a market maker in gilts, who quotes prices at which they would buy and sell. Also known as a *Primary Dealer*.

Gilt-Edged Stocks
Bonds issued by the UK government. Treasury bills are excluded. Capital gains and losses arising on disposal of gilts are exempt from Capital Gains Tax. The two main types are *Conventional* and *Index–Linked Gilts*.

Gilts
Abbreviated name for gilt edged stocks which are UK government issued fixed interest securities or index–linked securities.

Gilts Strip
An instrument created by breaking a gilt up into its constituent parts – capital and income. An example of a zero coupon bond.

Give Up
The process of giving a trade to a third party who will undertake the clearing and settlement of the trade.

Global Bond
Bonds distributed in both the Euromarkets and in one or more domestic markets.

Global Certificate
A single certificate recording the total issue of a bond. The certificate is held at a Central Depository, which maintains a record of individual bondholders.

Global Clearing
The channelling of the settlement of all futures and options trades through a single counterparty or through a number of counterparties geographically located.

Global Custodian
A global custodian provides clients with multi–currency custody, settlement and reporting services which extend beyond the global custodian's and client's base region and currency; and encompasses all classes of financial instruments.

Global Depository Receipts
See *American Depositary Receipts.*

Global Master Repurchase Agreement (GMRA)
Master agreement for repos and buy/sell–backs.

Globally Registered Share
A share that is quoted on more than one exchange.

GLOBEX
The overnight trading system operated by Reuters and the Chicago Mercantile Exchange (CME), which was developed in 1992.

GMP
See *Guaranteed Minimum Pension.*

Going Concern
One of the four fundamental accounting concepts. The company will continue to operate for the foreseeable future.

Good Delivery

A delivery of securities which meets all the contractual and regulatory requirements, including the type and number of shares, acceptable physical form and registration type, proper transfer deeds when necessary, etc. In certain markets, good delivery may consist of a form of undertaking from the seller attesting to the expected time of delivery of the securities. In general, payment is made only upon the determination of good delivery.

Good for The Day (GTD)

Good for the Day, an order type. The order must be filled during the day or it is cancelled. Contrast with a GTC (Good Till Cancelled) order which, if not filled on one trading day, is carried forward until it is either filled or cancelled by the investor. Orders are GD unless otherwise specified. See *GTC*.

Good Till Cancelled (GTC)

A limit order which stays effective until either it executes or is deleted by the broker which placed it.

Goodwill

Good reputation of a business which can be calculated as part of its asset value. It assists the ability of the business to generate profits and cash in the future.

Government Bonds

Bonds issued by a government to finance its borrowing requirements.

Government Securities Clearing Corporation (GSCC)

Clearing organisation for US Treasury securities.

Grantor

1. Person who grants a property to another.
2. An options writer. Term used by the LME. See *Writer*.

Gratis Issue
See *Bonus Issue*.

Greenshoe Option
A way to stabilise a new issue. The manager takes a short position in the stock which is covered by an option on new shares to be issued by the company. If, after the issue, the share price rises above the exercise price of the option, the manager can close the position by exercising the option on the company. This enables it to access the market for additional funds on the issue. If the share price falls below the exercise price of the option, the manager will let the option lapse and close his position by buying shares in the market. This will create additional demand for the shares and act as a stabilising mechanism.

Grey Market
Forward trading in new issues between market participants during the period from the announcement of a new issue to the closing date. Trades are dealt on a 'when issued' basis to cover the possibility that the issue might be withdrawn.

Gross
1. Before tax has been paid.
2. A position which is held with both the bought and sold trades kept open.

Gross Basis
The difference between the price of an asset and its implied price given by the price of a futures contract.

Gross Domestic Product (GDP)
Measure of a country's output which calculates the value of goods produced within that country.

Gross Income Yield
The income return on an investment before tax has been deducted.

Gross National Product (GNP)
Measure of a country's output comprising GDP as adjusted for net inflows or outflows of income with other countries.

Gross Redemption Yield (GRY)
The Gross Redemption Yield (or Yield to Maturity) of a bond is the return a bond earns on the price at which it was purchased if held to maturity. The calculation takes into account any capital gain or loss over the full period and assumes that all interest payments are reinvested. (In the case of index linked bonds, the redemption price and future interest payments are not known so certain standard assumptions are made regarding future inflation rates).

Gross Settlement
Each trade is settled separately from any other. There is no netting. Also called *Trade–for–Trade Settlement*.

Grossed–Up Net Redemption Yield
The post–tax return on an asset to its redemption date, to which a notional tax rate is added to aid comparisons with the yield on other assets.

Grossing up
The process of calculating the gross income from a figure net of taxation.

Group
Where one company controls one or more other companies, they are collectively a group.

Group Personal Pension (GPP)

An arrangement made for the employees of a particular employer to participate in a personal pension scheme on a grouped basis. GPPs are not separate schemes, merely collecting arrangements.

Growth Stock

Shares in a company with a low dividend yield and high investor expectations of future capital growth.

GTC

See *Good Till Cancelled*.

Guarantee Fund Contributions

Made by the clearing members of a clearing house operating a mutual guarantee. The guarantee fund will be used in the event of a default of a clearing member causing losses. It must be exhausted before the resources of the clearing house are used.

Guarantee Stock

The lender's performance of its obligations is guaranteed by a third party. Often arises if a subsidiary company raises external finance and the bond is guaranteed by its holding company.

Guaranteed Annuity

Annuity which is guaranteed to make payments for a minimum period even if the annuitant dies during that period. Payments continue after that period if the annuitant is still alive.

Guaranteed Bond

Bonds on which the principal or income or both are guaranteed by another corporation or parent company in case of default by the issuing corporation.

Guaranteed Fund

A fund which guarantees to return at least the original sum invested to the investor after a set period (normally 5–7 years), and any further profits if the fund has traded successfully.

Guaranteed Income/Growth Bond

Normally single premium life assurance policies that provide a guaranteed fixed level of income or growth over a pre–determined period.

Guaranteed Minimum Pension (GMP)

The minimum pension which an occupational pension scheme has to provide as one of the conditions for contracting out of SERPS, unless it is contracted out through providing protected rights. For employees leaving service within two years of joining, their employer's scheme can pay a contributions equivalent premium to the State scheme to buy them back into SERPS. Employees with over two years service in the scheme have to be granted a preserved pension revalued in line with the National Average Price Index.

Guaranteed Stop

The investor is guaranteed that the stop order will be filled at the stop level specified and not at the prevailing market price when the stop is filled. Such an order involves large risks for the broker, and therefore such orders are rare and incur high charges.

GUI

Graphical User Interface. The term GUI is used to refer to the Windows™ based system supplied by CRESTCo which allows interactive connection to CREST or CGO via one of the approved networks.

H

Haircut
The discount applied to the value of collateral used to cover margins.

Hang Seng Index
Index of the Hong Kong Stock Exchange.

Hard Commodities
Commodities such as tin or zinc. Futures on them are generally traded on the London Metal Exchange.

Hard Currency
A currency whose exchange rate seems to be rising against other currencies. See *Soft Currency*.

Hard Disclosure
Disclosure made by an IFA, to a potential investor, of his entitlement to receive commission from an AUT Manager on investments being made. This includes initial and renewal commission and must be made in pounds and pence.

Hard Stock

A security in high demand and therefore special in the repo market.
Also called *Hot Stock*.

Headroom

The credit that is available to a member during the CREST processing
day, based on the difference between the member's credit limit (ie, cap)
and its net payment obligation. Headroom (and the cap) is dynamic,
varying throughout the day as the result of transactions settling.

Hedge

Protect against the risks arising from potential market movements in
exchange rates, interest rates or other variables. See *Arbitrage,
Speculation.*

Hedger

A person who uses the markets to reduce the risk of their underlying
position.
Example: a coffee grower may sell coffee futures to guarantee him a
fixed selling price for his coffee.

Hedge Ratio

The number of units of an asset that should be bought to hedge one unit
of liability. See *Delta.*

Hedging

Use of investments to protect or minimise a potential loss to an existing
position or known commitment.

Herstatt Risk

The risk on and FX transaction where there is a non simultaneous
exchange of the different currencies.

High Net Worth Individuals

Specifically, individuals who have a current certificate signed by their accountant or employer stating that their previous year's income was not less than £100,000 or that their net asset (excluding their home) throughout that time was not less than £250,000; and who have signed a statement acknowledging their status and their ability to receive exempt financial promotions in respect of securities in unlisted companies.

High Yielding Bond

Also called a junk bond. Any bond which is not of investment grade.

Higher Rate of Tax

The rate of tax above the basic rate, to which higher earners are liable. See also *Basic Rate of Tax* and *Taxable Income*.

Historic Pricing

System for pricing units where buyers and sellers trade on the basis of prices set at the last price fix before their dealing instruction was received. See *Forward Pricing*. Contrast with Forward Pricing.

Historic Rate Rollover

A forward swap in foreign exchange where the settlement exchange rate for the near date is based on a historic off–market rate rather than the current market rate. It is prohibited by many regulators.

Historic VaR

A method of calculating VaR by applying historic price movements to the current portfolio of instruments. See *Monte Carlo Simulation, Variance, Co–variance*.

Historic Volatility

The standard deviation of the change in the price of the underlying over a designated time period.

Historical Loss Analysis
The process of identifying previous loss events and attributing them to operational risk issues.

Historical Simulation
The simplest method of VaR calculation that uses actual historic returns in risk factors to estimate risk exposure in the future.

Hit
Deal on a bid price quoted by another party.

HKE
The holding company of the Hong Kong Futures Exchange, The Stock Exchange of Hong Kong Ltd and The Hong Kong Securities Clearing Company Ltd.

Hold in Custody (HIC) Repo
A repo in which the party who receives cash does not deliver the securities to the counterparty but segregates them in an internal account for the benefit of the cash provider.

Holder (Options)
The beneficial or legal owner of an asset. Buyer of an option. See *Writer*.

Holding Company
A company which owns more than 50% of the shares of another company is its holding company.

Home/Host

Firms must follow the rules of their domestic authorising body (home) for all aspects of their ISD business except conduct of business rules. Home conduct of business rules apply to all business undertaken in the authorising state. The conduct of business rules of the host state apply when services are provided in that state.

Home State Regulation

Under the Investment Services Directive (ISD), an investment business is authorised in the place of its head office and registered office. This home state authorisation entitles it to conduct business in any member state of the European Union.

Horizontal Spread

An option spread where one option is bought and another sold. The sold one has the same strike price as the bought but a different expiry date. The spread will be constructed with either all calls or all puts on the same underlying asset. This spread is sometimes known as a *Time Spread* or a *Calendar Spread*.

Host State

Under the ISD any member of the European Union where an investment business established in any other EU state is now conducting business.

Host State Regulation

Any European investment business operating outside its home basis is regulated by its host for its Conduct of Business.

Hot Stock

See *Hard Stock*.

House Account

Also called a principal account or transaction. An account or transaction designated for the firm's own purposes, rather than for those of its segregated customers.

Hybrid Security

A security that has the characteristics of both debt and equity.

I

ICAEW

See *Institute of Chartered Accountants in England and Wales.*

Icing

Reserving stock before borrowing it on the stock lending market.

ICM

See *Individual Clearing Member.*

ICO

See *International Coffee Organisation.*

ICOM

See *International Currency Options Market.*

ICSA

See *Institute of Chartered Secretaries and Administrators.*

ICSD

See *The International Central Securities Depository.*

IDB
See *Inter–Dealer Broker*.

Identification Rules
Rules which determine which shares are deemed to be sold for Capital Gains Tax purposes, when only part of a holding is being sold.

IDR
International depository receipt. See *American Depository Receipt*.

IFA
See *Independent Financial Adviser*.

IFEMA
See *International Foreign Exchange Master Agreement*.

Illiquid SEAQ Securities
See *Less Liquid SEAQ Securities*.

Immobilisation
The practice of using physical certificates as evidence of total ownership, while recording the specific investors' proportional holding by book–entry. Immobilisation may be based on fungible certificates (which can sometimes be withdrawn for physical holding) or on jumbo certificates.

Immobilised Securities
Securities which are stored collectively in a vault in order to eliminate physical movement of securities or documents of title when transfer of ownership takes place. All movements of immobilised securities subsequently occur by book entry transfer.

Immunisation

This is the process by which a bond portfolio is created that has an assured return for a specific time horizon irrespective of changes in interest rates. The mechanism underlying immunisation is a portfolio structure that balances the change in the value of a portfolio at the end of the investment horizon (time period) with the return gained from the reinvestment of cash flows from the portfolio. As such immunisation requires the portfolio manager to offset interest–rate risk and reinvestment risk.

Implied Repo Rate

The rate of return before financing costs implied by a transaction where a longer–term cash security is purchased and a futures contract is sold (or vice versa).

Implied Volatility

The level of volatility that the current market price of a derivative is implying.

IMRO

See *Investment Management Regulatory Organisation.*

Inc.

Short for 'incorporated'. A US corporation.

Incentive Compensation

A fee paid to the investment adviser determined by fund performance in relation to specified market indices

Income

Dividends or distributions received from an investment.

Income Allocation Date
Date by which income attributable to units in authorised trusts must have been computed and dispatched to unit holders.

Income Bonds (National Savings)
National Savings product which pays regular income.

Income Drawdown
The drawing of regular amounts from a pension fund as an alternative to annuity purchase. Found in personal pensions, some SSASs, and a very small number of EPPs. In theory, available for AVCs, too.

Income Fund
A fund whose objective is to provide income on a regular basis.

Income Protection
Cover that provides a regular income if the insured is disabled as defined under the policy. Also called *Permanent Health Insurance*.

Income Share
Income shareholders in an investment trust company have the right to all the income received from the underlying portfolio and distributed as dividends and a fixed repayment of capital when the company is wound up.

Income Statement
See *Profit and Loss Account*.

Income Stock
Shares which yield above average income. Normally the basis for income unit trusts.

Income Tax
The tax that is charged on all income as defined by tax laws. Includes, as well as income from employment, dividends, interest, rental income, pension receipts and retirement annuities receipts.

Income Units
Investors holding such units are entitled to receive regular income payments. The payments are usually made twice a year, but can be quarterly or monthly.

Income Yield
The annual income expressed as a percentage of the purchase cost. See *Flat Yield*.

Incorporation
The process of creating a company in accordance with the legislation of the country concerned.

Indemnity Guarantee Policy
Insurance taken out by mortgage providers to cover loans which represent a high percentage of the purchase price of a property.

Independent Clearing Organisation
The independent organisation is quite separate from the actual members of the exchange and will guarantee, to each member, the performance of the contracts by having them registered in the organisation's name.

Independent Financial Adviser (IFA)
Adviser not employed by a single firm who can select from all companies' products ie. pensions, unit trusts etc when providing 'best advice' to their client.

Independent Guarantee

A guarantee operated by clearing houses where losses caused by clearing member defaults are first covered by the defaulting clearing member's assets (if any), and then by the clearing house's resources. There is no guarantee fund contributed to by the clearing members with this type of guarantee, unlike the mutual guarantee where such a fund exists. See *Mutual Guarantee.*

Independent Intermediaries

See *Independent Financial Adviser.*

Index

A figure calculated from the share prices of a specific number of shares on a Stock Exchange.

Index Arbitrage

The purchase or sale of a basket of different shares and the simultaneous sale or purchase of an index derivative based on the shares in the basket.

Index Fund

Also known as a tracker fund and is a type of unit trust which invests in the component parts of a particular index. Charges tend to be relatively low.

Index–Linked Bonds

Bonds which have their coupon and principal index linked, usually to the Retail Price Index. The return on the bond will therefore rise in line with inflation.

Index–Linked Gilts

Gilt edged securities where both the annual interest and the capital at redemption are revalued in line with the Retail Price Index.

Index Swap
Sometimes the same as a basis swap. Otherwise, a swap where payments on one or both of the legs are based on the value of an index, such as an equity index.

Index Tracking Funds
A fund that is run by a computer algorithm to track a particular set of stocks.

Indexation Allowance
An allowance deducted from a capital gain calculated from the cost of acquisition and the percentage increase in the RPI from the month of acquisition to the earlier of the month of disposal or April 1998.

Indexation Relief
The adjustment made to reflect inflation when calculating a capital gain for tax purposes.

Indexed Repo
The repo rate is linked to an external specified index such as LIBOR.

Indirect
An exchange rate quotation against the US dollar in which the dollar is the base currency and the other currency is the variable currency.

Indirect Loss
The loss associated with the opportunity costs of a risk being realised.

Indirect Market Participation
Non–broker/dealers, such as institutional investors, who are active investors/traders.

Indirect Market Risk Factors

The factors that have an indirect bearing on an instrument's price, such as economic events, political and environmental effects.

Indirect Quote

In the foreign currency market, an indirect quote is expressed in terms of US$1 and the order currency amount varies. Thus a US dollar/Swiss franc quote is indirect. The quote will give the number of francs which $1 will buy or the number of Swiss francs needed to buy $1.

Individual Clearing Member

A clearing member of a clearing house who is able to clear for the firm and its clients only. General Clearing Members can clear for the firm, its clients and other investment businesses.

Individual Savings Account (ISA)

Introduced in April 1999 and have taken the place of Personal Equity Plans (PEPs) and TESSAs. An ISA is a scheme of investment with no tax liability on income or capital gains tax arising from assets held within the scheme. It is not an investment in itself, but a wrapper put around one on more investments, and may comprise components which fluctuate in value eg. stocks and shares.

Industrial and Provident Society

A society which is a bona fide co–operative society intended to be conducted for the benefit of the community (and not conducted with the objective of making profit), mainly for the payment of interest, dividends or bonuses or money invested, deposited with or lent to the society.

Industrial Assurance
A class of business where the premiums are physically collected in cash from the policyholder by an agent of the life office. Relatively rare now as most companies have found it an inefficient method of doing business.

Industry Standardisation for Institutional Trade Communications (ISITC)
Set up to standardise communication between Fund Managers and their Custodians.

Inflation
A persistent rise in prices in an economy.

Inflation Risk
The risk that the real value of an investment and its income falls because of inflation.

Inheritance Tax (IHT)
The tax that is levied on a person's estate after their death.

Initial Capital Requirement
The amount of initial capital that a firm must have on authorisation and also the amount of Own Funds that it must have at all times.

Initial Charge
The initial charge on a unit trust is made when the units are sold to the investor. The charge is a percentage of the bid price, and covers the manager's start–up costs including commissions.

Initial Margin
Collateral deposited when opening a position (eg, writing an option or trading a future).

Initial Offer Price

The price at which units are available to the public in a new trust for a limited period which may not exceed 21 days.

Initial Public Offering (IPO)

The primary market of the stock market. See *Primary Market*.

Initial Rate of Return (IRR)

The discount rate that when applied to a series of cashflows produces a net present value (NPV) of zero. Also known as the DCF yield.

Initial Yield

An estimated figure which indicates how much income a new unit trust buyer might expect to receive in the first year of his investment. This is not the only basis of preparing an estimate. Estimated gross yield is calculated before allowing for tax credit amounts.

Injunction

A court order telling someone not to do something.

Inland Revenue

The government department responsible for the administration and collection of tax in the UK.

Input

The first stage of settlement, after the trade has been agreed between two CREST members. Each inputs a settlement instruction, detailing the transaction, via the GUI or a bespoke interface to a CREST network.

Insider Dealing (Criminal Justice Act 1993)

A crime committed when an individual in possession of unpublished price sensitive information and knowingly connected with a company attempts to deal in its shares; or when the information is communicated to a third party in the expectation that it will be acted upon.

'In Specie' Dealings

An ACD can arrange for the issue of shares in return for certain investments, and this, for example, would be a method of converting an investment trust into an OEIC. Similarly, the ACD can agree with a shareholder for shares to be redeemed by way of a transfer of a suitable proportion of the OEIC's portfolio of equal value.

Instant Auction

Also called continuous auction, this is an order driven system of trading used on the Tradepoint Stock Exchange. Buy and sell orders are instantly matched by the system if the prices at which the buyer and seller are prepared to deal agree.

Institute of Chartered Accountants in England and Wales (ICAEW)

The designated professional body responsible for chartered accountants.

Institute of Chartered Secretaries and Administrators (ICSA)

The professional body of company secretaries and registrars.

Institutional Investors/Shareholders

An organisation whose primary purpose is to invest assets managed on behalf of others. Includes pension funds, investment companies, insurance companies and banks. They own in excess of 80% of UK equities.

Instrument
Used to describe a form of financing mechanism such as bonds, bills of exchange etc. The term is normally used to describe the actual document.

Instrument of Incorporation
Legal document which sets out the constitution of and internal regulations of an OEIC. Broadly similar to a Companies Act company's memorandum and articles of association.

Insurable Interest
A legally recognised interest enabling a person to insure another. In a life assurance contract, the insured must stand to be financially worse off on the death of the life assured to an extent capable of valuation and as a result of a legally recognised relationship.

Intangible Assets
In the balance sheet of a company intangible assets are a sub–category of fixed assets which are not physical and cannot be touched, eg, goodwill, brands. Not all intangible assets are shown on the balance sheet because some are too difficult to measure accurately.

Integrated Risk Management (IRM)
A philosophy that provides a firm with the ability to understand and address any risk in any area in the most effective way.

Integration
The third stage of money laundering – provision of apparent legitimacy to criminally derived wealth. See *Placement and Layering* .

Intended Settlement Date
The date on which a transaction will settle, if the associated stock and/or cash is available.

Interbank Market
A market in which banks deal between themselves. See *LIBOR*.

Interbank Rate
Interest rates at which banks will take and place cash deposits with each other. Other forms of borrowing might be based on these interbank rates. See *LIBOR, LIBID, EUROIBOR*.

Inter–Dealer Broker
A member firm of the London Stock Exchange authorised by the Exchange to act as an intermediary between two market makers who wish to buy and sell stock, but wish to remain anonymous.

Interest
Payment made for the use of money over time.

Interest Accrual
Interest earned but not yet paid on a bond. When a bond is sold, the purchaser has to compensate the seller for interest accrued up to the date of sale. This is achieved by adding an interest accrual to the clean price being quoted in the market, to give the dirty price payable by the purchaser. See also *Clean Price* and *Dirty Price*.

Interest Cover
An accounting ratio which measures a company's profits relative to its interest charge in the profit and loss account. It is usually defined as profits before interest and tax divided by interest charges. The higher the ratio, the less 'gearing' a company has. See also *Gearing* and *Gearing Ratio*.

Interest In Possession
Broadly, the legal right to income from, or enjoyment of trust property.

Interest Payment

A benefit distribution in which a cash payment is made to holders of certain types of stock issued by the company. The rate of interest and the interval for payment are determined within the original terms of issue of the stock. The company's agent pays the interest on the dates specified by these terms.

Interest Rate Cap

An option product where the holder (buyer) is guaranteed a maximum borrowing cost over a specified term at a rate of his choosing. A premium is required.

Interest Rate Collar

An option product where the holder (buyer) is guaranteed a maximum and minimum borrowing cost over a specified term at rates of his choosing. A premium may be required, but may net to zero. Involves the simultaneous trading of caps and floors.

Interest Rate Floor

An option product where the holder (buyer) is guaranteed a minimum yield on a deposit over a specified term at a rate of his choosing. A premium is required.

Interest Rate Futures

Based on a debt instrument such as a Government Bond or a Treasury Bill as the underlying product and require the delivery of a bond or bill to fulfil the contract.

Interest Rate Guarantee (IRG)

Effectively an option on a forward rate agreement. An IRG can be either a borrower's option (ie, a call on an FRA) or a lender's option (ie, a put on an FRA).

Interest Rate Parity
Formula, based on the interest rate differential between two currencies, which calculates the theoretical forward exchange rate.

Interest Rate Risk
The risk that the value of a fixed interest security will fall with a rise in interest rates. It is also the risk that the income from a variable interest investment will fall with a fall in interest rates.

Interest Rate Swap (IRS)
An agreement to exchange interest related payments in the same currency from fixed rate into floating rate (or vice versa) or from one type of floating rate to another.

Interest Yield
See *Flat Yield*.

Interim Accounting Period
One or more periods ending on dates prior to the end of the fund's annual accounting period in respect of which interim distributions of income are paid.

Interim Bonus
The bonus rate applying to claims that arise before the next official declaration date.

Interim Claim
See *Tax Claims*.

Interim Dividend
A dividend paid by a company during the course of its financial year. See *Final Dividend*.

Intermarket Spread

A transaction involving the purchase of a future on one asset and the sale of a future on another, usually related asset such as purchasing a crude oil future and selling a gas oil future. These spreads are entered into in order to profit from a change in the price differential between the two products.

Intermediaries Offer

A system for primary issues on the London Stock Exchange. Stock is made available to brokers who can take it on behalf of clients.

Intermediary

An institution or individual which takes loans or deposits and lends money to clients, examples include financial advisers, solicitors, etc.

Intermediate Customer

Type of customer who is assumed to understand the working of the business and financial world and to whom only limited protections are provided in their relationship with investment businesses. Could be large corporate customers or individuals with expertise.

Internal Detective Controls

Controls that detect errors after they have occurred but before a potential loss is realised in the outside world, ie, they detect the internal effect in order to prevent the consequence.

Internal Environmental Causes

Environmental causes of operational risk arising from a firm's business strategy.

Internal Measurement Approach (IMA)

A category of Advanced Measurement Approaches used to calculate the capital charge for operational risk.

Internal Rate of Return (IRR)
Discount rate at which an investment has a zero net present value.

International Bank for Reconstruction and Development (IBRD)
An international organisation established at Bretton Woods in 1944, to control the financial requirements for the re–building of war–torn Europe. Its function has evolved into financing the development of LDCs. Known colloquially as the World Bank.

International Central Securities Depository (ICSD)
This is a central securities depository which clears an settles international securities or cross–border transactions in domestic securities, either directly or indirectly to local CSDs.

International Coffee Organisation (ICO)
A trade organisation active in the coffee markets.

International Currency Options Market (ICOM)
Standard documentation for netting foreign exchange option settlements.

International Depository Receipt
See *American Depository Receipts.*

International Equity
An equity of a company based outside the UK but traded internationally.

International Foreign Exchange Master Agreement (IFEMA)
A master agreement for foreign exchange spot and forward deals.

International Monetary Fund (IMF)

An organisation set up by the Bretton Woods agreement in 1944 to oversee the fixed exchange rate regime (now defunct) and to provide borrowing facilities to allow corrective action to be taken to alleviate exchange rate pressure in deficit countries.

International Organisation for Standardisation (ISO)

A worldwide federation of national standards bodies mandated to develop and promulgate standards for communications, including various numbering systems associated with international commerce. See *British Standards Institution.*

International Petroleum Exchange (IPE)

Market place for trading energy product derivatives.

International Primary Markets Association (IPMA)

A professional association which oversees the market practices and procedures for the primary or new issue eurobond markets.

International Securities Identification Number (ISIN)

A coding system developed by ISO with the purpose of creating one unique number on a global basis for identifying securities.

International Securities Markets Association (ISMA)

Founded in 1969 as the Association of International Bond Dealers, The investment exchange responsible for the market place in international securities such as Eurobonds. Trades undertaken are reported into a system known as TRAX. Recognised as a designated investment exchange by the FSA.

International Securities Services Association (ISSA)

An organisation consisting of international banks, ISSA was set–up in 1979 to promote progress in worldwide securities administration. (Formerly known until May 1996 as the International Society of Securities Administrators.)

International Swaps and Derivatives Association (ISDA)

The professional association for swaps dealers. ISDA documentation is used for a range of derivatives deals.

Interpolation

The process of estimating a price or rate for value on a particular date by comparing the prices actually quoted for value dates earlier and later than the date required.

Inter–Professional Business

Inter–professional business is where the firm is either dealing, arranging or advising in respect of an investment between market participants. This, in turn, is defined as a share, bond, warrant, derivative or contract for differences where the other party to the transaction is a market counterparty. Conduct of Business rules do not apply as they have a separate Code of Conduct.

Intervention

The process whereby a central bank acts to influence the exchange rate for its currency by buying it to support its value or selling to weaken it.

Intervention Order

Notice from the FSA to one of its regulated firms where immediate action is required to prevent serious damage being done.

Inter Vivos Trust

A trust created during the lifetime of the settlor.

Intestate
Deceased person not having made a will.

In–The–Money
Any option with intrinsic value. For a call the strike price will be below the current market price (of the underlying stock) and for a put the strike will be above the current market price.

In–The–Money Warrant
A warrant with intrinsic value. See *Intrinsic Value*.

Intra–Day Exposure
See *Daylight Exposure*

Intra–Day Margin
An extra margin call which the clearing organisation can call during the day when there is a very large movement up or down in the price of the contract.

Intramarket Spread
Two futures over the same underlying with different maturity dates are traded – one is bought and the other is sold.

Intrinsic Value
The amount an option or warrant would be worth if it expired immediately. This will come to either the positive difference between the strike and the underlying price, or zero.

Introduction

A way to obtain a listing for shares. If a company wants its shares to be listed and it already has a wide range of shareholders so that the marketability of the shares, once listed, can be assumed, it is allowed to apply for a listing by means of introducing the shares to the market. If the existing number of shareholders is too small for the marketability of the shares to be assumed, the company will be required to make a share issue to increase the number of shareholders. See also *Offer for Subscription, Offer for Sale, Intermediaries Offer* and *Placing.*

Inverted Yield Curve

See *Negative Yield Curve.*

Investigation

Carried out by the FSA Inspection Team when a member firm is suspected of misconduct by the Monitoring Department.

Investment

General meaning is any product in which money is spent with the aim of receiving more money back at a later date. FSMA 2000 defines it in terms of specified activities which are regulated by the Act.

Investment Advertisement

Announcement inviting persons to enter into an investment agreement.

Investment Bank

A bank specialising in capital market dealing, origination and distribution of securities and in corporate finance activities.

Investment Business

Dealing, advising or managing investments. Those doing so need to be authorised.

Investment Company with Variable Capital (ICVC)

Name given by FSA to describe organisations such as OEICs.

Investment Management Association (IMA)

Formed by a merger of the Association of Unit Trust and Investment Funds (AUTIF) and the Fund Managers Association (FMA).

Investment Management Regulatory Organisation (IMRO)

Investment Management Regulatory Organisation Limited was the self regulatory organisation which regulated the activities of fund managers, unit trust groups, occupational pension funds, merchant banks, clearing banks and venture capitalists. Its functions were subsumed into FSA from midnight 30 November.

Investment Manager

A firm who, acting on behalf of a customer, either: manages an account or portfolio in the exercise of discretion (ie, a discretionary manager) or has accepted responsibility on a continuing basis for advising on the composition of the account or portfolio (ie, an advisory manager).

Investment Protection Committee (IPC)

Committees of the ABI and NAPF set up to monitor their positions as shareholders.

Investment Services

The activities of dealing, arranging and managing under the Investment Services Directive. When these activities are undertaken in qualifying instruments they are within the scope of the Directive.

Investments

General meaning is any products in which money is spent with the aim of receiving more money back at a later date.

Investment Services Directive (ISD)
European Union Directive implemented in the UK in January 1996, the objective of which is to harmonise standards of regulation and therefore allow firms established in any EU member state to conduct investment business in any other EU state.

Investment Specific Risk
The risks associated with a particular investment. Diversification is used to reduce it. This risk is separate from general market risk.

Investment Trust (Company)
Quoted companies which invest in the shares of other companies. They are close–ended and their prices may fluctuate somewhat independently of the value of their underlying assets so their market value can be less (discount) than net asset value. They can also be more (premium) than net asset value.

Investors Compensation Scheme
Scheme run by FSA to compensate private customers in the event of the default of the authorised investment business through whom they invested.

Investors Protection Scheme
Fund set up under the Building Societies Act 1986 to pay compensation in respect of deposits held at a building society that goes into liquidation.

Invisibles
See *Current Account*.

Invoice Amount
The amount calculated under the formula specified by the exchange which will be paid in settlement of the delivery of the underlying asset.

IOSCO
International Organisation of Securities Commissions.

IPC
See *Investment Protection Committee.*

IPE
See *International Petroleum Exchange.*

IPMA
International Primary Market Association. Responsible for regulating the issue of Eurobonds.

IPO
See *Initial Public Offer.*

IRG
See *Interest Rate Guarantee.*

IRS
See *Interest Rate Swap.*

Irish Stock Exchange
A Recognised Investment Exchange (RIE), providing a market place for Irish registered securities.

Irredeemable Stock
A fixed interest stock (eg, gilts) which shows no date at which the government has to redeem it.

Irrevocable Payment
A payment instruction that cannot be cancelled by the sender.

ISA

See *Individual Savings Account.*

ISA Manager

See *Account Manager.*

ISD

See *Investment Services Directive.* Also the abbreviation for *Intended Settlement Date.*

ISDA

See *International Swaps and Derivatives Association.*

ISD Firm

An investment firm subject to the regulation of the Investment Services Directive.

ISIN

See *International Securities Identification Number (ISIN).*

ISITC

See *Industry Standardisation for Institutional Trade Communications.*

ISMA

See *International Securities Market Association.*

ISO

See *International Organisation for Standardisation.*

Issue

Stocks or bonds sold by a corporation or government entity at a particular time.

Issue Price
The price at which a new issue is made.

Issuer
An entity (Sovereign country, supranational, banking or corporate) that raises cash through issuing negotiable securities.

Issuer Risk
The risk of default when one institution holds debt securities issued by another institution.

Issuing
The process an institution will go though for the issuance of debt paper.

Issuing Agent
Agent (eg, bank) which puts original issues out for sale.

Issuing House
An institution that facilitates the issue of securities.

iX
Name of the exchange which would have resulted from the proposed merger between the London Stock Exchange and the Deutsche Börse. Projected abandoned in 2001.

J

Japan Securities Depository Centre (JASDEC)
A central depository for Japanese shares, similar to the US DTC.

JATS
Jakarta Automated Trading System.

Jensen's Alpha
The amount by which a stock or portfolio outperforms the market as predicted by the Capital Asset Pricing Model.

JET
Johannesburg Electronic Trading.

JGB
Japanese government bond.

Joint Life Policy
Life policies jointly effected by two life assureds, usually husband and wife.

Joint Money Laundering Steering Group (JMLSG)
Group representing 14 trade bodies which has produced guidance notes on the standards expected to comply with the Money Laundering Regulations.

JSE
Johannesburg Stock Exchange.

Judgemental Analysis
See *Fundamental Analysis*.

Junk Bond
High–risk bonds which have a poor credit rating with a relatively high risk of default. Coupon rates are therefore higher than would be expected for creditworthy borrowers.

K

Kassenverein
Depository banks for securities within the German clearing system.

KATS
Dealing system for the Korean Stock Exchange.

Kas–Associate
Settlement bank for the Netherlands.

KELER
Clearing and depository for the Budapest Stock Exchange.

Kerb
A trading method on the LME. Open outcry transactions can occur in all metal futures at the same time. Kerb trading takes place twice a day, at the end of the first and second trading sessions. Each of the two trading sessions has two rings which immediately precede the kerb trading. See also *Ring*.

Key Features Document
A document drawn up for all potential investors explaining the features of a packaged product, eg, the objective of the fund, the risks, the effect of charges containing essential to enable individuals to determine whether they should invest and what their rights are.

Key Person Insurance
Insurance of a person who is vital to the continued profitability of a business.

Key Risk Indicators (KRIs)
Objective measurement criteria that measure a firm's ongoing risk status.

Knock–In Option
An option which is activated if a trigger level is reached. See *Barrier Option, Knock–Out Option*.

Knock–Out Option
An option which is cancelled if a trigger level is reached. See *Barrier Option, Knock–In Option*.

Know Your Customer (KYC)
The FSA Conduct of Business Rules requiring investment advisers to take sufficient steps, before taking on a customer, to determine the financial position, investment objectives of the client and sources of their funds.

Korea Securities Depository
CSD and clearing organisation for the Korean Stock Exchange.

L

Lamfalussy Recommendations

Six standards for netting systems published by a committee of the Bank for International Settlements, headed by Alexandre Lamfalussy.

LAPR

Life assurance premium relief.

Lapsed Rights

In a rights issue, rights for which call payments have not been made by acceptance date.

Large Exposure Requirement (LER)

Part of the financial resources requirement for ISD firms.

Large Exposure Risk

Achievement of capital adequacy by allocation of more capital if total exposure to any one counterparty is a particularly large proportion.

Last Notice Day

The final day that notification of delivery will be possible. On most exchanges all outstanding short futures contracts are automatically delivered to open long positions.

Last Trading Day

Often the day preceding last notice day which is the final opportunity for holders of long positions to trade out of their positions and avoid ultimate delivery.

Launch

The announcement that a new bond is to be issued.

Layering

The second stage of money laundering, in which the money is passed through a series of transactions to obscure its origin. See *Placement* and *Integration*.

LCH

See *London Clearing House*.

Lead Manager

The Institution responsible for putting together a new issue and taking responsibility for its distribution.

Legacy

A gift to a beneficiary under a will or the rules of intestacy.

Legacy Currencies

The currencies of the member states participating in euro. The legacy currencies ceased to be legal tender by end February 2002.

Legal Risk
The risk of loss due to lawsuits brought by one or more contracted parties. These lawsuits may result in fines, damages or out–of–court settlement and may have consequential effects on a firm's reputation and future business.

Legal Title or Ownership
Legal title to property is held by the person in whose name the property is registered.

Legatee
The recipient of a legacy.

Lender of Last Resort
A central bank function which provides liquidity to the banking system by lending overnight funds.

Lender's Option
See *Interest Rate Guarantee*.

Lending
1. Allowing someone to use money for an amount of time.
2. An example of a 'carry' which takes place on the LME, this is a sale of near–dated futures and purchases of longer dated futures. On other markets such an intramarket spread trade it is known as 'selling the spread'. See also *Borrowing, Carrying* and *Intramarket Spread*.

Less Liquid SEAQ Securities
A SEAQ stock with a normal market size of 500. Because they have less liquid trading than other SEAQ securities, details of trades in them done by market makers are not usually displayed on SEAQ, enabling the market maker to cover their position in the stock. See also *Maximum Publication Level* and *Block Trading*.

Lesser SEAQ Size

The quantity of shares up to which a reduced size market maker must
be prepared to deal for stocks in which they are registered. Generally it
is 50% of the Normal Market Size.

Letter of Acceptance

Also called a Letter of Allotment. If investors apply for shares in a new
issue and their application is successful, they will receive a letter of
acceptance as evidence of their ownership of the shares in the short
term.

Letter of Allotment

See *Letter of Acceptance*.

Letter of Credit

A written undertaking of a bank made at the request of a customer (eg,
importer) to honour the demand for payment from a seller (eg,
exporter) if the terms and conditions of the credit are met.

Letter of Request

A form sent by a personal representative to the registrar of a company
requesting that the shares of the deceased be re–registered in the name
of the personal representative.

Letters of Administration

The formal permission issued by the probate registry authorising the
administrator to administer the estate.

Level Term Assurance

A policy under which a fixed sum assured will be paid out if the life
assured dies during the term of the policy.

Leverage

The magnification of gains and losses by only paying for part of the underlying value of the instrument or asset; the smaller the amount of funds invested, the greater the leverage. See *Gearing*.

Liabilities

Amounts owed by a company to suppliers of goods, to bankers and to bondholders.

LIBID

London Interbank Bid Rate – the interest rate at which banks bid (borrow) for cash deposits in the interbank market.

LIBOR

London inter–bank offered rate, the rate at which banks are willing to lend to other banks of top creditworthiness. Generally used to mean both the interest rate at any time, and specifically the fixing at a particular time (generally 11:00 am).

Lien

Right to seize assets under control in order to satisfy debts. Might be used by a custodian who would sell the securities held in custody to settle fees owed to them.

Life Assured

The person whose death will trigger a payment under the terms of a life insurance policy.

Life Interest

The interest of the life tenant in a trust.

Life Interest Trust

A trust where a beneficiary (the life tenant) has the immediate right to the income or to enjoy the trust property, either for life or for a given period.

Life Tenant

The beneficiary of a life interest entitled to the income from the trust either for their lifetime or for a limited period; the life tenant has the life interest in the property.

LIFFE

The London International Financial Futures and Options Exchange. Market place for trading derivatives on financial instruments, and on soft commodities such as coffee and sugar.

LIFFE CONNECT™

LIFFE's electronic dealing system. See *CONNECT™*.

LIMEAN (London Interbank Mean Price)

The average of LIBOR and LIBID.

Limit (Up or Down)

The maximum price increase/decrease from the previous day's closing price allowed by exchange rules.

Limit Order

Type of order input into SETS or an options order in which a buy or a sell price is specified. If not completed immediately the balance is displayed on the screen and forms the Order Book.

Limit or MOC Order

Limit or market on close. An order may be filled at or better than the limit during the trading day, but, if it is not already traded, it must be filled at the prevailing market price during the official closing period.

Limited Liability

A benefit of share ownership whereby the liability of a shareholder for the debts of a company is limited to the capital subscribed.

Limited Price Indexation (LPI)

The requirement to increase pensions and payments under a final salary scheme by 5% pa or RPI if less.

Line of Credit

A commitment by a bank to make loans to a borrowers up to a specified maximum during a specified period.

Line Order

An order in which a customer sets the maximum price he is willing to pay as a buyer or the minimum price he is willing to accept as a seller.

Linked Forex

When the currency contract is purchased to cover the local cost of a security trade.

Liquid Memorandum Account (LMA)

The record of the cash resource held by a payment bank with the Bank of England that is available for use in settling transactions in CREST.

Liquidation

The formal process of closing down a company. The assets are sold, the liabilities and preference shares are repaid and any balance of assets is paid to the ordinary shareholders.

Liquidator

Named person responsible for closing a company, converting its assets to cash and distributing those assets to investors according to a legally defined priority, starting with creditors and ending with ordinary shareholders.

Liquidity

Ease with which an item can be traded on the market. The ease with which shares can be converted into cash, ie, the ease with which they can be sold, or cashed in, and the speed with which the proceeds are received. Liquid markets are often described as deep.

Liquidity Risk

The risk that a bank may not be able to close out a position because the market is illiquid.

Listed Company

Company which has been admitted to listing on a stock exchange and whose shares can then be dealt on that exchange.

Listed Money Market Institution

An institution which undertakes transactions in the money markets and satisfies the criteria laid down by the FSA for listing. They are exempt from authorisation with respect to their money market activity.

Listed Security

A security listed on a major stock exchange.

Listing

Status applied for by companies whose securities are then listed on a stock exchange, eg, the London Stock Exchange and available to be traded.

Listing Authority
Organisation which drafts the Listing Rules and grants the status of listing, enabling the shares to be publicly traded. Until May 2000 the London Stock Exchange was the Listing Authority, but from that date the FSA has taken over the role.

Listing Particulars
Detailed information that must be published by a company applying to be listed.

Listing Rules
Rule book for listed companies which governs their behaviour.

Lloyd's of London
The London insurance market, which uses capital subscribed principally by corporate bodies to underwrite risks. Now regulated by the FSA.

Lloyd's Member's Agent
Agent responsible for advising a Name and handling their day–to–day affairs at Lloyd's.

Lloyd's Member's Funds
The assets of a Name available to meet any liabilities. these comprise the Lloyd's Deposit, the Personal Reserve and the Special Reserve.

Lloyd's Member's Premium Trust Funds
Trust fund comprising the premiums received by a syndicate and out of which claims and expenses are paid and ultimately any profit.

Lloyd's Names
Participants in the Lloyd's insurance market who provide the underwriting capacity. A Name may be either an individual Name or a corporate Name, but is now more likely to be the latter.

LMA
See *Liquid Memorandum Account.*

LME
See *London Metal Exchange.*

Loan Back
A loan from the life office or other lender under a pension plan.

Loan Sales
The practice of a firm making a loan to a company and then selling the loan to other institutions or investors.

Loan Stock
Fixed interest stock issued by a company or corporation. Can have a variety of features such as cumulative, preference, redeemable.

Local
An individual member of an exchange who trades solely for his or her own account.

London Clearing House (LCH)
A Recognised Clearing House (RCH) under the FSA, it has responsibility for the clearing and settlement of derivative transactions effected on LIFFE, LME and IPE, and securities transactions on virt–x.

London Code of Conduct
The rules and guidelines which regulate and control the activities of the wholesale money markets and foreign exchange markets in London.

London Gold Fix
The opening fixing of a price for gold which takes place twice daily in London, it is effected by a foundation of four members under the chairmanship of NM Rothschild.

London Interbank Bid Rate (LIBID)
See *LIBID*.

London Interbank Mean Rate
Known as LIMEAN. The average of LIBOR and LIBID.

London InterBank Offer Rate (LIBOR)
See *LIBOR*.

London International Financial Futures and Options Exchange (LIFFE)
See *LIFFE*.

London Metal Exchange (LME)
Market for trading in base metal derivatives such as copper, tin, zinc etc.

London Silver Fix
See *London Gold Fix*. The Silver Fix takes place once a day.

London Stock Exchange (LSE)
Market for trading in securities. The LSE is a Recognised Investment Exchange and as such regulates the operation of the market place.

Long
Being the owner of an open bought position.

Long Coupon
A bond on which the first coupon payment period (only) is longer than the normal period.

Long–Dated
Gilts with more than 15 years until redemption.

Long Hedge

The purchase of a futures contract in anticipation of actual purchases in the cash market. Its aim is that any increase in the cash price on the subsequent cash market purchase is offset by a profit on the futures position. Also known as a *Consumer's Hedge*.

Long Position

The term used to indicate that an investor or trader holds a quantity of bonds that has not been sold.

Longs

Abbreviated name for gilt edged securities with more than 15 years left until final redemption.

Long–Term Care Insurance (LTC)

Insurance taken out to cover the cost of caring for individuals who are unable to perform, say, two or three activities of daily living.

Loss Distribution Approach (LDA)

A category of the Advanced Measurement Approach used to calculate the capital charge for operational risk.

Loss, Given Default (LGD)

The estimated loss that a firm would incur at a specific time if a counterparty defaulted.

Lot

Alternative term for one option or futures contract.

Low Cost Endowment

Form of endowment policy which combines with a decreasing term assurance. Usually used to provide a low cost method of funding eventual repayment of a mortgage.

Low Cost Whole Life

A low–cost whole of life with–profits policy, in effect combining a with–profits whole life policy with a decreasing term assurance element to provide a guaranteed minimum level of cover.

Low Start Endowment

A low–cost endowment with premiums starting at a low level and rising gradually over a number of years (eg, five years) to the full premium. Normally aimed at house buyers.

Lower Rate of Tax

This rate of tax was replaced in the fiscal year 1999/2000 by the starting rate of tax.

LME

See *London Metal Exchange*.

LSE

See *London Stock Exchange*.

M

M0
Narrowest measure of the money supply comprising notes and coins.

M2
Measure of the money supply comprising M0 plus sight deposits.

M4
Measure of the money supply comprising M2 plus all bank and building society deposits.

Maastricht Treaty
The treaty on European Union which amended the Treaty of Rome. The Maastricht Treaty established key criteria which member countries needed to achieve in order to be eligible for EMU.

Making a Price
Market maker offering a selling and buying price for a security (bid and ask prices).

Maintenance Margin

An American way of margining. When a position is opened, initial margin is called as normal and is credited to a maintenance margin account. However, variation margin debits and credits are debited and credited directly against the maintenance margin account rather than payable/paid daily. When the balance in the account falls below a predetermined level (usually two thirds of the initial margin payment), the customer must fund the account back up to this level. The system is also sometimes operated by brokers in the UK for their customers. See also *Margin*.

Managed ISA/PEP

May have contained qualifying shares, corporate bonds, unit trusts, investment trusts or combinations of the three. Whilst the manager decided which assets to hold within the pooled investments, the investor often had the choice of selecting the trusts. May also include cash and/or insurance component.

Managed Unit Trust

See *Fund of Funds*.

Management Buy–Out

The purchase of most or all of a companies share capital by its senior executives or management.

Management Fee

The amount paid to fund managers for their services.

Management Group

The primary group consisting of lead manager, co–lead manager(s) and co–managers, that leads a new issue of bonds.

Manager

Person authorised under FSMA 2000 to run the investment decisions of an authorised unit trust.

Manager's Box

See *Book/Box*.

Managing

Buying and selling investments for customers' portfolios either on a discretionary or advisory basis.

Managing Agents (Lloyd's)

Agent appointed by a Lloyd's syndicate to manage the syndicate on behalf of the Names.

Mandatory Event

A corporate action which affects the securities without giving any choice to the security holder.

Mandatory Offer

When an investor either obtains or consolidates control in a company which is covered by the Takeover Code, they must make a mandatory offer to buy out all the other shareholders. See also *Control* and *Consolidation of Control*.

Mandatory Quote Period

Time of day during which market makers in equities are obliged to quote prices under London Stock Exchange rules.

Manufactured Dividend

A payment of an amount equal to a dividend payment made by a borrower of securities to a lender of securities, so that the lender receives the coupon amount from the bonds that it would have received had it not lent or repoed out the bonds.

Many–to–Many (MTM)
A CREST transaction type created by dual input complex delivery instructions, through which up to four stock movements and two cash movements can be moved between two participants. It can be used for taking up rights in a rights issue.

MAOS
Dealing system of the Prague Stock Exchange.

Mapping
Representing a position in terms of other standardised instruments in the variance/covariance approach to VaR.

Margin
Collateral paid to the clearing house by the counterparties to a derivatives transaction to guarantee their positions against loss. Initial margin is collateral placed by one party with a counterparty or clearing house at the time of a deal, against the possibility that the market price will move against the first party, thereby leaving the counterparty with a credit risk.
In a loan, margin is the extra interest above a benchmark such as LIBOR required by a lender to compensate for the credit risk of that particular borrower.

Margin Call
A request by one party in a transaction for variation margin to be transferred by the other. See Margin.

Margined Value
The margined value of securities in a linked account is equal to the value of those securities as determined by the reference price, less the margin which the relevant payment bank has set for those securities.

Mark to Market

The process of revaluing an OTC or exchange–traded product each day. It is the difference between the closing price on the previous day against the current closing price. For exchange–traded products this is referred to as variation margin.

Market

Description of any organisation or facility through which items are traded. All exchanges are markets.

Market Abuse

Offence introduced by FSMA 2000, which is enforced by the FSA and for which can apply to all UK markets. There are three possible offences: abusing information, misleading the market and manipulating the market.

Market Capitalisation

The total value of a company's issued securities at their current market prices. This figure should include all the different types of security issued by the company, but is often used in relation to the equity market capitalisation. The market capitalisation of a company is the market price per share multiplied by the number of shares in issue. The market capitalisation of a stock market is the sum of the market capitalisations of all the companies quoted on the exchange.

Market Counterparty

A person dealing as agent or principal with the broker and involved in the same nature of investment business as the broker.

A large corporate customer can opt up to market counterparty status. This is defined as:

- A company with a share capital of £10m or more; or
- A company which meets any two of the following:
  - Balance sheet total of e12.5m;
  - Net turnover of e25m;
  - Average number of employees of 250.

Market Economy

An economic system where individuals have complete freedom to buy and sell whatever goods and services they wish.

Market Forces

Supply and demand allowing buyers and sellers to fix the price without external interference.

Market–if–Touched (MIT)

An order which becomes a market order if a specified price is achieved. A buy MIT order is placed below the current market price; a sell MIT is placed above. Once the market reaches the specified price, the order is traded at the prevailing market price. Usually a MIT order opens rather than closes a position. MIT orders differ from stop orders in their relationship to the underlying price.

Market Maker

A trader who quotes bid and offer prices in the market and is normally under an obligation to make a price at all times.

Market Match

An electronic trade matching system for international equities on the London Stock Exchange operated by Thomson.

Market Order

Type of order input into SETS. Only available during the opening and closing periods.

Market Place Service (MPS)
A dealing service offered by OM London Exchange that lets less active members place orders by contacting market officials on the telephone, as opposed to using the computerised trading system, Click.

Market Portfolio
A portfolio made up of all the securities in a specified market.

Market Price
In the case of a security, the market price is usually considered as the last reported price at which the stock or bond has been traded.

Market Proxy
Generally an index which includes most of the securities in a market. Used to measure the performance of the market portfolio.

Market Risk
The risk that the value of a position will fall because of changes in market rate/prices.

Market Risk Limit
See *Stop–Loss Limit*.

Market Value
The price at which a security is trading.

Marketing Operation
An issue of shares to raise cash, eg, *Offer for Subscription, Offer for Sale, Intermediaries Offer, Placing* or *Rights Issue*. An Introduction is not a marketing operation because it does not involve the issue of shares.

Marking to Market
See *Mark to Market*.

Master Agreement

This agreement is for OTC transactions and is signed between the client and the broker. It covers the basic terms under which the client and broker wish to transact business. Each individual trade has a separate individual agreement with specific terms known as a confirm.

Matador Bond

A peseta bond issued in Spain by a non–Spanish issuer.

Matched Bargain

See *Order-Driven.*

Matched Book

This refers to the matching by a repo trader of securities repoed in and out. It carries no implications that the trader's position is matched in terms of exposure, for example to short–term interest rates.

Matched Transaction

The successful result of two CREST members each inputting their side of a transaction where key fields (matchable fields) are entered with matching (ie, identical or corresponding) information. See also *Dual Input Transaction* or *Non–matching Transaction.*

Matching

The process whereby a settlement system compares and attempts to combine settlement instructions in order to achieve an agreed transaction record which can then go on to be settled.

The second stage of settlement processing, after input during which CREST authenticates the settlement instruction and attempts to match it immediately after input with a corresponding instruction from the counterparty.

Matching Concept
See *Accruals*.

Matching Rules
See *Share Identification Rules*.

Material Interest
1. When a firm's own position may conflict with the best interest of a customer. This can be managed in various ways including an independence policy. The interests of the customer must be placed above those of the firm.
2. A beneficial holding of 3%+ of the shares of a public company. Once an investor obtains such a holding, they must tell the company within two business days. They must also disclose, within two business days, when the holding moves to the next full percentage point.

MATIF
The French International Financial Futures Exchange.

Maturity (Date)
The partial or final repayment of the outstanding debt by the issuer/borrower (on a particular date).

Maxi ISA Account
An account offered and managed by a single approved ISA manager.

Maximum Investment Plan (MIP)
A unit–linked endowment policy with the minimum sum assured necessary for it to be a qualifying policy.

MCSD
Clearing house and depository for the Egyptian Stock Exchange.

Mean
The average of a set of values, calculated by dividing the sum of all the values in the population by the total population.

Medium Dated
Gilts due to be redeemed within the next 7–15 years.

Mediums
Abbreviated name for gilt edged securities officially classified as having 7 – 15 years left until final redemption.

MEFF
Spanish derivatives exchange, a recognised overseas investment exchange.

Member Firm
A firm that is a member of a stock exchange. A London Stock Exchange (LSE) member firm is one that acts either in a single or a dual capacity. Also see *Broker Dealer*.

Memorandum
The document which forms the basis of a companies registration, giving details of its address, powers and objects. See *Articles of Association*.

Merchant Bank
A (now somewhat old fashioned) term for a UK bank which is primarily involved in matters such as portfolio management, bills of exchange acceptance, mergers etc, rather than retail banking business.

Mergers and Acquisitions (M&A)
Divisions of securities houses or merchant banks responsible for advising on takeover activity. Usually work with the corporate finance department and is often kept as a single unit.

Merval
Trading and settlement organisation for the Buenos Aires Stock Exchange. The trading system is called SINAC.

Middle (Mid) Price
The price half way between a buying and selling price. This is the price for a share taken at close of the previous days business published in the Financial Times. Alternatively, a page of SETS or SEAQ which gives the current mid–price of stocks. If the colour of the price is blue, it means that the most recent price movement has been upwards. If it is red, it means that the most recent movement was downwards.

Mine
On receipt of a price this is a quick way of stating that you wish to buy the base currency.

Mini ISA Account
An account which comprises of one component of an ISA.

Minimum Funding Requirement (MFR)
The minimum funding requirement is the minimum amount of funds that should be in a pension scheme at all times, in order to meet the scheme's liabilities if it were to be discontinued.

Minimum Income Guarantee
This is a means tested benefit that helps people with low incomes in retirement and is calculated by reference to a person's total income from all sources. It is an increase to the basic pension to provide a minimum income.

Minimum Quote Size
The minimum amount at which a normal market maker is allowed to quote for a SEAQ security. It is defined as 1 x the normal market size (NMS).

Minority Interests
These arise when a company has a subsidiary in which it does not own all of the shares. The shareholders excluding the holding company are referred to as the minority interests.

Misconduct
Failure to comply with the law or rules of the FSA.

Misleading Statement
Giving false information about an investment in order to affect its value.

Mismatch
Where short and long positions do not complement one another.

MIT
See *Market–if–Touched*.

Mixed Economy
Economy which relies on a mix of market forces and government involvement.

MMTS
Dealing system for the Budapest Stock Exchange.

Model
A series of mathematical processes that will produce an estimate of the 'fair value' of a financial instrument, eg, 'Black Scholes' or the binomial model.

Model Code (for Director's Dealing)
Part of the Listing Rules that relates to directors dealing in their own company's securities. Prohibits them from doing so during the two months before results are announced.

Model Risk
The risk that the computer model used by a bank for valuation or risk assessment is incorrect or misinterpreted.

Modified Dietz
Simplified method for calculating the time–weighted rate of return.

Modified Duration (MD)
A measure closely linked to duration, this can be used to predict a change in price for a bond given a change in interest rates. Defined as duration divided by (1 + the gross redemption yield of the bond).

Modified Following
The convention that if a settlement date in the future falls on a non–business day, the settlement date will be moved to the next following business day, unless this moves it to the next month, in which case the settlement date is moved back to the last previous business day.

MOF
The Ministry of Finance, (Japan)

MONEP
The Paris options market.

Monetary Offer
A provision of the City Code that requires a formal bid to be made for a company's ordinary share capital once 30% of that company's voting capital is held by the bidder. A mandatory bid must be made at a price at least equal to the highest price paid by the bidder for the target company's shares over the last 12 months.

Monetary Policy
The setting of short term interest rates by a central bank in order to manage domestic demand and achieve price stability in the economy. Monetary policy is also known as stabilisation policy.

Monetary Policy Committee (MPC)
Committee chaired by the governor of the Bank of England, which sets interest rates.

Money Broker
Formerly, a member firm of the London Stock Exchange authorised to act as an intermediary for stock loans between a market maker who wishes to borrow stock and an authorised institution who has stock to lend. As of January 1996, stock borrowing and lending intermediaries act in this role.

Money Laundering
The process where criminals attempt to conceal the true origin and ownership of the proceeds of their criminal activities and to legitimise these proceeds by introducing them into the mainstream of financial activities.

Money Laundering Regulations Act 1993
The regulations place the legal obligation on investment houses, etc, in the UK to report suspicious movements of cash. Failure to comply renders the individual liable to a fine and/or imprisonment.

Money Laundering Reporting Officer (MLRO)
The senior employee who implements the anti–money laundering rules and is responsible for reporting suspicions to the National Criminal Intelligence Service.

Money Market
A reference to the market where short–term instruments such as certificates of deposit, bankers' acceptances, repurchase agreements are traded. There is no physical market location.

Money Market Basis
An interest rate quoted on an ACT/360 basis.

Money Market Fund
A unit trust which invests in deposits and other money market instruments, eg, Treasury Bills.

Money Market Securities
Debt securities with a maturity of less than one year.

Money Market Scheme
An authorised fund that invests primarily in assets that comprise cash or near cash investments as defined in the Financial Services (Regulated Schemes) Regulations 1991.

Money Purchase Scheme
See *Defined Contribution Scheme.*

Money Purchase Underpin
A minimum benefit, eg, capital allowances, provided in a defined benefit scheme, calculated on a money purchase basis.

Money Rate of Return
Annual return as a percentage of asset value.

Money Supply
Measure of the money available in the economy.

Money Weighted Rate of Return (MWR)
The internal rate of return (IRR) that equates the value of a portfolio at the start of an investment period plus the net new capital invested during the investment period with the value of the portfolio at the end of this period. The MWR, therefore, measures the fund growth resulting from both the underlying performance of the portfolio and the size and timing of cashflows to and from the fund over this period.

Money Weighted Return
Calculates the average rate of return on money invested using the same rate of return on each sum invested. It can be distorted by the timings of cash inflows and outflows out of the portfolio. See also *Time Weighted Return*.

Monitoring
Procedure whereby the FSA receives regular reports from regulated firms and checks compliance with the rules.

Monopolies and Mergers Commission (MMC)
See *Competition Commission*.

Monte Carlo Simulation
A statistical model used to calculate VaR.

Monti Titoli
Central Securities Depository for Italian securities.

Moody's Investment Services
Located in New York City with its parent, Dun & Bradstreet, Moody's is one of the best known popular bond rating agencies in the U.S. The other agency is Standard and Poor's. See *Rating (Credit)*.

Mortgage

Form of secured borrowing. Used mainly in the context of loans taken for the purpose of house purchase.

Mortgage–Backed Security

Security backed by an investment company that raises money from shareholders and invests it in stocks, bonds or other instruments (unit trust, investment fund, SICAV – BEVEK).

Mortgage Code

Voluntary code of practice drafted by the Council of Mortgage Lenders, which regulates the behaviour of its members in the provision of mortgage services.

Mortgage Debenture Stocks

A debenture secured by a fixed charge on the borrower's property assets.

MPL

See *Maximum Publication Level.*

MPS

See *Market Place Service.*

MQP

See *Mandatory Quote Period.*

MQS

See *Minimum Quote Size.*

MTA

Dealing system of the Milan Stock Exchange.

Multilateral Netting

The agreement to net payments in the same currency between a group of banks.

Mutual Collateralisation

The deposit of collateral by both counterparties to a transaction.

Mutual Funds

An open ended investment company or trust which combines the contributions of many investors with similar objectives.

Mutual Guarantee

A guarantee operated by clearing houses. Losses caused by a clearing member's default are covered firstly by the defaulting clearing member's assets (if any), and then from the guarantee fund contributed to by the clearing members. Only once this guarantee fund has been exhausted does the clearing house use its own resources to meet losses.

Mutual Life Office

Insurance companies which are effectively 'owned' by their with–profits policyholders.

My Risk

On receipt of a price this is a quick way of stating that you acknowledge that it could change before you accept it.

N

N2
Midnight 30 November 2001. Date on which the FSA assumed full powers and previous regulators ceased to exist.

Naked Option
An option bought or sold for speculation, with no offsetting existing position behind it. See *Covered Option*.

Naked Writing/Options
The seller does not own the stock corresponding to the call option which he has sold and would be forced to pay the prevailing market price for the stock to meet delivery obligations, if called.

Names
Individuals of Lloyds of London who join together in syndicates to write insurance business. Their liability is unlimited and therefore all their personal wealth is at risk. Now a much less important source of capital at Lloyd's than it used to be.

NASDAQ
See *National Association of Securities Dealers Automated Quotation System*.

National Association of Pension Funds (NAPF)
Trade association of pension funds through which they can voice their opinions collectively.

National Association of Securities Dealers Automated Quotation System (NASDAQ)
A US screen–based dealing system. It is owned and operated by the National Association of Securities Dealers (NASD) which is an American securities industry self–regulatory organisation. Companies listed on NASDAQ are often smaller, newer companies, especially in the higher technology sector.

National Central Securities Depository (NCSD)
A CSD which deals specifically with (and is usually based in the country of) domestic instruments eg. CREST for the UK and Ireland.

National Criminal Intelligence Service (NCIS)
Organisation to whom suspicions of money laundering are reported.

National Currency Unit
See *Legacy Currency*.

National Insurance Contributions (NICs)
A form of tax theoretically used to fund the social security system although in fact there is no link between the amounts received and amounts paid. The payment structure is split into Classes with differing amounts paid by employees, their employers and the self–employed.

Nationality Declaration

A statement of compliance from a purchaser of shares in a company whose Memorandum and Articles of Association specify a limit to shareholders who are not of specified nationality.

National Savings

Government department which provides savings products to the public with the objective of raising funds for the government. Most transactions are conducted through main branches of post offices.

National Savings Certificates

Certificates which are held for five years by an investor before being redeemed. No interest is paid over the five years. On redemption, all the proceeds are free of tax. If the certificates are redeemed early, the proceeds are tax free, but the effective interest rate achieved is fairly low. If the certificates are not redeemed after five years, they continue to accrue tax free interest but again at a fairly low rate of interest (referred to as the general extension rate). They are issued by the UK government's National Savings department.

National Savings Stock Register (NSSR)

Selection of gilts purchasable through Post Offices at very low commission. Income tax is not deducted at source from dividends.

National Securities Clearing Corporation (NSCC)

An organisation providing settlement and clearing facilities in the USA.

National Securities Depository

Depository for the National Stock Exchange in India.

NC

A trade condition for indicating non–central settlement, ie, not for settlement in CREST.

NCBO
Applied to a transfer meaning No Change of Beneficial Owner.

NCM
See *Non–Clearing Member*.

NCS
Dealing system for EURONEXT.

NDF
See *Non–Deliverable Forward*.

Near Cash
Assets which may be converted into cash very quickly, eg, Treasury Bills and certificates of deposit.

Nearby Month
The first available month for derivatives trading.

NECIGEF
CSD for the Netherlands.

Negative Correlation
An inverse, or opposite relationship between two factors.

Negative Skewness
A downward movement is more likely than an upward one.

Negative Yield Curve
A yield curve that slopes downwards. Also called inverted yield curve. See *Normal Yield Curve*.

Negotiable
A security which can be bought and sold in a secondary market.

Negotiable Security

A security whose ownership can pass freely from one party to another. Negotiable securities are, therefore, tradeable.

Net Asset Value (NAV)

This is the value of the underlying shares held in the portfolio based on quoted mid–market prices, together with other assets, less liabilities, divided by the number of shares in issue. NAV is quoted in pence per share.

Net Assets

The difference between assets and liabilities.

Net Assets Per Share

Also known as net worth per share, this is an accounting ratio, defined as net assets divided by the number of shares in issue. Its purpose is to compare the net assets per share with the share price. The share price will either be at a premium to net asset value or a discount. Usually, a discount to net asset value indicates a company which, for some reason, is less popular.

Net Current Assets

Current assets less current liabilities. This is also called the working capital of the company.

Net Current Liabilities

See *Net Current Assets*.

Net Debt

Total loans less cash balances.

Net Debt to Equity Ratio

See *Gearing Ratio*.

Net Income Yield
The income return on an investment after tax has been deducted.

Net Present Value (NPV)
The economic value of a known set of future cash flows calculated by discounting the cash flows at the rates applicable to the future periods to produce a present value for each cash flow

Net Redemption Yield (NRY)
After tax equivalent of the Gross Redemption Yield. This is the measure which should be used by taxpayers in selecting the gilt in which to invest.

Net Relevant Earnings (NRE)
Self–employed earnings or earnings from a non–pensionable employment less certain deductions. NRE is used to determine the maximum contributions to a retirement annuity or personal pension plan. See *Earnings Cap*.

Net Settlement Limit
Limit on the net value of transfers which can be made out of a CREST Personal Members account in any one day.

Net Worth
See *Shareholders' Funds*.

Netting
Trading partners offset their positions thereby reducing the number of positions for settlement.

Network Provider
An organisation accredited by CRESTCo to provide network communication services to users. Current network providers are SWIFT and Syntegra.

New Issues
Issue of shares arising from the flotation of a company on the stockmarket.

New York Stock Exchange (NYSE)
The NYSE is the world's largest stock exchange. Dealing takes place on the floor of the Exchange or through a computer system called SuperDot.

NFA
National Futures Association. The US regulator responsible for the futures markets.

NICs
See *National Insurance Contributions*.

NIEC
CSD in the Netherlands.

Nikkei 225 Index
Index of the Tokyo Stock Exchange. Most widely quoted Japanese stock index. Consists of 225 shares listed on the Tokyo Stock Exchange.

Nikkei Dow Index
Main share index in Japan.

Nil Paid Rights Price
Ex–rights price less the subscription price.

Nil Paid Shares

New shares offered to existing shareholders by way of a rights issue can normally be bought and sold in a nil paid form up to a week before the call is due. The price is usually, but not necessarily, the difference between the call price and the price of existing shares. See *Rights Issue* and *Fully Paid Shares*.

NMS

See *Normal Market Size.*

No Netting Off

One of the fundamental accounting principles. Amounts of individual assets and liabilities must be disclosed separately in a set of accounts rather than netted off against each other. A company with cash deposits and an overdraft must not show a net figure in the accounts. Each must be disclosed separately.

No Par Value (NPV)

Shares which do not possess a nominal or par value. Such a method of not expressing a par value is not allowed in the UK where securities must be given a nominal value. In the US however, the issue of shares of no par value is quite common. One problem with par value is that special rules apply to the raising of new money when existing securities stand at a discount on par value, which makes the raising of new money difficult in such circumstances.

Nominal

The quantity or amount of securities irrespective of its market value.

Nominal Rate Of Interest

Actual rate of interest paid which comprises the real rate plus inflation. See *Real Rate of Interest.*

Nominal Value (or Par Value)

The face value of a share as against its market value. For example, a company may have an issued capital of £10 million, divided into 40 million shares of 25p. Par values may be of any amount. They have no real significance, being purely a matter of law and book keeping.

Nominal Value of a Bond

The value at which the capital, or principal, of a bond will be redeemed by the issuer.

Nominated Advisor

Firm appointed to advise AIM company directors on their responsibilities. Role can be combined with that of a nominated broker.

Nominated Broker

Firm appointed to assist dealing in AIM securities.

Nominee

Legal arrangement whereby securities are held by a third party on behalf of the beneficial owner. For administrative reasons, securities are more than likely to be held in a nominee name.

Nominee Company

A company set up to hold shares on behalf of other companies or individuals. Used by custodians and stockbrokers to hold shares on behalf of their customers or clients.

Non–Accelerating Inflation Rate of Unemployment (NAIRU)

That level of unemployment that is consistent with a stable inflation rate. Also known as the natural rate of unemployment or the long run Phillips curve.

Non—Callable
Cannot be redeemed by the issuer for a stated period of time from date of issue.

Non—Certificated Shares
Shares for which no certificate is issued to the holder.

Non—Clearing Member
A member of an exchange which does not undertake to settle its business. This type of member must appoint a clearing member to register all its trades at the clearing organisation.

Non-Competitive Bid
In an auction, bidding for a specific amount of securities without mentioning a price. Usually, the price paid will be equal to the average of the accepted competitive bids.

Non—Contributory Pension Scheme
Occupational Scheme funded entirely by the employer.

Non—Core Services
Activities, such as giving advice on ISD instruments, which are passportable if the firm is already authorised to perform a core activity (dealing, arranging, managing).

Non—Cumulative Preference Share
If the company fails to pay a preference dividend the entitlement to the dividend is simply lost. There is no accumulation.

Non—Deliverable Forward
Foreign exchange forward outright deal traded as a contract for differences. Instead of delivering one currency and receiving the other, the rate dealt is compared with the spot rate at maturity and the difference only is settled, usually in the base currency.

Non–Discretionary Dealing
Client takes decisions to buy/sell investments.

Non–Discretionary Securities Lending
A form of securities lending where the custodian seeks approval for each loan from its client on a case–by–case basis.

Non–Executive Director
Director who does not have an operational responsibility within the company.

Non–Fungible
Securities which have the same security code and which are identifiable by separate certificate numbers. These securities are not interchangeable. See *Fungible*.

Non–ISD Firm
A firm that was authorised to conduct investment under the Financial Services Act 1986 but is not covered by the Investment Services Directive, eg, commodity derivative brokers.

Non–Matching Transaction
A transaction that requires single–sided input only, including the following types: OAT, REG, STD, STW, TFE, TTE, USE, BDR and ADJ. See also *Matched Transaction*.

Non–Profit Insurance
A policy which does not participate in the profits of the life office. A non–profit whole of life policy pays out only a fixed sum assured whenever death occurs. A non–profit endowment policy pays out a fixed sum assured on maturity or earlier death. Most term assurance policies are non–profit policies.

Non–Qualifying
With respect to unit trusts or investment trusts where more than 50% of the underlying comprise shares in companies, regardless of where incorporated, which are quoted on a recognised stock exchange. A maximum of £1,500 of the annual allowance may be invested in such funds.

Non–Qualifying Policy
A policy that does not qualify for full tax relief and where the proceeds on maturity, surrender or death may be subject to higher rate tax.

Non-Readily Realisable Investment
Shares not traded on a recognised or designated investment exchange or are not traded frequently and units in unregulated collective investment schemes.

Normal Bonus
Also known as a reversionary bonus. The bonus added each year to a with profits policy. Once declared this bonus cannot be withdrawn.

Normal Distribution
Symmetric bell–shaped distribution defined by its mean and standard deviation. Basis for much probability analysis.

Normal Market Size (NMS)
Minimum size in which market makers must quote on LSE.

Normal Profit
The required rate of return for a firm to remain in business taking account of all opportunity costs.

Normal Yield Curve
A yield curve that slopes upwards. Also called positive yield curve. See *Negative Yield Curve.*

Nostro
Italian word for 'our', usually associated with accounts maintained by banks held with other banks in another currency and country. See *Vostro*.

Nostro Account
One bank's foreign currency account with another bank.

Nostro Reconciliation
Checking the entries shown on the bank's nostro account statement with the bank's internal records (the accounting ledgers) to ensure that they correspond exactly.

Not Completed
The status given an unmatched settlement instruction.

Not Ready
The status given a matched settlement instruction that has not yet reached its settlement due date.

Note
Bonds issued with a relatively short maturity are often called notes.

Notice of Cancellation
In circumstances where the right to cancel exists, this document, which explains those rights must be sent within 14 days of the agreement.

Notifiable Interest
A holding of 10% or more (including non–beneficial interests) in the shares of a public company. Once an investor has such a holding, they must notify the company within two business days. They must also notify the company when the holding moves to each next full percentage point.

Notified Point

Regular point chosen by ACD, within two hours of valuation point of an OEIC, by which a decision is made to issue or cancel shares.

Notional

Contracts for differences require a notional principal amount on which settlement can be calculated.

Novation

The process where registered trades are cancelled with the clearing members and substituted by two new ones – one between the clearing house and the clearing member seller, the other between the clearing house and the clearing member buyer.

NPV

See *Net Present Value*.

NYMEX

New York Mercantile Exchange.

NYSE

See *New York Stock Exchange*.

O

OASYS
Trade confirmation system for US brokers operated by Thomson Financial Services.

OAT
1. French government bond issued with a maturity between 7 and 30 years.
2. Also an Own Account Transfer in CREST/CGO – a transfer of stock between two accounts under the same CREST/CGO participant.

Obligation Netting
An arrangement to transfer only the net amount (of cash or a security) due between two or more parties, rather than transfer all amounts between the parties on a gross basis.

Obligor
A party that has a financial obligation to another party.

Obligor Default Rates
The likelihood of a default event occurring.

Occupational Pension Scheme

Pension scheme run by an individual employer for the benefit of its employees. Could be contributory or non–contributory. Maximum pension payable is limited by Inland Revenue rules.

Occupational Pensions Board (OPB)

A statutory body responsible for issuing contracting out and appropriate scheme certificates for pension schemes which meet the statutory requirements. The OPB supervises schemes to ensure that GMPs and protected rights are secure and ensures that equal access and preservation requirements are satisfied.

Occupational Pensions Regulatory Authority (OPRA)

Regulator for Occupational Pensions.

Odd Lot

A quantity of shares which is not an exact multiple of a board lot. Will often be at a disadvantageous price to a board lot.

OECD

Organisation for Economic Co–operation and Development.

OEICs

Open Ended Investment Companies (pronounced OIKs). New corporate structure introduced in 1997. It is a form of collective investment vehicle. Its share capital can expand or contract.

Off

A quick way of stating that the last price quoted by a market maker is no longer valid.

Off–Balance Sheet

A transaction whose principal amount is not shown on the balance sheet because it is a contingent liability or settled as a contract for differences.

Off–Balance Sheet Transaction

A transaction which affects the assets or liabilities or an organisation, but is not required by accounting standards to be reported as such.

Off–The–Page Advertisement

Advertisements which appear in the press and which contain application forms for purchasing units. If used the investor does not have rights to cancel the investment.

OFEX

An off–exchange share matching and trading facility established by J P Jenkins Limited to enable London Stock Exchange member firms to deal in the securities of unlisted and unquoted companies. Securities traded on OFEX are not deemed to be quoted, listed or dealt on the London Stock Exchange or subject to its rules.

Offer

The rate at which the market or a dealer is willing to sell.

Offer Basis

Circumstances where the trust manager has set the offer price of an authorised unit trust at the highest level allowed by FSA rules.

Offer for Sale

Method for a company to issue shares and come to the market for the first time. Anyone can apply for shares through the publicly available application forms.

Offer for Subscription
An issue of shares by a company. Investors are invited to subscribe for the shares directly with the company. Used when obtaining a listing for the first time on the Stock Exchange. See also *Offer for Sale, Intermediaries Offer, Placing, Introduction* and *Marketing Operation.*

Offer Price
The price at which a dealer will sell securities – also called the *Ask Price.*

Offer–to–Bid
Performance comparison unique to the unit trust industry.

Offer–to–Bid Basis
The usual form of unit trust performance appraisal – the opening price used for the calculation is the then current offer price and the closing price is the then current bid price.

Office of Fair Trading (OFT)
Government department which administers the Fair Trading legislation and advises the Secretary of State for Trade and Industry on whether or not a proposed takeover should be referred to the Competition Commission for full investigation.

Official Listing
Companies granted an official listing for their securities by the Listing Authority (now part of the FSA) can issue shares to the public and have them traded in the secondary market under Stock Exchange rules. The official listing enables the company to raise large sums of money and enables investors to trade shares in the company easily. A company must comply with strict regulatory requirements designed to protect investors in order to obtain a listing. Only relatively large companies will seek one. See also *Alternative Investment Market.*

Offset

Obliterating a futures/option position by undertaking an opposite transaction. A sale offsets a Long Position, a purchase offsets a Short Position. Sometimes known as a *Closing Trade*.

Offshore Fund

A collective investment scheme based outside the UK.

Offshore Investment

Any investment made by an individual who is resident or domiciled in one country, into an investment medium based in another country. An investment centre which is offshore is not subject to UK tax or regulations.

OMGEO

Joint venture between Thompson Financial Services and the DTCC providing trade confirmation services.

Omnibus Account

Single account held in a depository or with a sub custodian for all assets held by a client of that depository or sub custodian. See *Pooled Nominee Account*.

OM London Exchange

The Swedish market operating in London where Swedish equity and index derivatives are traded. Formerly known as OMLX.

OMLX

See *OM London Exchange*.

OMX

The Swedish equity index.

On–Balance Sheet
A transaction whose principal amount is shown on the balance sheet.

On–Exchange/Off–Exchange
Any transactions conducted on a RIE are termed 'on–exchange', whereas those on any other market are known as 'off–exchange'. The latter are subject to special reporting FSA rules.

One Eighth Measure
The alteration in interest rates necessary to produce a change in price of a bond of $£^1/_8$. The lower the one eighth measure, the more volatile the bond price is to changes in interest rates.

One–Off Test
The criteria by which an investor may be always treated as a market counterparty.

One Sided Confirmation
Only one party to the transaction, usually the broker or dealer, submits trade details to a centralised trade confirmation system. The other counterparty merely affirms or rejects the trade.

One Way Agreement
A customer agreement sent by the firm to the customer and no formal acknowledgement by the customer is required.

OPEC
Organisation of Petroleum Exporting Countries, an organisation to which many of the major oil producing countries belong.

Open
Market positions that have not been offset, ie, still capable of delivery.

Open Economy
A country where there are few restrictions on trading with other countries.

Open Ended Fund
Type of organisation such as Unit Trusts or OEICs which can expand without limit. Where the total of units on offer can rise or fall according to customer demand.

Open Ended Investment Companies (OEICs)
See *OEICs*.

Open Interest
The number of contracts outstanding with the market in a particular instrument.

Open Market Option
The right to take the accumulated fund from a personal pension scheme or retirement annuity plan in order to purchase an annuity from another life office.

Open Offer
This is an offer to existing shareholders to subscribe money to buy further shares, usually at a discount to the market price. Although set out on a pro rata basis, shareholders may subscribe for any amount of shares.

Open Outcry
The style of trading whereby traders face each other in a designated area such as a pit and shout or call their respective bids and offers. Hand signals are also used to communicate. It is governed by exchange rules.

Open Position
A position held with a clearing house (or other counterparty) or a trade that has not been counteracted by an equal and opposite trade.

Open Repo
A repo in which the term (length) is not specified at the outset. It can be terminated at any time by either party giving notice.

Opening
Undertaking a transaction which creates a position.

Opening Leg
The first half of a repo transaction.

Opening Order
An order type which requires the order to be filled during the official opening period in the market at the prevailing market price, as opposed to the opening price.

Opening Purchase
A purchase where rights or obligations are established. With an option sale, the buyer becomes the holder of the option.

Opening Sale
A sale where rights or obligations are established. With an option sale, the seller becomes the writer of the option.

Opening Trade
A bought or sold trade which is held open to create a position.

Operational Controls
Activities that are inserted into a process to protect it against specific operational risks.

Operational Risk
The risk to an organisation of failures in the systems, procedures and routines in the dealing support areas.

Operational Risk Policy
A framework for operational risk management.

Operations Risk
The risk of direct or indirect loss in the transaction processing and settlement activities resulting from inadequate or failed internal processes, people and systems or from external events. This can alternatively be described as operational risk that occurs within the Operations function.

Opportunity Cost
The cost of foregoing the next best alternative course of action. In economics, costs are defined not as financial but as opportunity costs.

Optimisation
See *Passive Fund Management*.

Option
An option gives the holder the right (but not the obligation) to buy or sell a fixed quantity of an underlying asset on or before a specified date in the future. There are two basic types of traded option – puts and calls. The buyer of a call option has the right to buy the underlying asset at a given price. The seller (also known as the writer) has the obligation to sell shares to him, if the option is exercised. Conversely, the buyer of a put option has the right to sell the underlying asset at the given price. The writer of a put option is obliged to buy stock from the holder if the option is exercised.

Option Premium
The sum of money paid by the buyer, for acquiring the right of the option. It is the sum of money received by the seller for incurring the obligation, having sold the rights, of the option. It is the sum of the intrinsic value and the time value.

Optional Dividend
Dividend that can be paid either in cash or in stock. The shareholders entitled to the dividend make the choice.

Options On Futures
These have the same characteristics as an option, the difference being that the underlying product is either a long or short futures contract. Premium is not exchanged as the contracts are marked to market each day.

Order Book
See *Stock Exchange Electronic Trading System (SETS).*

Order Book Security
A security which the Exchange has admitted to trading on the order book.

Order-Driven
Dealing system in which prices are determined by the direct flow of buying and selling orders.

Ordinarily Resident Outside UK
A person who for tax purposes is deemed not to live in the UK. Agreement letters and risk warnings do not need to be signed by such people if the firm has reasonable grounds to believe that they do not wish to consent to writing.

Ordinary Business Investor

Customer of an investment business which is a business entity and which meets the size criteria such that it does not have to be given the same levels of protection as a private customer.

Ordinary Resolution

A shareholders' resolution to be voted on at the *Annual General Meeting* or *Extraordinary General Meeting*. A majority of votes cast at the meeting is needed for the resolution to be passed. Most resolutions are ordinary resolutions. See also *Special Resolution*.

Ordinary Shares

Shares which are the risk capital of the company. These shares carry no guarantees and reflect the success (or failure) of the company. The ordinary shareholders are the true owners of the company who are entitled to the balance of the income of the company after all expenses have been paid.

OTC

See *Over-The-Counter.*

Out of Pocket Expenses

Market charges which are charged to the client without taking any profit.

Out–Of–The–Money

A call option whose exercise price is above the current underlying share price or a put option whose exercise price is below the current underlying share price. This option has no intrinsic value.

Outright

Simple foreign exchange transaction involving the purchase of one currency for another at a specific exchange rate.

Outsourcing

The transfer of an aspect of a firm's business to a third party who will carry the risk exposure for a fee.

Out–Trade

A trade which has been incorrectly matched on the floor of an exchange. These types of trades should normally be resolved by the end of the business day on which they were traded.

Overborrowed

Liabilities (borrowings) are of longer maturity than assets (loans). See *Overlent*.

Overcollateralised

The value of collateral exceeds that of cash lent against it.

Overdraft

A loan on individuals current/banking accounts which enables them to withdraw extra funds up to an agreed limit and for a specific period of time.

Overlent

Assets (loans) are of longer maturity than liabilities (borrowings). See *Overborrowed*.

Overnight

A deal from today until tomorrow (the next working day). Also known as O/N or today/tomorrow.

Overnight Indexed Swap (OIS)

A swap in which one leg is based on an index for the overnight or tom/next interest rate.

Overnight Limit
The largest size position that a dealer is permitted to take overnight.

Overnight Money
Money placed on the money market for repayment for the next day.

Overseas Tax Relief
If someone has an overseas source of income liable to UK tax on which they have already paid overseas tax, they may be able to claim overseas tax relief, reducing the amount of UK tax which is due on the income. This is to prevent individuals suffering unfairly high rates of taxation on their income, when both UK and overseas tax is taken into account.

Oversubscribed
Applications have been received for more shares than are available in a new issue.

Over–The–Counter (OTC)
Generic name for trading in any product outside a formal exchange. In contrast to exchange traded products which are standardised but offer greater liquidity.

Over–The–Bridge
The electronic link between Euroclear and Cedel which allows book entry movements of securities between customers of either clearing house.

Own Account Transfer (OAT)
A transaction type abbreviated OAT, used to move securities between member accounts belonging to a single member. OATs cannot be used to move securities between members.

Own Funds

Part of a firm's funding obligations, which oblige it maintain own funds at the level of the initial capital requirement at all times. To arrive at a firm's own funds, the current value of initial capital is reduced by any intangible assets and then increased by certain subordinated loans and by any revaluation reserves. The definition therefore permits funding from other sources to count towards its requirement.

P

Packaged Products
Investments which evolve from a range of other investments such as life assurance, pensions and unit trusts.

Paid In Surplus
See *Share Premium Account*.

Paid–Up Benefit
A preserved benefit which is secured for an individual member under an insurance policy where the premiums have stopped being paid for the member.

Paid–Up Policy (PUP)
A policy that was a regular premium policy but has been converted to a PUP at the policyholder's request. No further premiums are paid and the benefits previously guaranteed are accordingly reduced.

Pair–Off
Netting of consideration and stock in the settlement of two trades in the same security to allow settlement solely of net differences.

PAL

Provisional allotment letter. See *Rights Issue.*

Panel on Takeovers and Mergers (POTOM)

A non–statutory body comprising City institutions which regulates takeover activities.

Paper Interface

The mechanics by which investors who have certificated holdings settle transactions, once the company has become a CREST participant. It also includes the way in which CREST members convert certificated holdings into dematerialised holdings (ie, stock deposit). See *CREST Courier and Sorting Service.*

Par

The par rate of bonds in most cases equals £100. For shares it can be any amount.

Par Value

See *Nominal Value.*

Parallel Shift

A parallel shift is a change in the level of the yield curve, where all points along the yield curve move by exactly the same amount. For example a 10 basis point upward parallel shift in the yield curve means that all points along the term structure (all maturity points) have moved up in yield by 10 basis point. By definition this means that the shape of the yield curve remains the same after the parallel shift has taken place.

Pari Passu

Equal in all respects (Latin). A corporate action in which a line of stock is issued by a company which is identical to the existing class of security (except perhaps that it does not qualify for a recent dividend or has some other restriction).

Part IV Permission

Permission granted by the FSA, under Part IV FSMA 2000, to allow firms to conduct particular types of investment business.

Participant

A person who has a business relationship with CREST and who communicates with CREST via the gateway computer of a user (who may or may not be the same legal entity). There are several participant types, including:

- the CCSS
- CREST System Controller
- member
- network provider
- payment bank
- registrar
- regulator
- product provider
- overseas CSD.

Participant Transaction Status

All participants in a transaction have a participant transaction status. It is a single–letter code providing an indication of the status of the input for that participant. Each principal is able to view its own and its counterparty's participant transaction status.

Participating Preference Shares

See *Preference Shares*.

Partly Paid Bonds

Bonds in which a proportion of the price is not due immediately payable, but falls due on a fixed date in the future.

Partnership Insurance
An insurance policy which pays out on the death of a partner, normally allowing the survivors to buy the deceased partner's interest in the business.

Party Transaction Status
The transaction status which reflects the input status of one party to a transaction type, designed to reflect the logical stage in a member's input. Sometimes referred to as 'party status'.

Passive Investment Management
Investment management which is not seeking to outperform the market, but only looking for a fair return for the risk involved, ie, the market average return.

Pay As You Earn (PAYE)
A system whereby employees have income tax deducted at source from their salaries. An employer has to deduct tax from an employee and submit these amounts to the Inland Revenue.

Pay Date
In a benefit distribution, the date on which the benefit is distributed by an issuer.

Paying Agent
The financial institution appointed by the borrower and responsible for making due interest payments and principal repayments to bondholders against presentation of the coupon or bond certificate.

Payment Bank

A CREST participant who is obliged by contract with each CREST member, each payment bank and CREST to guarantee payment for securities delivered to their customers through CREST. Settlement of these obligations takes place outside CREST although the system creates and records the obligations.

Payment Type

The payment type defines the mechanism by which such obligations are to be settled:
- central payments: for payments in sterling or euro the payment obligations settle across accounts with the Bank of England;
- bilateral payments: for payments in US dollars, the payment obligations settle between the payment banks directly and on a bilateral basis.

Payment versus Payment (PvP)

The simultaneous payment and receipt of the currencies involved in a foreign exchange deal.

Perfected Interest

An obligor retains ownership of collateral, but the lender has certain rights of ownership in the event of default.

Penny Share

The FSA now defines a penny share as a ready realisable security in relation to which the bid offer spread is 10% or more of the offer price but not a) a government and public security, b) a share in the company quoted in the FTSE 100, or c) a security of a company with market capitalisation of £100m or more.

Pension Fund

Provider of pensions. Status requires Inland Revenue approval.

Pension Plan

Pension scheme. A fund that is established for the payment of retirement benefits to its beneficiaries.

Pensioners' Bond

National Savings Product exclusively available to those aged 60 or over. A lump sum investment is made which then provides a monthly income.

PEP (Personal Equity Plan)

See *Personal Equity Plan.*

P/E Ratio

See *Price to Earnings Ratio.*

Performance Attribution

The process of determining how much each of asset allocation, sector choice, and security selection contributed to the overall performance of the portfolio.

Periodic Charge

See *Annual Management Charge.*

Permanent Health Insurance (PHI)

Policies designed to replace income in the event of the policyholder being unable to work due to illness.

Permanent Interest Bearing Shares (PIBS)

Permanent Interest–Bearing Shares are issued by building societies and pay a fixed rate of interest for an indefinite period (they are irredeemable). PIBS repayment rank behind all other creditors for capital.

Permitted Person

Someone who has applied to the FSA under Paragraph 23 of Financial Services Authority rules for permission to carry out deals in the course of non–investment business (eg, treasury department of conglomerate).

Perpetual Bond

A bond which has no maturity date.

Personal Account (PA) Dealing

Transactions conducted by employees for their own account and not for a customer or for their employer.

Personal Account Notice

A written summary given to all member firm employees detailing the rules on own account dealings.

Personal Allowances

The amount of annual income that each person is allowed to earn which is not liable to income tax. The amount differs according to whether a person is married or single and according to age.

Personal Equity Plan (PEP)

An investment plan managed by a plan manager, approved by the Revenue, and managed in accordance with PEP regulations. PEPs were discontinued after April 1999, but those taken out prior to that date may still be maintained.

Personal Identification Number (PIN)

A unique numerical number which is keyed into a computer machine to gain access, eg, ATM.

Personal Investment Authority (PIA)
The SRO who held responsibility for regulating firms advising on and arranging deals in life assurance and personal pensions, friendly society investments, unit trusts and investment trust savings schemes. Subsumed into the FSA at the beginning of December 2001.

Personal Member
A sponsored CREST membership where the investor is an individual.

Personal Pension Plan (PPP)
An Inland Revenue approved scheme under which individuals who are self–employed or in non–pensionable employment can make pension contributions for retirement and/or life assurance benefits. Employers can also contribute to PPPs. Payments into the scheme are limited by Inland Revenue rules.

Personal Representative
Persons authorised to administer the estate of a deceased person. May be executor or an administrator.

Physical Delivery
Delivery of definitive or material certificates in a security. More commonly, ownership of securities is transferred by book entry transfer. Also applies to deliveries of underlying commodities in an options or futures contract.

Physical Securities
Securities represented in the form of certificates.

PIA
See *Personal Investment Authority.*

Pillar 1

The rules in the New Basel Capital Accord that define the minimum ratio of capital to risk weighted assets.

Pillar 2

The supervisory review pillar of the New Basel Capital Accord, which requires supervisors to undertake a qualitative review of their bank's capital allocation techniques and compliance with relevant standards.

Pillar 3

The disclosure requirements of the New Basel Capital Accord, which facilitate market discipline.

PIN

See *Personal Identification Number.*

Pips

See *Points*.

Pit

The designated area on the market floor where a particular contract is traded. It may be termed a ring in some markets, eg, LME.

Placement

The first stage of money laundering, in which the money is placed in the banking system. See *Layering* and *Integration*.

Placing

Procedure used for new issues where a securities house contacts its own clients to offer them stock.

Plain Vanilla or Vanilla Swap

A swap which has a very basic structure.

Plain Vanilla Transaction
A straightforward transaction.

Plan Sponsor
The company or entity whose employees are the beneficiaries of the pension plan (scheme).

PLC
Public Limited Company (UK).

Points
Also known as Pips. The last two decimal places in an exchange rate.

Poison Pill
Strategic move by a company that is the target of a take–over to make its stock less attractive to an acquirer. As a defence, the company can issue Poison Pill Rights.

Polarisation
The situation in which firms selling long–term financial products must either act as a company representative and only sell that one company's products or act as an independent financial adviser and choose a recommendation from all companies' products.

Policy Protection Board
Organisation established under the Policyholders Protection Act 1975 to ensure compensation and continuity of cover for holders of long–term insurance products.

Pooled Nominee Account
Investors' securities are registered in the name of the nominee. The details of the beneficial owners are maintained in the records of the nominee rather than the records of the issuer's registrar.

Portfolio
Collection of financial assets which is designed to achieve a specific investment objective.

Portfolio Balance Model
The theory of exchange rate determination which concentrates on the analysis of capital investment flows.

Portfolio Valuation
Regular valuation report sent to a client for who the firm acts as investment manager and the portfolio comprises securities.

Position
The quantity of bonds held by an investor. See *Long* and *Short Position*.

Position Reconciliation Process
The process of ensuring that all managed positions are the same as those being settled.

Position Risk
Used in capital adequacy calculations. See *Market Risk*.

Positioning
See *Cash Funding*.

Positioning Process
The process of ensuring that there is sufficient cash or stock available to fulfil the contract.

Positive Yield Curve
See *Normal Yield Curve*.

Post–Settlement Stage
The third stage of a transaction's lifecycle involving the movement of, and control over, cash and physical assets.

Potential Exposure
The likely maximum loss (for a specified confidence level) in the event of default at a particular point in time.

Potential Future Exposure
The risk of an increase in credit exposure due to a movement in external market conditions.

Potentially Exempt Transfers
The law believes that the estate should include not only what was owned at death, but also assets given away relatively recently before death. Anything given away more than seven years before death is completely excluded from the estate, and anything given away within the three years before is completely included (at the value at the date of transfer). For deaths between three and seven year after transfers the amount of tax that would have been payable had it been owned at death is reduced on a sliding scale.

POTOM
See *Panel on Takeovers and Mergers.*

Pound Cost Averaging
A feature of the regular investment of a fixed sum. Because the fixed sum buys more units when the price is lower and fewer when it is higher, the effect is to make the average price paid for the units bought more advantageous than investing a lump sum at one time.

Power of Attorney
The legal authority for one party to sign for, and act on behalf of another party.

Practitioner Panel

Panel representing the providers of financial services, which the FSA must set up and consult when implementing new rules.

Pre–Emption Right

The right of a shareholder whereby a company making a new issue of shares must offer the shares to the existing shareholders in proportion to their existing holdings. Also called a rights issue.

Preference Shares

Shares which carry rights to a fixed amount of dividend and return of capital in priority to ordinary shares.

Preferred Stock

See *Preference Shares*.

Premium

The price that an option buyer pays and a writer receives when trading an option.

Present Value

The amount of money which needs to be invested (or borrowed) now at a given interest rate in order to achieve exactly a given cashflow in the future, assuming compound re–investment (or re–funding) of any interest payments received (or paid) before the end. See *Future Value*.

Preserved Benefits

The benefits payable at a later date when an individual stops being an active member of a pension scheme. Preserved pensions from a final salary occupational scheme relating to service since 1 January 1985 generally have to be increased by RPI or 5% per annum whichever is the lower (limited price indexation – LPI). LPI applies for all preserved benefits for those who left a scheme on or after 1 January 1991.

Pre–Settlement Risk
The risk that an institution defaults prior to settlement when the instrument has a positive economic value to the other party.

Pre–Settlement Stage
The second stage of a transaction's lifecycle involving the capture and agreement of transaction–specific data.

Prepayments
Cash paid by a company for a service not yet received. The cash paid is shown as a prepayment in the company's Balance Sheet.

Price
The cash amount payable or receivable per minimum nominal amount of a security.

Price (Conversion) Factor
The price at which a bond would trade, per 1 nominal, to yield the notional coupon of the futures contract on the delivery day (or the first day in the deliverable month if this applies).

Price Differential
The accrued return on the cash involved in a repo.

Price Driven
See *Quote-Driven*.

Price Level Risk
The risk of potential adverse changes in the price of a financial instrument.

Price to Earnings Ratio (P/E Ratio)

The price to earnings ratio is a measure of the market's (investors')
valuation of a company. By evaluating how much higher the share price
is than the company's current profits (earnings) this provides an
approximate measure of the share's desirability amongst investors.

Price Uncertainty

The uncertainty of knowing whether market prices will move in a
favourable or adverse direction.

Pricing Rate

See *Repo Rate*.

Prima Facie

At first sight. For instance, a portfolio's past performance provides
prima facie evidence of a portfolio manager's skill and investment style.

Primary Charge

See *Initial Charge*.

Primary Dealer

See *Gilt Edged Market Maker.*

Primary Issue

An issue of new shares when a company is first admitted to an
Exchange.

Primary Market

Initial launch of a company's shares when they first become available
for trading on the Stock Market.

Primary Requirement
The part of the Financial Resources Requirement that is calculated arithmetically according to the firm's current activities. It is made up of a base requirement; a position risk requirement and a counterparty risk requirement; a foreign exchange requirement and a large exposure requirement. See *Secondary Requirement.*

Prime Broker
A one–stop back office service for, eg, Hedge Funds.

Principal
The nominal amount of a bond due to be repaid at maturity.

Principal Protected Product
An investment whose maturity value is guaranteed to be at least the principal amount invested initially.

Principal–To–Principal Market
A market where the clearing house only recognises the clearing member as one entity, and not the underlying clients of the clearing member.

Principal Trading
When a member firm of the London Stock Exchange buys stock from or sells stock to a non–member for its own account, ie, not as an agent.

Principal Value
That amount inscribed on the face of a security and exclusive of interest or premium. The amount is the one used in the computation of interest due on such a security.

Principles for Businesses
FSA's 11 principles for investment businesses that underpin the regulatory structure in the UK. See *Statements of Principle* for equivalent applicable to individuals.

Priority

The means by which the order of items queued for settlement can be altered; higher priority instructions take a resource (a security or available headroom) before lower priority instructions.

Private Customer

Classification of those customers who are financially unsophisticated and require most protection within the rules. The FSA 1986 and FSMA 2000 were primarily designed for the benefit of private customers.

Private Investor

An individual who holds shares solely for their own benefit.

Private Limited Company

This form of company is not permitted to issue shares to the public and has limited liability.

Private Medical Insurance (PMI)

Also known as medical expenses insurance, it provides cover for private medical treatment.

Private Placement

Issue of securities that is offered to a limited number of investors.

Privatisation

Process whereby the government puts state owned industries into the private sector, eg, water, electricity. Usually involves an offer for sale of its shares.

Probability Density

The likelihood of any one of a series of numbers occurring.

Probability Distributions

Mathematical functions that describe the probabilities of possible outcomes occurring. They are depicted as graphs with the "probability of occurrence" on the vertical axis and the "possible outcome" on the horizontal axis.

Probability of Default (PD)

The estimated likelihood that a counterparty will default on an obligation.

Probate

The formal permission issued by the probate registry authorising the executor to administer the estate.

Probate/Confirmation

Legal document nominating executors and detailing total value of the estate.

Probate Value

The value of an individual's estate at death.

Process

A set of activities that allows the firm to deliver its product to the customer. A process takes a collection of inputs and turns them into desired outputs by adding value to them.

Product Particulars

Factual information about the investment, which must accompany notices of the right to cancel. The purpose is to ensure that the investor knows what he or she is acquiring. Details include the investment objectives, dealing procedures, charges, the yield, dealing spread and the name of the trustee.

Product Provider

Part of a group which, under the polarisation rules, can only promote its own products.

Profit and Loss Account

Financial statement showing how the profit of the company has arisen over a period of time, usually a year, leading up to the balance sheet date. Under US reporting, the profit and loss account is called the income statement.

Profit Margin

$$\frac{\text{Profit}}{\text{Sales}} \times 100\%$$

Profit Sharing Scheme

Profits of a company given to their employees in the form of shares. Employees may be given share options where they can purchase shares at a fixed price or they may be able to buy shares under a save–as–you–earn scheme.

Project A

The after–hours trading system used by the Chicago Board of Trade.

Project Risk

The risk that the failure or partial failure of a project to meet its objectives leads to financial loss.

Program Trade
One of a number of trading strategies which involve the simultaneous purchase or sale of a number of different shares.

Prohibition Order
Order issued by the FSA barring an individual from working for an authorised person.

Promissory Note
A written promise to pay.

Property Bond
Single premium insurance policy where the funds are invested in property.

Proposal Form
Form used to apply for a life policy.

Proprietary Office
Life offices that are owned by shareholders. If the life office runs a with–profits fund, the shareholders and with–profits policy holders share the profits: normally 10% to shareholders and 90% to policyholders.

Proprietary Trader
A trader who deals as a principal for an organisation such as an investment bank taking advantage of short–term price movements as well as taking long–term views on whether the market will move up or down.

Prospectus

1. A formal document giving all relevant details about a new issue of shares.
2. Every OEIC is required to have a prospectus which fulfils a similar role to that of the scheme particulars of a unit trust. It contains details which investors and professional advisers would reasonably require before making a judgement about the merits of investing in a company. See Listing Particulars.

Protected Rights

The benefits under an Appropriate Personal Pension Scheme from the contributions paid by the DSS for a member who has contracted out of SERPS. Also the benefits secured from the minimum payments than must be made to contract an employee out of SERPS.

Proxy

A person appointed by a shareholder to vote on their behalf at company meetings.

Proxy Voting

Voting on company issues by a representative (the proxy) of the shareholder.

PSA

See *Public Securities Association.*

PSNCR

See *Public Sector Net Cash Requirement.*

PTM Levy

A flat–rate levy on agency bargains which is collected to finance the Panel on Takeovers and Mergers (POTOM).

Public Offer
An offer to sell shares to the public, usually on the flotation of a company on the stock market.

Public Order Member
A member of a futures exchange who can undertake transactions for customers.

Public Placement
An issue of securities that is offered through a securities house to institutional and individual clients.

Public Sector
Areas of the economy which are owned by central and local government.

Public Sector Borrowing Requirement (PSBR)
See *Public Sector Net Cash Requirement.*

Public Sector Net Cash Requirement (PSNCR)
If the government spends more than it receives from tax and other revenues, the shortfall is known as the Public Sector Net Cash Requirement. This shortfall was until June 1998 known as the Public Sector Borrowing Requirement (PSBR).

Public Securities Association (PSA)
See *Bond Market Association.*

Purchase Fund
A fund set aside by the borrower and used to repurchase a specified amount of its bonds at or below a specified price.

Purchase Price
See *Offer Price.*

Purchasing Power Parity (PPP)
A theory for the determination of exchange rates based upon the relative value of a basket of internationally traded goods and services in different countries.

Pure Endowment
A policy which pays out only if the life assured lives until the maturity date.

Put
A bondholder's right to sell the bonds back to the borrower in accordance with pre–agreed terms.

Put Option
A deal giving one party the right, without the obligation, to sell an agreed amount of a particular instrument or commodity, at an agreed rate, on or before an agreed future date. The other party has the obligation to buy if so requested by the first party. See *Call Option*.

Put Through
Selling and rebuying a share to change the beneficial owner. Occurs in Spain and Greece.

Q

Qualifying Corporate Bonds

Non–convertible bonds which are denominated in Sterling. Exempt from capital gains tax.

Qualifying Individual

A person who meets the requirements of the PEP/ISA Regulations to hold a plan or to hold or subscribe to an account.

Qualifying Investment

Securities meeting the requirements of the PEP/ISA Regulations for unrestricted investment within a PEP/ISA.

Qualifying Policy

A life assurance policy which meets rules set out in Taxes Act 1988. Qualifying policies taken out before 14 March 1984 may qualify for life assurance premium relief (LAPR). Policy proceeds on death or maturity are free of personal tax.

Qualifying Securities

A term used with specific meaning in the PEP/ISA Regulations to refer to any loan stocks issued by a company, whether secured or unsecured, which qualify for inclusion in a PEP or stocks and shares ISA.

Quarterly Accounting

The arrangement whereby withholding tax on coupons is paid shortly after the end of the calendar quarter.

Quasi–Coupon Date

The date on which a coupon would be due on a bond assuming it is a conventional bond and not a strip.

Quote-Driven

Dealing system where some firms accept the responsibility to quote buying and selling prices, moving these prices to stimulate business.

Quoted

Colloquial term for a security that is listed on the Stock Exchange.

Quoted Currency

The currency in a foreign exchange deal, the amount of which is equated to one unit of the 'base currency'.

R

Range Forward
A forward outright with two forward rates, where settlement takes place at the higher forward rate if the spot rate at maturity is higher than that, at the lower forward rate if the spot rate at maturity is lower than that, or at the spot rate at maturity otherwise. See *Collar*.

Ranking
A method of assessing risk by estimating the likelihood of it being realised and the magnitude of its impact. This information is usually depicted graphically.

Rating (Credit)
An indication of the credit quality of a bond. The ratings are prepared and updated by independent agencies such as Moody's Investors Services and Standard & Poor's.

RCH
Recognised Clearing House under the Financial Services Act (FSA).

Readily Realisable Investments

These are packaged products, or securities listed on an EEA exchange, or securities "regularly traded" on one of those exchanges or any Recognised Investment Exchange or Designated Investment Exchange.

Real Effective Exchange Rate

Effective exchange rate adjusted for inflation differences between countries.

Real Rate Of Interest

Amount by which the nominal rate of interest exceeds inflation. See *Nominal Rate of Interest*.

Real-Time

Indices of some stock market prices are said to be calculated in real time. Data is fed into a computer and a new share price index is calculated as soon as changes occur.

Real-Time Financial Promotions

Financial promotions, which are either by telephone, personal visit or "other interactive medium". Does not include email.

Real-Time Gross Settlement (RTGS)

The settlement mechanism of a payment system involving the movement of funds between accounts over the books of the central bank in real time.

Realised Profit

Profit which has arisen from an actual sale or other disposal of assets.

Rebate

The fee payable by a borrower of stock in the stock loan market.

Rebate–Only Personal Pension

An Appropriate Personal Pension Scheme funded solely by rebates of National Insurance contributions (and tax relief and additional payments/incentives) paid by the DSS to a pension provider for an employee contracted out of SERPS.

Recall

A request to return repoed securities if the repo is an open transaction.

Receiver

Person appointed to wind up a company.

Receiving Agent

An organisation appointed by a company to assist it in administering a corporate action, for example, a takeover or a rights issue by receiving acceptances/applications from investors.

Reciprocal Rate

Exchange rate quoted with base and variable currencies reversed.

Reclaim

The process by which a non–resident investor obtains a refund of taxes previously withheld from income when the taxes were withheld in error or, more frequently, when the investor is qualified for local tax reduction under the provisions of a double taxation treaty. Some tax authorities require individual reclamation filing for each dividend and after each payment, while others allow for yearly filing for the aggregate reclamation amount. Some markets do not allow the reclamation. These markets make the benefits of double taxation agreements available only by reduced withholding, which must be requested prior to the income payment.

Recognised Clearing House (RCH)
Status granted by the FSA to organisations that it believes are acceptable to provide clearing and settlement facilities in the UK. LCH and CRESTCo are the only ones with the status.

Recognised Collective Investment Schemes
Non UK–based unit trusts which FSA has recognised as being adequately regulated and which can be marketed freely in the UK, subject to adherence with UK marketing standards.

Recognised Investment Exchange (RIE)
Status granted by FSA to UK exchanges which it believes are acceptable in the quality of market services they provide.

Recognised Overseas Investment Exchange
An overseas exchange which can operate as an exchange in the UK.

Recognised Stock Exchange
A Stock Exchange approved by the Inland Revenue under the Taxes Act.

Reconciliation
The comparison of a person's records of cash and securities position with records held by another party and the investigation and resolution of any discrepancies between the two sets of records.

Reconstitution
The process of reconstituting a bond from its component cashflows.

Record Date
This date, set by the company, determines those shareholders who are entitled to receive a specific benefit on their shareholding. This may include dividends, rights or in some instances, incentives.

Record Day
See *Books Closed Day*.

Recovery Rate
The amount a firm recovers as a result of an obligor's foreclosure, liquidation or re–structuring.

Recovery Stock
Shares in a company whose profits have fallen substantially but are expected to recover in the future.

Redeemable Security
A security issued with a known maturity, or redemption, date.

Redemption
The repayment of the principal amount of a bond by the borrower.

Redemption Charge
See *Exit Charges*.

Redemption Date
The date on which the borrower will repay the capital on a loan stock or the government will repay the capital on a gilt.

Redemption Price
See *Bid Price*.

Redemption Yield
The total annualised return on owning a fixed interest security, made up of annual income plus any gain or minus any loss to redemption.

Reduction in Yield Factors
The reduction in yield on an investment arising from the impact of charges.

Refer

The practice whereby a trader instructs a broker to put 'under reference' any prices or rates he has quoted to him, meaning that they are no longer 'firm' and the broker must refer to the trader before he can trade on the price initially quoted.

Reference Price

The list of the previous business day's closing bid and offer prices for securities maintained in the system and taken from an external information provider.

Referral

The Secretary of State for Trade and Industry refers a proposed takeover to the Competition Commission who then investigates further.

REG

The transaction type for registrar adjustment.

Regional Custody

A term used to describe the custody of securities traded within a geographical region, eg, European countries only or Far Eastern countries only.

Register

The legal record of company shareholders.

Register Update Request (RUR)

An instruction generated by CREST for a registrar, requesting that the register be changed to reflect a movement of stock between member accounts in CREST.

Registered Securities

Shares or bonds whose ownership is recorded on a central register as opposed to bearer securities.

Registered Title
Form of ownership of securities where the owner's name appears on a register maintained by the company.

Registrar
A quoted company usually appoints a registrar to manage its shareholder records. This company is responsible for the administration of the share register, distributing shareholder information on behalf of the company and paying dividends to shareholders.

Registrar Adjustment (REG)
The transaction type used by registrars to change a stock balance in the system as a result of an event (corporate action or other kind of event) that is external to the system.

Registrar of Companies
Government official whose department is responsible for keeping records of all companies.

Registrar's Service Level Agreement
The agreement between CREST participating registrars and CRESTCo which defines the standards under which registrars operate.

Registration
The process whereby a company's register is amended to reflect transfer of its securities. It is the final stage of settlement processing, after settlement.

Regression Analysis
Statistical method for finding the 'line of best fit'.

Regular Income Plans
The use of several income–oriented unit trusts to provide an investor with either a monthly or quarterly income.

Regular Member

A type of broker on the Tokyo Stock Exchange.

Regular Premium

Policies where the premiums are paid at regular intervals, usually monthly.

Regulated Activities

The activities (investment business) which must be regulated under the provisions of FSMA 2000. The legislation describes a range of specified activities in a range of specified investments.

Regulated Collective Investment Schemes

Those schemes, which can be freely marketed in the UK. UK schemes would either be Authorised Unit Trusts (AUTs) or Investment Company with Variable Capital (ICVCs) and overseas schemes trusts would have to be recognised by FSA.

Regulated Unit Trusts

Those trusts which can be freely marketed in the UK. Any trusts based in the UK would be authorised by FSA and overseas trusts would have to be recognised by them.

Regulatory Capital

The capital that a financial institution must set aside against assets (loans) as stipulated by the national regulatory authority.

Regulatory Decisions Committee (RDC)

Committee of FSA responsible for most enforcement matters.

Release Date
Third anniversary of date on which shares were appropriated to participant in profit sharing scheme.

Relevant Discounted Security
A security which is issued at a discount to the redemption value where the size of the discount is greater than either:
i.   15% of the redemption value, or
ii. $1/_2$% of the redemption value per year for each year of the life security.

RELIT
Settlement system used in France for corporate securities and OATS.

Remainderman
The beneficiary of a life interest trust entitled to the trust property when the life interest comes to an end; the remainderman has the revisionary interest.

Renewable Term Assurance
Type of term assurance where the policy is renewable at the end of its original term without further medical examination.

Renewal Commission
A fee (typically 0.5%) paid to IFAs, usually on an annual basis, out of the fund manager's charge. It is paid on funds which remain in the unit trust. The purpose is to encourage long term investment and remunerate the IFA for servicing the client. Also known as trail commission.

Renounceable Document
A document for which legal title can be transferred to another person.

Renunciation Form

The form which may appear on the back of a unit trust certificate or may be separate and which the holder(s) signs when selling units back to the managers. The form is the formal transfer of legal title to the managers of the units being redeemed.

Repatriation

The specific act of bringing capital sent to a foreign location or income earned from that investment back into the investor's home country.

Repayment Mortgage

Form of mortgage where the monthly payments made are a combination of interest and capital.

Replacement Cost

The mark to market loss which would be incurred if it was necessary to undertake a new transaction to replace an existing one, because the existing counterparty defaulted.

Replacement Risk

The risk of losing an unrealised profit should the counterparty default.

Repo Rate

The return earned on a repo transaction expressed as an interest rate on the cash side of the transaction.

Repo (Sale and Repurchase)

Transaction in gilts, where the gilt is sold with a price and date fixed for its re-purchase. UK government allowed gilts to be traded on the repo market in 1996. Repos can also be transacted for bonds and equities.

Reportable Transactions

Any product traded off-exchange by a member firm.

Reporting Risk

The risk of decisions being taken on the basis of incorrect, incomplete or badly specified reports.

Repricing

At a variation margin call, when a repo is closed–out and restarted to reflect margin delivery. See also *Mark to Market*.

Repurchase Agreement (Repo)

See *Repo*.

Reputational Risk

The risk that an organisation's reputation will be damaged.

Request for Proposal (RFP)

As a first step in making major changes to its custody arrangements, an institution will send a questionnaire (the RFP) to a selection of global custodians. The RFP enables the custodians to provide basic details of their services, deadlines and costs.

Reserve Bank Transfer System (RITS)

Central Securities Depository (CSD) for Australian Government Bonds.

Reserves of a Company

The share premium account and the retained earnings of the company.

Residence

The status determining the extent to which a person is taxed in a country with a global system to taxation. Residence is determined according to periods of physical presence in the country.

Residual Securities (CREST)

UK and Irish securities which are not eligible for settlement in CREST.

Residual Settlement

Settlement which takes place outside CREST. If both the transferee and transferor are CREST members, CREST can facilitate residual settlement using the CCSS and CREST payment instructions.

Residual Transaction (RES)

The transaction type used by CREST members to confirm and report a trade in residual securities. Only the cash, but not the stock, can be settled in CREST.

Resolution

A proposal put to shareholders at a general meeting.

Retail Price Index (RPI)

Monthly Index that shows the movement of retail prices in the UK.

Retail Sales

The gauge for monitoring the level of retail demand in the UK. If there is a high demand for goods then prices may rise.

Retained Benefits

Retirement or death benefits due to an employee from a previous period of employment or self–employment. These may have to be taken into account in calculating maximum approvable benefits under an occupational scheme.

Retained Earnings

The accumulated retained profits, or earnings, of the company.

Retirement Annuity Plan (RAP)

Also known as Section 226 or RAC. Contracts issued on or before 30 June 1988 for self–employed people and employees with non–pensionable earnings. Maximum pension contributions are based on net relevant earnings. RAPs are not subject to the pension cap, but lower percentage contribution limits apply.

Return on Capital Employed

$$\frac{\text{Profit}}{\text{Capital Employed}} \times 100\%$$

Reuters

A news agency that provides instant access to bond and equity prices and news information via monitors located in subscribers' offices. There are some 100,000 subscribers in approximately 120 countries.

Revaluation Reserve

An official one–off increase in the value of a currency in terms of other currencies.

Reverse

The opposite stance of a counterparty to a Repo Agreement. The Reverse is a purchase of bonds with the simultaneous sale back to the repo counterparty for future settlement.

Reverse Repo

Purchase of gilt where the price and date for its re–sale is fixed at the same time.

Reversing

Entering into a Reverse Repo.

Reversionary Bonus

Normally declared as a percentage addition to the sum assured (and existing bonus) payable on a policy. Once it is attached to a policy it cannot be withdrawn or reduced in value. See *Normal Bonus*.

Revisionary Interest

The interest of the remainderman in the trust. See *Remainderman*.

Revocable Payment

A payment instruction that can be cancelled unilaterally by the sender.

RIE

See *Recognised Investment Exchange*.

Right Of Offset

Where positions and cash held by the Clearing Organisation in different accounts for a member are allowed to be netted.

Rights Issue

Rights issues are capital raising exercises by companies in which existing shareholders are given the right to buy the new shares normally at a discount to the market price for the existing shares.

Ring

The designated area on the market floor where a particular contract is traded. It may be termed a pit in some markets, eg, LIFFE.

Ring Member

A category of LME membership where members can place traders in the ring and trade metal contracts by open outcry.

Risk

Risk is best defined as the degree of exposure to change of a portfolio. This may be exposure to a change in the market (known as market risk) or to movement in a specific stock (specific risk). Systemic risk is defined as exposure to the stability of the financial system. There are also risks associated with currency and interest rate exposure.

Risk–Adjusted Return On Capital (RAROC)

A VaR measure developed by Bankers Trust that allows risk to be factored into the evaluation of financial returns.

Risk, Counterparty

Risk of non–fulfilment of a trade contract due to inability or unwillingness of the counterparty to complete the transaction.

Risk Factor

An environmental effect that influences the price of a financial instrument or value of a portfolio.

Risk Management

The implementation of a strategic process that reduces the likelihood of risks being realised to acceptable levels.

Risk Measurement

Risk measurement is concerned with understanding the size of a risk by trying to predict a future event using past knowledge.

Risk Models

Basis of the approach FSA takes in determining its approach to satisfying itself about the risks posed by any investment business. All firms are assessed according to a standard risk model and then rated according to the results.

Risk, Operational
Risk of loss due to clerical errors, organisational deficiency, delays, fraud, system failure, non–performance by third party providers and similar events.

Risk, Settlement
Risk that a party will default on one or more delivery or payment obligations to its counterparty or to a settlement agent.

Risk, Systemic
The risk that the inability of one institution to meet its obligations when due will cause a large number of other participants or financial firms to be unable to meet their obligations when due (chain reaction).

Risk Warning
Document outlining the risks that must be dispatched and signed by private customers before they deal in derivatives.

Risk–Weighted Assets
See *Capital Adequacy Ratio*.

RITS
See *Reserve Bank Transfer System*.

Rollercoaster Swap
A swap in which the notional principal amount varies up and down over the life of the swap.

Roll Over
Transferring a position from one delivery month to another, usually closing the nearby month to open a position in a far month.

Rolling Settlement

A trade is settled a specific number of days after the date of the trade. Usually denoted as T+n, where n is the number of business days. Thus T+3 means settlement 3 business days after the trade day.

Roll Up Fund

An offshore fund which distributes no income.

Rotation

The process by which all series of options on an underlying stock are sequentially quoted. On LIFFE all series are rotated at the opening and at the close of business, but a rotation may be requested at any other time.

Round Lot

The minimum amount for which dealer's quotes are good. See *Board Lot*.

Round Trip

An opening transaction and its corresponding closing trade are known as a round trip. Dealing charges are sometimes quoted on a round trip basis.

RPI

See *Retail Price Index*.

RPIX

Index that shows the underlying rate of inflation in the UK, by excluding mortgage payments from the RPI.

RTGS

Real Time Gross Settlement system, an interbank system to eliminate interbank risk during the day.

Running Yield

See *Flat Yield*.

Running a Book

Firms which are buying and selling stock for themselves hoping to profit from price differences are said to run a book in that stock.

RUR

A Register Update Request is an instruction to a registrar from CREST indicating that a transfer or Own Account Transfer has taken place in CREST and requesting that the register be amended accordingly.

RVP

RVP stands for receipt versus payment. See *Delivery versus Payment*.

S

S&P 500
Standard & Poor's capitalisation weighted index of 500 stocks. The index represents price trend movements of the shares of US public companies.

Safe Custody Repo
The borrower of cash keeps hold of collateral pledged, placing it in a segregated client account.

Safekeeping
Holding of securities on behalf of clients. They are free to sell at any time.

Saitori
A member of the Tokyo Stock Exchange who acts as an intermediary between brokers.

Sale and Repurchase Agreement
A repo trade. See *Repo*.

Sale of Rights Nil Paid
The sale of the entitlement to take up a rights issue.

Same–Day–Funds
The term used to describe a cash payment of which the receiver has constructive use on the day of receipt, ie, funds that can be used immediately to fund a clean payment to a third party.

Same–Day–Settlement
A transaction where trade execution and settlement take place on the same day.

Sampling
A method of indexing in which a sample of shares is held which, statistically, should perform like the index.

Samurai Bonds
A Yen bond issued in Japan by a non–Japanese issuer.

SATURNE
Settlement system for BTANs and BTFs operated by the Banque de France.

Save As You Earn Employee Share Scheme
A scheme which qualifies for treatment under the provisions of the Income & Corporation Taxes Act 1988, enabling employees to acquire shares in the company for which they work with advantageous tax treatment and at a special price.

Savings Certificates
National Savings product which provides a tax–free sum. A lump sum investment is required and maximum benefits are obtained if the certificate is held for five years.

Savings Plan
Schemes run by unit trust groups enabling investors to purchase units conveniently on a regular, usually monthly, basis. Similar schemes are offered by some investment trusts.

Sawtooth Risk
A swap in which the notional principal amount varies up and down over the life of the swap, with an overall upward or downward trend.

Sawtooth Swap
A swap in which the notional principal amount varies up and down over the life of the swap, with an overall upward or downward trend.

SAX
Dealing system of the Swedish Stock Exchange.

SAXESS
Swedish Exchange Trading System.

SAYE
See *Save As You Earn Employee Share Scheme.*

SBLI
Stock Borrowing and Lending Intermediary.

Scaling Down
When applying for shares in a company joining the stock market, investors may only receive a proportion of their application if there is an oversubscription and a refund cheque will be sent. See *New Issues.*

SCANS
Clearing and settlement system for Malaysia.

Scenario Analysis

A subjective method of highlighting potential risk issues in order to allow preventative action to be taken.

Scheme of Arrangement

A corporate action in which a company replaces one or more of its lines of security with other securities, cash or a combination of securities and cash.

Scheme Particulars

A detailed document which must be available for every authorised or recognised unit trust, giving full particulars of the fund and how it operates.

SCL

Settlement organisation and custodian of Spanish securities.

SCLV

Spanish Clearing House.

Screen–Based Trading

A method of trading which takes place by the dealers inputting their bids and offers into screens linked to a computer system. There is no exchange floor and the traders operate the computer screens from their own offices.

Scrip Dividends

A company may offer its shareholders additional shares instead of a cash dividend.

Scrip Issue

An issue of new shares to existing shareholders in proportion to their existing shareholdings. Also called a *Bonus Issue* or *Capitalisation Issue*.

SCORE
Dealing system for the Kuala Lumpur Stock Exchange.

SD Indeval
Clearing House and Depository for the Mexican market.

SDRN
See *Stock Deposit Reference Number.*

SDRT
See *Stamp Duty Reserve Tax.*

SEAQ
See *Stock Exchange Automated Quotation System.*

Seasoned Bonds
Bonds that have been traded in the secondary markets for some time (90 days for eurobonds).

Seat
The term given to describe the membership of an exchange which entitles the holder to execute business on the exchange and in certain cases carries voting rights. A Seat must be held in order to be a member of an exchange and they can be purchased from the exchange or can be leased from other member firms, depending upon availability.

SEATS Plus
An order–driven system used on the London Stock Exchange for securities which do not attract at least two firms of market makers and also used for all AIM securities.

SEC
See *Securities and Exchange Commission.*

SEC Rule 17(f)5
Compliance regulation for US mutual funds registered under the Investment Company Act of 1940. Rule 17(f)5 establishes the conditions under which a mutual fund may hold foreign cash and securities outside the United States.

Secondary Issue
An issue of new shares by a company which is already listed; examples are rights issues and scrip issues.

Secondary Market
Market place for trading in existing securities. The price at which they are trading has no direct effect on the company's fortunes but is a reflection of investors' perceptions of the company.

Second Banking Co-ordination Directive (2BCD)
European Union directive that permits credit institutions (banks) to be authorised in any one member state and offer services in any other.

Second Order
A sensitivity measure that accounts for a changing relationship between the value of the portfolio/instrument and the associated risk factor (or a curved line if expressed as a graph).

Secondary Requirement
The part of the Financial Resources Requirement that is at the discretion of the FSA to allow for weaknesses within the firm. See *Primary Requirement*.

Second Section
The second tier market of the Tokyo Stock Exchange.

Section 32 Policy

Schemes provided by insurance companies to receive transfer values to replace a member's entitlement to pension scheme benefits, normally when a member's pensionable service ends. Sometimes known as buy–out bonds.

Section 47

See *Misleading Statement*.

Secured Bond

A bond where the company has pledged assets to back the bond. In the event of default the assets are then available to repay the bond.

Secured Limit

A secured limit in respect of a cap is the lower of the margined value of the securities held in a linked account and of any monetary limit last input as such by the relevant payment bank to the CREST system.

Secured Loan Stock

Loan stock issued by a company, usually secured on the assets of the company.

Securities

Tradeable financial instruments such as, for example, equities and bonds.

Securities and Exchange Commission (SEC)

The body for overall regulation of financial institutions in the USA.

Securities and Futures Authority (SFA)

Formerly the Self Regulating Organisation (SRO) for dealers in securities, financial and commodity derivatives and corporate financiers. Its functions were subsumed into FSA from midnight 30 November 2001.

Securities and Investments Board (SIB)
Original overall regulator under the FSA 1986.

Securities Borrowing
A method by which market makers are able to borrow securities in order to make up a shortage in those securities and in exchange for a fee.

Securities House
General term covering any type of organisation involved in securities although usually reserved for the larger firms.

Securities Institute
The UK professional body for qualified and experienced practitioners engaged in a wide range of securities and other financial services businesses.

Securities Lending
Authorised institutions lend their assets and, when permitted, those of their clients to market makers through a network of intermediaries in exchange for a fee.

Securities Scheme
An authorised fund that invests primarily in transferable securities as defined in the Financial Services (Regulated Schemes) Regulations 1991.
Within the ISA Regulations however, the term securities scheme is defined more widely to include the FSA definition (above) plus parts of an umbrella scheme that would be classified as securities schemes if they were themselves free–standing authorised funds.
Securities funds can be held as an investment only in the stocks and shares component of an ISA.

Securitisation
See *Asset Securitisation*.

Security Market Line
Line representing the relationship between expected return and market risk (measured by beta).

SEDOL
The local numbering system used on the London Stock Exchange for identifying securities on the Stock Exchange Daily Official List.

SEGA
Swiss central securities depository.

Segmentation
Use of a cluster of small identical policies rather than a large one.

Segregated Account
Account in which there is only the holdings of one client.

Segregation of Funds
Where the client assets are held separately from those assets belonging to the member firm. See *Designated Nominee Account*.

SEHK
Stock Exchange of Hong Kong.

Selective Marketing
See *Placing*.

Self Regulating Organisations (SROs)
Bodies which under FSA 1986 regulate specific sectors of the financial services industry. Now replaced by the single regulator, the Financial Services Authority.

Self–Administered Scheme

A scheme where the assets are invested by the trustees usually with the assistance of investment managers, instead of purchasing insurance policies.

Self–Assessment

The self assessment system applies both to income tax and capital gains tax. The onus is on the taxpayer to complete a return of all of their income and gains and then create the legal charge to tax. The figures submitted by the taxpayer will be used, but the Inland Revenue has the right to investigate any situation where it believes that the figures may be wrong or that there is undeclared income.

Self–Invested Personal Pension (SIPP)

A personal pension under which the member can control the investments and invest in, eg, unit trusts, stocks and shares.

Self–Select ISA

The investor makes all the decisions as to what is bought and sold within the ISA, particularly the stocks and shares component. An account manager is still required and would typically be a stockbroker.

Self–Trading

See *Crossing*.

Sell/Buy–Back

Simultaneous spot sale and forward purchase.

Selling Broker

The broker or dealer who represents the seller of the securities in market trades and settlements.

Selling Out
Process whereby on failure by the purchaser to pay for securities the seller sells to an alternative purchaser and any additional costs are passed on to the defaulting purchaser.

Selling Price
Price at which units are sold, inclusive of the initial and compulsory charges.

Semi–Strong Form Efficiency
Part of efficient market hypothesis. Market in which all publicly available information is reflected in security prices.

Senior Debt
Debt which ranks above other unsecured or subordinated debt in the event of the borrower's default.

SENN
Dealing system for the Rio de Janeiro Stock Exchange.

Sensitivity
The amount by which the value of a portfolio is vulnerable or sensitive to changes in interest rates.

SEQUAL
The checking system used in the UK for international equities.

Series
All option contracts on the same underlying stock with the same exercise price, expiry price and contract size belong to the same series.

SERPS

The State Earnings Related Pension Scheme which pays a pension according to the level of a person's earnings. Many companies contract out.

Service Companies

Authorised firms, which only make arrangements with a view to transactions in investments with market counterparties or intermediate customers. Only the financial promotions part of the Conduct of Business rules applies to them.

SETS

See *Stock Exchange Electronic Trading System*.

Settlement

The fulfilment of the contractual commitments such as payment of cash for securities: the conclusion of a securities transaction by delivery. Also known as another name for a trust.

Settlement Due Date

Intended settlement date – the earliest date a transaction can settle, as indicated in the mandatory and matchable field on settlement instructions for dual input transactions.

Settlement, Fixed

The pre–determined date(s) in a month when transactions are due to settle.

Settlement/Settlement Date

The day on which a trade is to be settled. See *Settlement, Fixed and Settlement, Rolling*.

Settlement Instruction

The mechanism within CREST for moving stock and/or money between participants whereby each counterparty transmits a settlement instruction to CREST, via the network, for matching. A generic settlement instruction is used by all participants, regardless of their role in the market; the type of transaction is indicated by entry of the three–character transaction type. CREST does not accept pre–matched instructions from other matching or trade confirmation systems.

Settlement Money

Money held under IMRO or PIA rules which has been paid by a client or a firm in respect of securities bought, but for which payment is not yet due. It must be kept separate from the firm's own money, but the client is not usually entitled to interest on it.

Settlement Queue

In the CREST settlement system, the sequences, one for each stock and one for credit (cash) into which matched transactions are entered once the intended settlement date has been reached. Once the transactions are on the queue, CREST assesses whether or not the resources (stock and cash) are available to settle them.

Settlement Risk

The risk that a counterparty defaults during settlement – a particular category of counterparty risk. See *Risk, Settlement*.

Settlement, Rolling

Settlement takes place on a certain number of days after the trade date, eg, Eurobond trades settle on the 3rd business day after trade (T+3). Shares in the UK normally trade T+5 or T+10.

Settlor

The person who sets up a trust.

SFA
See *Securities and Futures Authority (The)*.

SGX Sesdaq
Singapore trading system.

Shape
The quantity of shares to be delivered by the seller to the buyer. To split a bulk order into smaller constituent quantities.

Share
The unit of ownership of a company.

Share Buyback
The redemption and cancellation by a company of a proportion of its irredeemable ordinary shares subject to the permission of the High Court and agreement from the Inland Revenue.

Share Capital
The figure on the balance sheet representing the nominal value of the shares that have been issued.

Share Certificate
A certificate issued by a company to a shareholder stating either that a named person is the registered owner or that the bearer is the owner.

Share Exchange Facility/Schemes
A facility offered by some investment and unit trust managers to transfer an investor's existing shareholdings into a trust, OEIC or ISA.

Share Futures
Based on individual shares. Delivery is fulfilled by the payment or receipt of cash against the exchange calculated delivery settlement price.

Shareholder
The owner of a share in a company – the part–owner of a company.

Shareholder Insurance
Life assurance arrangements whereby shareholder directors in a small company take out policies which will pay out on the death of a shareholder director allowing the survivors to buy his shares.

Shareholders' Funds
The total of the share capital and the reserves of the company, shows how the shareholders have funded the company through subscribing for capital and through the retention of profits.

Shareholders' Rights
The legal rights of a shareholder such as the right to vote at meetings.

Share Identification Rules
The Inland Revenue identifies shares sold from a company's shareholding for calculating Capital Gains Tax Liability.

Share Matching Rules
Rules which specify how shares disposed of are matched up with acquisitions for the purposes of CGT.

Share Option
A right sold to an investor conferring the option to buy or sell shares of a particular company at a predetermined price and within a specified time limit.

Share Premium Account
The figure in the balance sheet that represents the excess of the issue price of shares over the nominal value. US accounts use the term 'paid in surplus'.

Share Split
A split of one share into a number of shares with a smaller nominal value. Also called *Subdivision*.

Share Yield
The share yield is a percentage of the quoted price of shares in an OEIC, representing the prospective annual income of the OEIC for its current annual accounting period, after deduction of all charges. The yield is expressed gross of tax.

Shogun Bond
Straight bond denominated in foreign currency, other than JPY, issued by a foreign issuer on the Japanese capital market.

Short
Having an obligation to a buyer to deliver stock the seller does not already own.

Short Coupons
Bonds or notes with a short current maturity.

Short Cover
The purchase of a security that has been previously sold short. The purpose is to return securities that were borrowed to make a delivery.

Short Date
A deal for value on a date other than spot but usually less than a month after spot.

Short–Dated Gilt
Gilts due to be redeemed within the next seven years.

Short Position
The result of a market maker selling shares or other securities which it does not have.

Short Sale
The sale of securities not owned by the seller in the expectation that the price of these securities will fall or as part of an arbitrage.

Short Selling
Selling stock that you do not own and is not yours to sell.

Short Termism
Allegation made against fund managers that they are traders on a short–term basis and are not willing to hold them for the long–term or to exert influence on management to improve corporate performance but prefer to sell the shares.

Short–Term Securities
Securities with a maturity of less than 12 months.

SIB
See *Securities and Investments Board.*

SIBE
Sistema de Interconnexion Bursátil Español. Spanish electronic dealing system linking the four Spanish stock exchanges.

SICOVAM
Central Securities Depository for French corporate securities and OATs.

Sight Deposits
Constituent of M2, the money supply measure, comprising current and all other instant access accounts.

Simple Interest
Interest calculated on the assumption that there is no opportunity to re–invest the interest payments during the life of an investment and thereby earn extra income.

Simple–Yield–to–Maturity
SYM accounts for the effect of the capital gain or loss on maturity of a bond as well as the current yield. Any capital gain or loss is assumed to be uniform over the life of the bond.

Simplified Defined Contribution Scheme (SDCS)
An occupational scheme fit to provide 'basic' benefits on a money purchase basis. The maximum contribution for each member is 17% of pensionable salary.

SINAC
Trading system for the Buenos Aires Stock Exchange. Operated by Merval.

Single Premium Bond
Non–qualifying life policies where the investor pays a lump sum to an insurance company and only a small proportion of it is used to provide life cover. The remainder is invested in unitised funds.

SIMEX
The Singapore International Monetary Exchange.

Single Currency Interest Rate Swap
An interest rate swap where the interest payments are exchanged in the same currency.

Single Pricing
Pricing system where unit trusts quote only one price instead of a bid and offer price. A sales charge is usually added when units/shares are purchased.

Sinking Fund
Funds put aside by a borrower to buy back its bonds in the market for cancellation.

SIS
SegaIntersettle, the Swiss Central Securities Depository.

SLD
The transaction which is automatically created by the revaluation process, consisting of one cash payment.

SLO
A stock loan agreement transaction type abbreviated SLO. Used to transfer stock from a lender to a borrower either free or against payment. When a SLO settles, CREST automatically generates a Stock Loan Return (SLR).

SLR
A transaction type abbreviated SLR, centrally–generated by CREST as a result of settling a member's instruction to settle a stock loan which mirrors (but reverses) the stock loan which generated it. SLRs cannot be input directly by CREST participants.

Small Company Tax Rate
See *Corporation Tax Rates.*

Small Self–Administered Scheme (SSAS)
A self–administered occupational scheme, normally with less than 12 members subject to special conditions for approval. At least one of the trustees must be a pensioner trustee; the trustees' powers are restricted with respect to borrowing money and investing in certain residential and other property.

SMATS
Korean trading system.

Social Security
The general name for the state system, which provides benefits for those in need.

Society for Worldwide Interbank Financial Telecommunications
See *SWIFT*.

Soft Commissions
The process of giving advice or providing other services in return for guaranteed business.

Soft Commodities
Description given to commodities such as sugar, coffee and cocoa. Most contracts are traded through LIFFE since its merger with the former London Commodity Exchange (LCE).

Soft Currency
A currency whose exchange rate is falling against other currencies as demand is weak. See *Hard Currency*.

Sole Proprietor
A business owned and managed by one individual who has unlimited liability for the liabilities of the business.

Sole Trader
See *Sole Proprietor.*

Solvency
The capacity to pay debts as they fall due.

Sophisticated Investor
Investor who has a signed statement from an authorised person verifying his level of understanding and who has signed a statement enabling them to receive financial promotions which are exempt from the usual requirements.

Sovereign Debt Securities
Bonds issued by the government of a country.

SPAN
Standardised Portfolio Analysis of Risk. A form of margin calculation which is used by various clearing organisations. SPAN calculates the effect of a range of possible changes in volatility and price on derivative portfolios.

Special
A security which for any reason is sought after in the repo market, thereby enabling any holder of the security to earn incremental income (in excess of the General Collateral rate) through lending them via a repo transaction. The repo rate for a special will be below the GC rate, as this is the rate the borrower of the cash is paying in returning for supplying the special bond as collateral. An individual security can be in high demand for a variety of reasons, for instance if there is sudden heavy investor demand for it, or (if it is a benchmark issue) it is required as a hedge against a new issue of similar maturity paper.

Special Cum

Terms of a bargain dealt during the ex period of a benefit distribution whereby the buyer receives the benefit entitlement, instead of the seller.

Special Drawing Right

The artificial basket currency of the IMF.

Special Ex

Trade condition, including that the trade price for a transfer is adjusted to reflect a deal with is dealt 'ex benefit' during a 'cum benefit' period ie. when the benefit goes to the buyer. CREST raises a claim between the members automatically, to create a transaction which enables the benefit amount to be transferred to the correct number.

Special Ex Date

The first date in the cum period from which special ex transactions can be agreed. It is set ten business days prior to the ex date.

Special Resolution

A resolution by shareholders at an AGM where 75% majority of votes cast is required for the order to be granted.

Specialist

A type of dealer on the New York Stock Exchange responsible for ensuring an orderly market in a range of stocks.

Specific

A repo in which the collateral is specified but not necessarily special.

Specific Risk

Risk that can be eliminated through diversification.

Specified Activities
The range of activities, which if undertaken in specified investments, must be regulated under the provisions of FSMA 2000.

Specified Investments
The investment products specified in FSMA 2000 for which providers of specified activities in them must be regulated.

Speculation
A deal undertaken because the dealer expects prices to move in his favour and thereby realise a profit. See *Hedge* and *Arbitrage*.

Speculator
The speculator is a trader who wants to assume risk for potentially much higher rewards.

Spline Method
The method by which a par yield curve is modelled, based on a series of polynomial equations spliced together.

Split–level Trust
Also known as a split capital trust, a type of investment trust which has been available since the mid–1960s. All splits have pre–determined winding up dates. Income shares are normally entitled to receive all or most of the income of the underlying investments. Capital shares are normally entitled to all surplus assets on winding up. Zero dividend preference shares ('zeros') offer a pre–determined growth of capital over a fixed period, but no income.

Splitting
An instruction that allows either counterparty in a DEL, SLO or SLR transaction type to re–shape an existing instruction within CREST either before or after matching.

Splitting Rights
Splitting the entitlement to rights shares and selling some nil paid and subscribing for the remainder.

Spot
An asset priced for instant delivery.

Spot-a-Week
A transaction from spot until a week later. Also known as S/W.

Spot Currency Transaction
A transaction completed in the foreign currency market for which delivery and settlement take place two business days after the day of the trade (T+2).

Spot Delivery
A delivery or settlement of currencies on the value date, two business days later.

Spot Month
The first month for which futures contracts are available.

Spot Month Margin
This is an additional rate of margin that is charged by the clearing organisation to ensure that customers have adequate funds for settlement upon delivery and also to discourage speculators in the delivery period. It covers the risk of a default during the delivery process. Spot month margins are charged in addition to initial margin.

Spot–Next
A transaction from spot until the next working day. Also known as S/N.

Spot Price
Cash price. Price of an asset for immediate delivery.

Spot Rate
The current exchange rate of a currency for delivery up to two business days after transaction date.

Spread
A trading strategy in which a trader buys one instrument and sells another, related instrument, with a view to profiting from a change in the price difference between the two. A futures spread is the purchase of one futures contract and the sale of another. An option spread is the purchase of one call (or put) and the sale of another.

SPS
Inland Revenue Savings and Pensions Schemes.

SPSS
Inland Revenue Savings, Pensions, Shares Schemes.

Square
Sales/assets exactly match purchases/liabilities.

SRO
See *Self Regulating Organisations*.

SSAP
Statement of Standard Accounting Practice. See *Accounting Standards*.

SSCCR
Shanghai Securities Central Clearing and Registration Corporation.

SSI

See *Standard Settlement Instructions.*

SSN

See *Stock Situation Notice.*

SSRC

Shenzhen Securities Registration Company – clearing organisation for the Shenzhen Stock Exchange.

Stabilisation

A price supporting process used on new issues of securities or bonds in order to maintain the price at level which may otherwise not prevail.

Stag

Someone who applies for a new issue of shares intending selling them (at a profit) as soon as secondary market dealings start.

Stakeholder Pensions

Low cost pension introduced in 2001. Maximum cost is 1% of the plan.

Stamp Duty

A UK tax on the physical transfer of certain certificated securities.

Stamp Duty Reserve Tax (SDRT)

A UK tax on the electronic transfer of certain securities (equities and convertible loan stocks).

Standard & Poor's 500

One of the Indexes of the New York Stock Exchange. See *Dow Jones Average.*

Standard Deviation (SD)
A means of measuring variability, uncertainty or volatility of return. It measures how spread out values are from the average (mean).

Standard Settlement
For the majority of securities this will be T+5 in CREST.

Standard Settlement Instructions
Instructions for settlement with a particular counterparty which are always followed for a particular kind of deal and, once in place, are therefore not repeated at the time of each transaction.

Stanza di Compensazione
Italian clearing organisation.

State–Controlled Economy
Country where all aspects of activity are controlled by the government.

State Second Pension (S2P)
Proposed replacement for SERPs, which will give employees earnings up to about £24,000 a better pension than SERPs with the most help going to those on the lowest earnings, which will be approximately £10,500.

Statements of Principle
Seven principles applicable to approved persons. Supplemented by Code of Practice.

Statement of Standard Accounting Practice
See *Accounting Standards*.

Status
The stage of settlement processing indicated by codes for transaction progress status, DBV progress status, and registration request status.

STD
The transaction type for stock deposits.

Stepped
A stepped coupon is one which rises or falls in a predetermined way over the life of an arrangement.

Stepped Preference Shares
Share in a split capital trust which provides a pre–determined amount of growth and pays a dividend.

STF
Stock transfer form, used to authorise a registrar to amend the register to reflect a transfer of certificated securities.

STIR Futures
Short term interest rate futures contract.

Stock
The US equivalent of a share.

Stock (Order)
An owner of a physical security that has been mutilated, lost or stolen will request the issuer to place a stop (transfer) on the security and to cancel and replace the security.

Stock Account
The CREST record of a member's holding of a particular security within a member account.

Stock Borrowing
Process by which a short seller borrows stock from an institution to settle the short sale. The stock is later re–purchased in the market and repaid to the institution.

Stock Borrowing and Lending Intermediary (SBLI)

An organisation authorised by the Inland Revenue to act as an intermediary between stock borrower (eg, market maker) and lender (eg, institution) to preserve anonymity. Formerly known as London Stock Exchange money broker.

Stock Deposit

A transaction (type STD) for the dematerialisation of certificated stock into a CREST member's account.

Stock Deposit Reference Number (SDRN)

A unique identifier on a CREST Transfer Form which links a stock deposit to its instruction in CREST.

Stock Deposit Transaction (STD)

Instruction to CREST to credit a firm's member account with shares which are the subject of a certificated sale.

Stock Dividend

See *Scrip Dividends*.

Stock Driven Repo

A repo initiated by a party who needs to borrow a specific security or repo out a specific security for funding purposes. It usually involves a round nominal amount of stock.

Stock Exchange

An organisation that provides facilities for companies and governments to issue securities to raise money and for those securities to be traded among investors.

Stock Exchange Automated Quotation System (SEAQ)

Electronic screen display system through which market makers in equities display prices at which they are willing to deal.

Stock Exchange Clearing House
Clearing House for the Tel Aviv Stock exchange.

Stock Exchange Electronic Trading System (SETS)
Computerised matching system through which traders in equities display prices and quantities of stock they wish to buy or sell.

Stock Exchange Yearbook
Stock Exchange manual which gives recent accounting information for listed companies.

Stockholder
See *Shareholder*.

Stock Index Futures / Options
Based on the value of an underlying stock index like the FTSE 100 in the UK, the S&P 500 index in the US and the Nikkei 225 and 300 in Japan. Delivery is fulfilled by the payment or receipt of cash against the exchange calculated delivery settlement price. These are referred to as either indices or indexes.

Stock Lending
An activity whereby holders of shares or bonds lend them to traders or market makers to facilitate the settlement of bargains and increase efficiency in the market.

Stock Loan (Agreement) (SLO)
A CREST transaction which transfers a specified security, against payment, from one member to another. When the stock loan settles, pre–matched stock loan returns are automatically created.

Stock Loan Return (SLR)

A pre–matched CREST standard transaction created on settlement of a stock loan (SLO). It is created with a settlement date of the next business day, with a priority of zero.

Stock (or Bond) Power

A legal document, either on the back of registered stocks and bonds or attached to them, by which the owner assigns his interest in the corporation to a third party, allowing that party the right to substitute another name on the company records instead of the originals owner's.

Stock Queue

A stock queue is a list of settlement instructions for sold trades and other outward delivery instructions that require stock from a member account. Each queue is security specific and relates to the member account from which the stock is to be delivered.

Stock Situation Notice (SSN)

A notice issued by the London Stock Exchange to advise member firms of the dates and details of a stock situation (corporate action).

Stock Split

A proportionate change in the number of shares in a company, without changing the total shareholders' equity. This increases the number of shares outstanding. Essentially, a firm splits its shares to reduce the market price and makes the shares more attractive to a larger pool of investors. The reverse action is referred to as a stock consolidation or reverse split. Note the difference between stock split and certificate split: the latter, a shareholder–initiated action, does not alter the value of each share.

Stock Transfer Form (STF)

Form defined by the Stock Transfer Act 1963 used to register the transfer of stock or registered securities from one name to another.

Stock Withdrawal (STW)
The transaction for changing dematerialised stock held in a CREST member's account to certificated stock.

Stockmarket
Description usually given to a stock exchange.

Stop Loss
A rate or price which if reached will trigger the closing of a position in order to limit loss. See *Take–Profit*.

Stop–Loss Limit
The specified maximum loss that a firm is prepared to make.

Stop Limit Order
An order that goes into effect where there is a trade at a specified price.

Stop Order
When a specified price level is reached, this type of order becomes a market order. A buy stop is placed above the market and a sell stop below the market.

STP
See *Straight–Through Processing*.

Straddle
The purchase of a call combined with the purchase of a put at the same strike (generally purchased with both at–the–money).

Straight Bond
A bond with a fixed coupon rate and no conversion or early redemption features.

Straight Debt
A standard bond issue, without right to convert into the common shares of the issuer.

Straight–Through Processing
Computer transmission of the details of a trade, without manual intervention, from their original input by the trader to all other relevant areas – position keeping, risk control, accounts, settlement, reconciliation.

Straits Times Index
Index of the Singapore Stock Exchange.

STRATE
New electronic settlement and depository organisation for the Johannesburg Stock Exchange (Share Transactions Totally Electronic).

Strategic Risk
The risk of loss due to a sub–optimal strategy being employed and associated with the way the institution is managed. For instance, a competitor or product strategy may be employed that fails to maximise the return on the investment made.

Stratified Sampling
A method of setting up a tracker fund in which a sample of shares is held which, statistically, should perform like the index to be tracked.

Street Name
Status of securities endorsed by the previous owner (which could be anyone "in the street"), but not registered in the new owner's name. As far as the issuer's register is concerned, the previous owner remains the owner and may be entitled to receive dividends, interest, bonus issues, rights etc.

Stress Testing
A means of testing the accuracy of VaR models against 'extreme' market event scenarios.

Strike Price/Rate
(Or exercise price). The price or rate at which the holder of an option can insist on the underlying transaction being fulfilled.

Strip
The purchase or sale of a series of consecutive interest rate futures contracts or forward rate agreements.

Stripped Bonds (Strips)
Bonds where the rights to the interest payments and eventual repayment of the nominal value have been separated from each other and trade independently. Facility introduced for gilts in December 1997.

Strong Form Efficiency
Part of efficient market hypothesis. Market in which all information is reflected in security prices.

Stump Period
A calculation period, usually at the beginning or end of a swap, other than the standard ones normally quoted.

STW
See *Stock Withdrawal*.

Style classification
Methodology for classifying shares into certain investment style categories.

Sub–Agent
See *Sub–Custodian*.

Sub-Custodian

A bank which provides clearance and safekeeping services in its domestic market on behalf of a global custodian based overseas.

Subdivision

A corporate action in which a company decides to increase the number of issued shares whilst simultaneously reducing the nominal value of each share so as to leave the total nominal value of the issued capital unchanged. For example, if a company replaces each share with two new shares, the value of each new share will be half that of the old. Sometimes called a 'stock split'.

Subdivision of Shares

If the price of shares increases substantially over a period, the ACD may 'split' the shares in the ratio of for example 4 for 1. The net result is a five-fold increase in the number of shares and a reduction in the price per share by a factor of 5.

Subordinated Loan Stock

A special type of loan stock which ranks after the other creditors, but before shareholders.

Subscription (Exercise of Warrants)

A corporate action in which holders of warrants may exercise their right to subscribe for ordinary shares in the company by exercising the warrant. Although warrants may be attached to other securities, they are usually detached, and traded as a separate line of stock. If not exercised by the final subscription date, the warrants lapse.

Subscription Limits

The maximum amounts (normally of cash) that an investor can put into each ISA component, depending on the type of ISA subscription (Maxi or Mini), in any particular tax year.

Subscription Price

Price at which shareholders of a corporation are entitled to purchase common shares in a rights offering or at which subscription warrants are exercisable.

Subsidiary

A company, at least 50% of which is owned by another company. See *Holding Company*.

Substantial Acquisition Rules (SARs)

Rules set out by the Panel on Takeovers and Mergers governing purchases of shares where the holding will be 15% or higher but below 30%.

Suitability

The appropriateness of investments considering a customer's attitude to risk, and financial and investment objectives.

Suitability Letter

Letter required in respect of various transactions in life policies or pensions, in which the firm explains its suitability for the investment needs of the client.

Sum Assured

The amount payable under a life policy.

SuperDot

Computer dealing system of the New York Stock Exchange.

Supranational

A governmental organisation formed with specific aims, such as the World Bank or the EBRD.

Supervisory Notice

Notice issued by the Regulatory Decisions Committee as an alternative to a warnings notice. It is preventative rather than disciplinary.

Surrender Value

The encashment value of a life policy before it becomes a claim by maturity or death.

Suspense Account

Account where client money is held if there are no clear instructions on which bank account to credit.

Suspension of Automatic

An interruption in order book trading triggered by the execution entry, deletion or expiry of an order that is 10% higher or lower than the base price. Trading may still occur outside the order book and limit orders may be entered pending the uncrossing which will re–start trading. Suspensions will normally last for 10 minutes.

Suspension of Listing

The complete suspension of a security listing either by the Listing Authority or at the request of the company concerned. All trading ceases and orders are removed from the order book.

Swap

Arrangement where two borrowers, one of whom has fixed interest and one of whom has floating rate borrowings, swap their commitments with each other. A bank would arrange the swap and charge a fee. Commodity, currency, equity and interest rate swaps are all commonly traded.

SwapClear

A clearing house and central counterparty for swaps.

SwapsWire

An electronic dealing system for swaps.

Swaption

An option to undertake a swap.

SWIFT

The Society for Worldwide Interbank Financial Telecommunication was founded in 1973 to service the payments needs of the banking industry through standardised, electronic messages. The securities markets became involved in 1987 with the acceptance of stock exchanges, brokers and depositories into the SWIFT network. Also, SWIFT is one of the approved CREST Network providers.

Switch

Sale of one stock and subsequent reinvestment into another stock.

Switching Discount

A discount, normally expressed as a percentage reduction in the offer price, given to investors upon switching from one fund to another within the same group.

SWORD

The London Clearing House delivery system for designated metal contracts, except silver.

SWX

The Swiss Exchange.

SYCOM

The overnight trading system operated by the Sydney Futures Exchange (SFE).

Syndicate
A group of securities houses who are placing a new issue of eurobonds under the authority of a lead manager.

Syndicated Issue
An issue method whereby new securities are sold to the clients of syndicate banks.

Syndicated Loan
A loan by a number of financial institutions to one borrower for a predetermined term and at a margin over short–term interest rates.

Syntegra
One of the approved CREST network providers, the systems integration business of British Telecom plc.

Synthetic Agreement for Forward Exchange (SAFE)
A generic term for ERAs and FXAs.

Synthetic Long Call
A long stock position combined with a long put.

Synthetic Long Put
A short stock position combined with a long call.

Synthetic Position
A hedging strategy which combines futures options and futures for potentially increased profit and price protection.

System Controller
The manager of the CREST system.

Systematic Risk
Risk that is inherent in any portfolio of securities. The risk that remains after a well–diversified portfolio of securities has been assembled.

T

T
Common abbreviation used to signify 'Trade Date'.

T+3
Settlement takes place three business days after the date of the transaction.

T+5
Settlement takes place five business days after the date of the transaction.

T+n
Trade is settled n business days after the day of trade. See *Rolling Settlement*.

TII
See *Treasury Inflation Indexed securities*.

TACT
See *Tel Aviv Continuous Trading*.

Tail
The interest rate gap between a deposit and a loan of differing maturities, representing interest rate risk.

Takeover
When one company obtains more than 50% of another company's shares.

Takeover Panel
See *Panel on Takeovers and Mergers*.

Take–Profit
A rate or price which if reached will trigger the closing of a position in order to ensure profit. See *Stop Loss*.

Talisman
The Stock Exchange computerised settlement system which was fully replaced by CREST in April 1997.

Talon
See *Coupon*.

Tangible Assets
Physical assets owned by a company or individual which can be touched such as machinery etc.

Tap
A sale of a government instrument, eg, a bond or treasury bill in response to demand.

Taper Relief (CGT)
An allowance deducted from a capital gain based on the period of ownership of an asset from the later of the date of actual acquisition or April 1998.

Tap Stock

A government bond which is issued in varying amounts at different times.

TARGET

The Trans–European Automated Real–Time Gross Settlement Express Transfer system that will handle the settlement of cross border payments of the euro.

Tariffable Unit (TU)

The unit of charging for CREST transactions (TU), based on the cost charged by CRESTCo to each counterparty for a movement of stock and cash between two memberships, with CREST matching input from both counterparties (ie, a standard stock/cash delivery (DEL).

Taurus

The proposed central settlement system, based on all securities being dematerialised. It was due to replace Talisman during the early 1990s but its development was abandoned in 1993.

Tax Avoidance

The legal use of tax concessions to reduce or dispose of a tax charge or debt.

Tax Claims

Interim Claim (PEP10): Form on which the plan manager claims back from the Inland Revenue the tax which has been deducted at source (at 20%) from the net dividends and distributions received on holdings in a PEP. Interim claims may be made monthly (in tax months 6th–5th).
Annual Claim (PEP14): The formal claim for all tax credits and adjustments for the whole of a complete tax year, subject to audit by the plan manager's external auditors.

Tax Credit

Income distributions, whether paid or reinvested, are treated as the top slice of income and carry a tax credit. A tax credit voucher is usually issued with the dividend or interest payment. Investors liable to tax at the basic rate or lower rate band will have no further liability to tax. Higher rate taxpayers will have a further liability to tax.

Non–taxpayers can no longer use the tax credit voucher to support a tax repayment claim as this benefit was withdrawn by the government in the late 1990s.

Tax Exempt Special Savings Account (TESSA)

TESSAs were deposit accounts or share accounts with a building society which were designated as TESSA for the purposes of section 326A of the Taxes Act. TESSAs are no longer available for new depositors.

Taxes Act

The Income and Corporation Taxes Act 1988.

Tax Reclaim

The process that a global custodian and/or a holder of securities performs, in accordance with local government filing requirements, in order to recapture a allowable percentage of taxed withheld.

Tax Year

The tax year runs from 6 April to the following 5 April.

Taxable Income

The total income in a year less allowances available at the marginal rate.

Taxable Pay

The amount of an individuals annual income on which tax is payable.

techMARK

Market for technology stocks opened by the London Stock Exchange in November 1999.

Technical Analysis

Analysis of past and current share prices in order to make investment decisions on the basis of trends in those prices. See *Charts*.

Technical Standards Committee (TSC)

The body recognised by BSI and ISO as representing practitioners in the UK Securities Industry in the setting of national and international standards in so far as they apply to the industry.

Tel Aviv Continuous Trading

The dealing system for the Tel Aviv Stock Exchange (TACT).

Tender Offer

Formal offer to buy made to holders of a particular issue by a third party. Detailed offer is made by public announcement in newspapers and sometimes by personal letter of transmittal to each stockholder.

Tenor

The length of time until a security matures.

Term

The length of time that a security has until it matures or its value can be redeemed.

Term Assurance/Insurance

A policy that pays out only if death occurs within a certain period. There is no savings element.

Term Loan
An advance by a financial institution for a given period, which has to be repaid, with interest, at regular intervals.

Term Repo
Repo trades (of a maturity over one day) with a fixed maturity date.

Terminable on Demand
An open repo that can be terminated on a daily basis.

Terminal Bonus
A bonus paid on death or maturity of a with–profits policy.

Termination Date
The end date of a swap.

Terms of Business
Documentation usually required from investment businesses to their customers, outlining the way in which the relationship will operate.

TESSA
See *Tax Exempt Special Savings Account.*

Testate
A person dying leaving a valid will.

Tested Telex
A telex message bearing a code number, for authentication purposes, calculated in accordance with a test key.

Testator
Person who has made a will.

TFE

The transaction type used by an escrow agent (receiving agent) to move stock from an escrow account, either to the original member's account or to the escrow agent's account.

Thailand Securities Depository Company

Central securities depository for Thailand.

Theoretical Value

The price of an option (or future) as computed by a mathematical model. If the assumptions used in the model are accurate then this will equate to the 'fair' value.

Thin Market

A market in which very few transactions occur.

Third Tier Rules

The minimum requirement set out by the FSA to reconcile safe custody holding positions at least on a semi–annual basis.

Thomson Report

An electronic transaction reporting system for international equities on the London Stock Exchange operated by Thomson.

Threshold Level

The value of an obligation above which collateral may be required, agreed between an obligor and a lender.

Tick

The minimum permitted price fluctuation in a futures or options contract.

Tick Size

For SETS securities, this will be set in bands depending on their price: 0.25p for shares priced below 500p per share, 0.5p for shares priced above 500p and up to and including 1000p per share, and 1.0p for shares priced above 1000p per share.

Tick Value

The value of a one point movement (0.01 per cent) in the price of an exchange traded financial future or option.

Tied Agent

An individual or business which only sells one company's products (such as life assurance) rather than advising independently on all the products available.

Time Decay

The rate at which the time value of an option deteriorates over its life.

Time Deposit

Deposit on an account held with a financial institution for a fixed term or with the understanding that the depositor can withdraw only by giving notice.

Time Spread

See *Horizontal Spread*.

Time Value

The portion of an options price that is not its intrinsic value.

Time Weighted Return

Calculates the rate of return for each period between each cash inflow and outflow and then calculates an average rate. It eliminates the timing effect of cash flows and is generally preferred to the money weighted return.

Timely Execution
To execute a client's order at a time that is in the best interests of the customer.

Tip Sheets
Publications giving recommendations on which shares to buy, sell and hold.

Title
The right to ownership and enjoyment of property.

TNT Express (UK) Limited
The organisation chosen to operate the CREST Courier and Sorting Service (CCSS) on behalf of CRESTCo.

Tokyo Stock Exchange
The Tokyo Exchange is the second largest (after NYSE) and is predominantly an order–driven market.

Tom Next
A transaction with value dates for tomorrow against the next day.

Tom/Spot Week
Money placed on the money market from tomorrow for repayment one week after.

Top–Down Management
A method of active portfolio management where different classes of security (cash, bonds, shares) are selected; then within each class different sectors are selected; and within each sector individual securities are selected.

TOREX
Dealing system of the Toronto Stock Exchange.

Total Margined Transaction Requirement
Amounts due to customers in respect of margined transactions.

Touch
The best prices available for a stock on the stockmarket, looking at all market makers.

Tracker Fund
A unit trust that invests in the companies which comprise a Stock Exchange index so as to follow the movements of the index.

Trade
A transaction dealt through a recognised investment exchange which is a contract to buy or sell an agreed quantity of stock at an agreed price. It is also called a trade or deal.

Trade Condition
A field, entered on an input instruction, used for agreeing special terms of the trade or specifying a non–settling condition. Trade and other conditions include:

- NC for non–central settlement, ie, not for settlement in CREST, although input of the transaction enable CREST to calculate SDRT and report the transaction to regulators.
- FD for form of delivery, if for foreign delivery.
- RO for result of option.
- GD for guaranteed delivery.
- RP for result of repo.
- BL for board lots (relates to securities registered in Hong Kong).
- PD for place of delivery, if not in country of incorporation.
- BN for bad names (relates to securities registered in the United States).

Trade Confirmation

The process by which the two counterparties to a trade input their instructions to a central system which compares them and, if the instructions agree, confirms them and passes them on for settlement.

Trade Date

The date on which an order to buy or sell a security is executed.

Trade for Trade Settlement

See *Gross Settlement*.

Trade Instruction Process

The process of agreeing delivery instructions with a third party.

Trade Matching

The matching by a clearing house of the trade details submitted by the two counterparties to a trade. Often combined with trade confirmation.

Traded Option

A term that usually refers to options dealt on a recognised exchange.

Tradepoint

Tradepoint was established in 1995 as a rival to the London Stock Exchange. Now merged into virt–x.

Trader

An individual who buys and sells securities with the objective of making short–term gains.

Trading Halt

A break in trading on Exchange in a security imposed by the Stock Exchange if a disorderly market has arisen. No trading is permitted on Exchange during a trading halt, but limit orders can be entered to the order book pending the uncrossing which will re–start trading.

Trading Permits

These are issued by exchanges and give the holder the right to have one trader at any one time trading in the contract(s) to which the permit relates.

Trail Commission

A commission usually paid annually for introducing IFAs to encourage long term investment. Also referred to as renewal commission.

Training and Competence

FSA sourcebook imposing obligations on firms in these areas. The firm's commitments to training and competence should be that:

a) its employees are competent;

b) its employees remain competent for the work they do;

c) its employees are appropriately supervised;

d) its employees' competence is regularly reviewed; and

e) the level of competence is appropriate to the nature of the business.

Tranche

One of a series of two or more issues with the same coupon rate and maturity date. The tranches become fungible at a future date, usually just after the first coupon date.

Transaction

1. Usually refers to the order to purchase or sell a security or to receive or pay cash.

2. Any instruction for matching and/or settlement of stock and/or cash within CREST. The term "transaction" includes instructions for cash–only transactions, and also reporting–only instructions for which no stock or cash movement is required.

Transaction Capture

The activity of capturing trades in back office systems.

Transaction Date
See *Trade Date.*

Transaction Progress Status
A three–letter composite transaction status, your Party transaction status, your counterparty's Party transaction status, and an overall transaction status. The first two letters indicate the current state of you and your counterparty's input. The final letter, the transaction status, summarises the status of the whole transaction.

Transaction Reference
The reference given to a transaction by the member on input, which must be unique to the member. The kind of reference used is entirely the user's choice – as long as it is unique to the user, and is no more that 16 character long.

Transaction Status
The one–letter code (with associated text description, where available) generated by CREST that summarises the status of the whole transaction and is visible to all parties to the transaction. It is the third letter in the Transaction progress status.

Trans–European Automated Real–Time Gross Settlement Express Transfer (TARGET)
See *TARGET.*

Transfer
An act, which transmits or creates an interest in a security, a financial instrument or money.

Transfer Agent
Agent appointed by a corporation to maintain records of stock and bond owners, to cancel and issue certificates and to resolve problems arising from lost, destroyed or stolen certificates.

Transfer Form

Document which owners of registered securities must sign when they sell the security. Not required where a book entry transfer system is in use.

Transfer In

Client transferring his PEP/ISA from another plan/account manager, without loss of tax benefits.

Transfer Out

Client transferring his PEP/ISA *to* another plan/account manager, without loss of tax benefits.

Transfer Value

The amount trustees pay to another pension scheme or an insurance company for an early leaver. They are capital sums intended to represent the present value of future pension benefits. Transfer values may be paid to a new employer's scheme, a Section 32 buy–out bond or a personal pension plan.

Translation Risk

Accounting or financial reporting risk where the earnings of a company can be adversely affected due to its method of accounting for foreign earnings.

Transparency

The degree to which a market is characterised by prompt availability of accurate price and volume information which gives participants comfort that the market is fair.

Transparent

A description of a market where investors have full immediate knowledge of the details of trades taking place.

TRAX

The International Securities Market Association's real time confirmation and risk management system used by brokers, market makers, institutional investors and fund managers to confirm trades in bonds and other securities.

Treasury

Arm of government responsible for all financial decisions and regulation of the financial services sector.

Treasury Bills

Short term government securities which pay no interest so are issued at a discount. Also known as T–bills and usually have a maturity of 91 days.

Treasury Bonds

Coupon bearing government securities with a maturity date greater than 5 years. Also known as T–bonds.

Treasury Inflation Indexed Securities

Securities issued by the US government.

Treasury Notes (US)

US government bond issued with 2, 3, 5 and 7 year maturity. Also known as T–notes.

Treaty Relief

Double tax relief given under the terms of a double tax agreement.

Trigger Level

See *Barrier Option*.

Trigger Option

See *Barrier Option*.

Tri–Party Repo
A repo in which an independent agent bank or clearing house oversees a standard two–party repo transaction. The responsibilities of the tri–party agent include maintaining acceptable and adequate collateral and overall maintenance of the outstanding repo trades.

Triple–A Rating
The highest credit rating for a bond or company where the risk of default (or non–payment) is negligible. See *AAA rating*.

Trust
An arrangement whereby people called trustees hold property for the benefit of others called the beneficiaries.

Trust Account Repo
See *Safe Custody Repo*.

Trust Deed
The legal document drawn up between the trustees and the managers containing basic details of the constitution of a unit trust.

Trustee
A person or organisation who is the owner of assets held in trust. They are responsible for safeguarding the assets, monitoring compliance with the trust deed and the activities of the trust manager.

Trust Instrument
The document creating the trust. This might be included in a will or it might be a separate trust deed.

Trust Property
The property put into trust by the settlor.

Trustee Investments Act, 1961

This Act laid down certain requirements which a security must meet before it can be bought by trustees. The object of the Act allowed trustees to invest in equity shares, giving their beneficiaries the prospect of capital growth.

TSA

Trading System for Amsterdam – the Dutch dealing system.

TSC

See *Technical Standards Committee*.

TSCD

Taiwan Securities Central Depository.

TSE

Tokyo Stock Exchange.

TTE

The transaction type used by members to move stock to an escrow account, eg, when accepting an offer in a takeover. The stock remains in the name of the member but is controlled by the receiving (escrow) agent.

Tunnel

See *Collar*.

Turn

See *Spread*.

Turnaround

Securities bought and sold for settlement on the same day.

Turnaround Time
The time available or needed to settle a turnaround trade.

Two Sided Confirmation
Both parties to a trade submit details to a centralised trade confirmation system.

Two Way (Customer) Agreement
A customer agreement which is sent to the customer and to which the customer has signified his assent in writing. The firm must be satisfied that the customer has a proper opportunity to consider its terms. Assent could be in the form of a copy of the agreement signed by the customer and returned to the firm or a signed letter of assent.

Two Way Price
Simultaneous prices in a stock quoted by a market maker, the lower at which he is willing to buy and the higher at which he is willing to sell.

U

Uberrima Fides
Utmost good faith.

UCITS
A European Directive governing 'Undertakings for Collective Investment in Transferable Securities'. It is designed to harmonise the operation of collective investment schemes which includes authorised unit trusts throughout the European Community, with a view to facilitating the sale of funds in other member states.

UK Listing Authority (UKLA)
Under EU regulations, each member–state must appoint a competent authority. The competent authority for Listing is the FSA. In this capacity the FSA is called the UK Listing Authority.

Ultra Vires
Outside the legal powers of an official or company.

Umbrella Funds

A single authorised unit trust scheme with any number of constituent parts, providing the opportunity for unit holders to switch all or part of their investment from one part to another. Each part may have an entirely separate portfolio.

Unauthorised Unit Trust

A unit trust which does not comply with FSA's criteria to make it authorised and which can only be marketed to sophisticated investors.

Uncertificated Transactions

Transactions involving dematerialised stock held in CREST.

Uncovered Sale

Selling an option without possessing the wherewithal to meet the obligations implicit in that sale. The writer of a call who does not possess the stock is said to be uncovered, as is the writer of a put who has no cash or near cash to pay for stock.

Uncrossing Auction

An automated auction of orders held on the order book.

Undated Gilts

UK government bonds which have no maturity date.

Undated Stock

An interest bearing security which has no final date of repayment of the principal sum.

Underlying

The financial instrument on which an option or future is based, sometimes referred to as 'the cash'.

Underlying Asset

The asset from which the future or option's price is derived. In the case of BIFFEX, this is the Baltic Freight Exchange Index.

Underlying Instrument

The instrument on which a futures or options contract is based.

Under Reference

The price must be reconfirmed before a counterparty can deal on it.

Undersubscribed

Circumstance when people have applied for fewer shares than are available in a new issue.

Undertaking for the Collective Investment in Transferable Securities

See *UCITS*.

Underwriters (of a share or bond issue)

Institutions which agree to take up shares in a new issue if it is undersubscribed. They will be paid an underwriting fee.

Underwriting (Insurance)

The procedure of assessing a risk and deciding whether to accept it and at what premium.

Underwriting Agreement

An agreement between the lead manager and the underwriters setting out the terms and obligations of each party to the agreement.

Underwriting Fee

The fee paid to institutional investors who agree to underwrite a new issue of securities.

Underwriting Standards
The standards that financial institutions apply to borrowers in order to evaluate their credit worthiness and therefore limit the risk of default.

Unemployment
The percentage of the labour force registered as available to work at the current wage rate.

Unemployment Benefit
State benefit to the unemployed who have an adequate NIC record.

Unfranked Income
All sterling bonds except prefs are deemed to be paying loan interest and so the interest is paid net of basic income tax, but the gross interest that the issuing company pays will be considered for tax purposes and could result in a further tax liability or refund to the company.

Unfunded Pension Scheme
A pension scheme where pensions are paid out of the current profits of the company.

Unilateral Arrangement (of collateral)
One party gives collateral to the other.

Unilateral Relief
Double tax relief given unilaterally by a country to its own residents for overseas tax where there is not a double tax agreement in force.

Unitised With–Profits
With–profits investments expressed as unit–linked policies. Benefits are based on unit holdings rather than on the sum assured payable at maturity or death.

Unit–Linked Policy

A policy where the value is linked to the value of units in a fund run by a life office or units of a unit trust. The units directly reflect values of the underlying assets of the fund. Whole of life, endowment, permanent health insurance and even term assurance policies may be unit–linked.

Unit Trust

A unit trust is a means of allowing an individual investor to participate in a large portfolio of shares with many other investors. Identical units are sold each representing a small fraction of the portfolio. As the number of units grows, the underlying portfolio is increased.

Unit Trust ISA

An ISA that contains investments only in one or more unit trusts.

Unit Trust Yield

The yield is a percentage of the quoted offer price of a unit trust, representing the prospective annual income of the trust fund for its current annual accounting period, after deducting all charges. The yield is expressed gross of tax.

Universal Whole Of Life Policy

Unit–linked whole of life policies with a wide range of benefits including death, accidental death, permanent disability, critical illness, permanent health insurance.

UNIVYC

Clearing settlement and depository organisation for the Czech market.

Unlisted Company

A company whose shares are not listed on the stock exchange. See *Alternative Investment Market*.

Unlisted Securities Market (USM) (UK)
The market, introduced by the UK Stock Exchange in 1980, open to companies which did not fulfil all the requirements of the Stock Exchange for a full quotation. No longer in operation. See *Alternative Investment Market*.

Unmatched Stock Event (USE)
The transaction type used by receiving agents during corporate actions for transferring stock and/or cash to members, or vice versa.

Unmatched Transaction
The result of an instruction not matching in CREST because: either only one party input a transaction instruction; or, although both parties input instructions, one or more of the matchable fields did not match. Certain types of transactions in CREST do not require matching.

Unrealised Profit
A profit which arises from the revaluation of an asset but where there is no actual sale.

Unregulated Collective Investment Schemes
Collective schemes that do not meet FSA's criteria and which therefore cannot be marketed to private customers.

Unsecured Loan Stocks
Domestic bonds which are not secured on any assets of the borrower.

Unsolicited Call
A personal visit or oral communication made without the recipient' s express invitation.

Unweighted Index
An index where all the parts of the index are equally weighted when calculating the index value.

Up–and–In Option

A knock–in option where the trigger is higher than the underlying rate at the start. See *Knock–In Option.*

Up–and–Out Option

A knock–out option where the trigger is higher than the underlying rate at the start. *See Knock–Out Option.*

Upside

The positive aspects of incurring risk.

Upstairs Trading

See *Block Trading.*

Up Tick

The last trade in a share is at a price higher than the one before.

User

An organisation with a gateway computer and network connection in order to communicate directly with CREST, on behalf of one or a number of participants.

User ID

The identification code used in the system for a particular user.

V

Value
See *Value Date*.

Value Added Tax (VAT)
A general tax on goods and services which was introduced into the UK in 1973.

Value–at–Risk (VaR)
The maximum loss that can occur with a specified confidence over a specified period of days. VaR is essentially a measure of the volatility of a bank trading book.

Value Chain
A number of processes that must occur to achieve a desired outcome.

Value Date
1. The date on which cash is credited to or debited from an account. It has the same meaning as settlement date.
2. The date that cash is received for stock sold.
3. The date from which interest begins.

Value Stock (Share)
Company shares undervalued by the market. Typically identified by low market to book ratio, low price earnings ratio, or high dividend yield.

Vanilla
See *Plain Vanilla*.

Vanilla Swap
Two parties enter into an agreement to exchange the difference between a fixed rate of interest and a nominated floating rate.

Variable Currency
The currency in a foreign exchange rate the amount of which is equated to one unit of the 'base currency'.

Variance/Co–Variance Simulation
See *Correlation Simulation*.

Variation Margin
Debits and credits on a margin account arising once a portfolio has been marked to market. Variation margin is calculated at the end of each business day by the London Clearing House.
Variation margin is a payment made, or collateral transferred, subsequently from one party to the other because the market price of the transaction or of collateral has changed. Variation margin payment is either in effect a settlement of profit / loss (for example in the case of a futures contract) or the reduction of credit exposure.

Vasicek Method
The method by which a zero–coupon yield curve is modelled, based on statistical methodology.

Venture Capital
Funds provided by, for instance, a bank, building society or specialised lending institution to an individual to start up or develop a business or company where a high degree of risk may be involved.

Venture Capital Trust (VCT)
A listed company which invests in small unlisted and AIM companies. The VCT regime was set up by the government in order channel private investors' money into small companies via the medium of a listed vehicle. VCTs enjoy generous tax reliefs but numerous tax regulations have to be complied with.

Vertical Spread
A combination of options, where one option is purchased and another is sold, both with the same expiry date. The spread will be a constructed with either calls or puts.

virt–x
A Recognised Investment Exchange (RIE) providing a screen–based stock market for UK registered shares, launched in 1995. Originally launched in 1995 as Tradepoint, virt–x was formed in 2001, by merger with the Swiss Stock Exchange.

Visibles
See *Current Account*.

Volatility
A measure of how much an underlying instrument is likely to fluctuate (or has fluctuated in the past) during a defined time period. See *Historic* and *Implied Volatility*.

Volatility Risk
The risk of price movements that are more uncertain than usual affecting the pricing of products.

Volume Sensitivity
A process cause of operational risk where the workload increases in proportion to increasing volumes.

Vostro
Italian for 'your' usually associated with accounts maintained by foreign banks held by other banks in another currency and country. The opposite to *Nostro*.

Voting Shares
Shares which entitle a holder to vote in the election of directors of a company.

VPC
The Swedish settlement system, facilitating cross border settlement of AstraZeneca shares, and the possibility of other Swedish securities.

W

Warning Notice

Notice that can be issued by the Regulatory Decisions Committee advising a firm or approved person that disciplinary action against them is taking place.

Warrant

An equity warrant offers the holder the right to buy underlying equity at a predetermined price on specified dates, or at any time, up to the end of a predetermined time period. A warrant differs from an option in that options usually have a life of less than 1 year. Warrants are usually issued by companies or by securities houses and have a life span of more than 1 year. The exercise of a company–issued warrant will result in an increase of the capital of that company.

Warrant Agent

A bank appointed by the issuer as an intermediary between the issuing company and the (physical) warrant holders, interacting when the latter want to exercise the warrants.

Warrant Fund

An authorised securities scheme which is permitted to invest more than 5% of the value of its property in warrants.

Warrant Scheme

An authorised fund, similar to a securities fund, that may include warrants up to 100% as defined in the Financial Services (Regulated Schemes) Regulations 1991.

Within the ISA Regulations however, the term "warrant scheme" is defined more widely to include the FSA definition (above) plus parts of an umbrella scheme that would be classified as warrant schemes if they were themselves free–standing authorised funds.

Warrant schemes can be held as an investment only in the stocks and shares component of an ISA.

Weak Form Market Efficiency

Part of efficient market hypothesis. A market in which all historical information regarding the security is reflected in its price.

Weekly Official Intelligence (WOI)

Weekly publication by the London Stock Exchange which provides (amongst other information) a summary of company announcements during that week.

When–Issued Trading

Trading a bond before the issue date; no interest is accrued during this period. Also known as the *Grey Market*.

Whole Life Assurance

A life policy which pays out on death, whenever it occurs.

Will

A written document signed by the testator and witnessed giving instructions as to the distribution of their estate on death.

Will Trust
A trust created by a will.

Winding Up
See *Liquidation*.

Window Dressing
Financial adjustments by companies for the purposes of accounting representation. A company may, for instance, raise a short–term loan in order to show their balance sheet in a favourable light.

Wire Transfer
A type of payment where the clearing house debits the participant's cash account and pays the funds externally to the beneficiary's account held by another bank See *Book Entry Transfer*.

Withdrawal
Rules which oblige providers of certain products to defer the commencement of the investment for a period of time during which the customer has the right to change his or her mind and withdraw from the agreement.

Withholding Tax (WHT)
Tax deducted from dividends on investments which are paid to foreign investors. This can be claimed back if there is a Double Taxation Agreement in place between the two countries.

With–Profits
Policies where policyholders receive a guaranteed sum assured plus a share of the investment profits of the life fund in the form of bonuses.

Worked Principal Agreement

An agreement by a member firm to effect, at some future time, as principal, either a transaction in an order book security or a portfolio transaction which includes order book securities, within agreed price and size parameters.

Worked Principal Notification

A notification of the details of a worked principal agreement.

Worked Principal Transaction

A transaction executed pursuant to a worked principal agreement.

Working Capital

See *Net Current Assets*.

Working Families' Tax Credit

This was introduced in October 1999 in an attempt to provide extra support for low earning families. It replaced family credit, which was a Social Security benefit and is administered through the tax system.

Working Member

A broker or underwriter who carries out the actual business (as a professional member) at Lloyd's of London.

World Bank

See *International Bank for Reconstruction and Development*.

Writer

The seller of an option (usually refers to an opening sale). See *Holder*.

X

XD

See *Ex–Dividend*.

XDC

The transaction type for cross border delivery confirm.

XDL

The transaction type for cross border delivery.

XDR

The transaction type for cross border delivery reversal.

Xetra

Computerised dealing system on the Deutsche Börse.

Y

Yankee Bond
A US dollar bond issued in the US by a non–US issuer, eg, a foreign bank.

Yellow Book
Colloquial name which was formerly applied to the Listing Authority Rules when supervised by the London Stock Exchange.

Yield
The yield on an investment is the interest or dividend income as a percentage of the capital value. This is also known as the running yield. The yield to redemption also takes into account the annualised capital profit (or loss) on holding a fixed interest security to redemption, ie, the investors have an annual average total return.

Yield Curve
A series of interest rates plotted against the time to maturity to which they apply. The graph below show the 'normal' shape of a yield curve.

Yield to Maturity
See *Gross Redemption Yield*.

Yours
A quick way of stating that you will sell the base currency.

Z

Zero Coupon Bonds

A deep discount bond where the coupon payable per annum is zero and the entire return of the bond is in the form of capital accrual from the original discounted price to the final redemption value at maturity of the bond.

Zero Dividend Preference Shares

Issued by split capital investment trusts these shares pay no income but promise to repay the shares at a higher level at a fixed date. The shares are very tax efficient and are frequently used for school fees planning.

Zone A

Under Basel rules, certain countries such as sovereign borrowers attract the lowest risk.

Securities Institute Publishing

Each publication provides a detailed overview and practical introduction to key topics within financial services.

Our range consists of re–worked and updated notes from our popular courses. These publications are a useful reference for everyone who needs to grasp the basics of a topic – fast!

To place an order or find out more, call now on *020 7645 0680.*

INTRODUCTION TO BOND MARKETS

Introduction to Bond Markets provides a comprehensive, authoritative description and analysis of the bond markets. The book considers basic 'plain vanilla' bonds and elementary bond mathematics, before looking at the array of different instruments available. Contents include:

- Bond Yield Measurement
- Corporate Debt Markets
- Eurobonds
- Introduction to Repo
- Risk Management
- Off–Balance Sheet Instruments
- Government Bond Markets
- Emerging Bond Markets.

410pp paperback, ISBN: 1 900520 79 6, 2nd edition

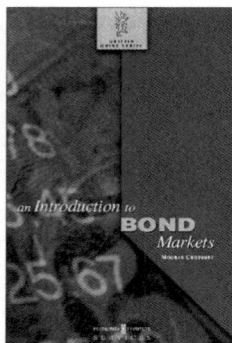

AN INTRODUCTION TO CORPORATE FINANCE
- Transactions and Techniques

Introduction to Corporate Finance provides readers with the key elements of corporate finance. The book introduces the principle techniques used in corporate finance, combined with practical experience and hands-on, numerically orientated case studies.

- Sources of Capital
- Flotations/Initial Public Offerings
- Mergers and Acquisitions
- Management Buy Outs
- Determining the Cost of Capital
- International Equity Offerings
- Valuing Securities
- Well illustrated with diagrams and tables, bullet points and summaries.

96pp paperback, ISBN: 1 900520 09 5, 1st edition

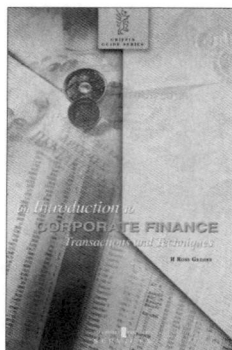

THE FUNDAMENTALS OF CREST

The Fundamentals of CREST gives a detailed overview of securities administration and settlement through the CREST system. It is illustrated throughout with diagrams and tables, bullet points and summaries.

- Handling Certificated Securities
- Corporate Actions and Claims
- Stock Loans and Collateral.

128pp paperback, ISBN: 1 900520 98 2, 2nd edition

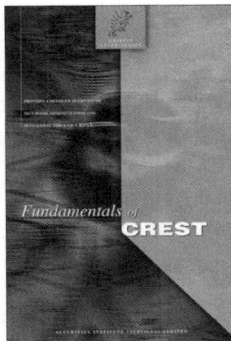

DICTIONARY OF FINANCIAL & SECURITIES TERMS

This updated and greatly expanded 2nd edition gives definitions of frequently used terms in the financial and securities industry. Also included is a comprehensive listing of abbreviations, acronyms and industry websites. Over 2,500 entries.

- What is BIFFEX?
- What does CDP stand for?
- What are the Conduct of Business Rules?
- What is the definition of Debt/Equity Ratio?

Included with the dictionary is a FREE CD–ROM version for users to load onto their PC for easy reference at home or at work.

400pp paperback, ISBN: 1 84307 023 5, 2nd edition

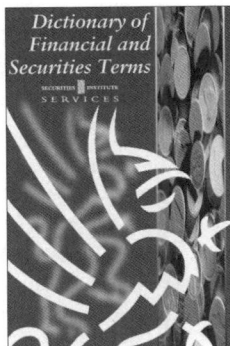

ECONOMIC & MONETARY UNION

Economic and Monetary Union (EMU) is the system that
links together the economies and currencies of the participating European countries. The European Central Bank
has become responsible for centralised monetary policy.
What does the Euro mean for you?

■ Convergence
■ Impact of the Euro on the markets
■ Preparing for the future.

28pp paperback, ISBN: 1 900520 31 1, 1st edition

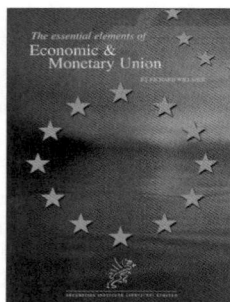

INTRODUCTION TO EQUITY MARKETS

Introduction to Equity Markets provides an overview of
the current financial services industry. The book
introduces the reader to different types of companies and
shares as well as analysis of UK markets. An overview of
dealing and settlement in some of the world's major markets is also featured. Contents include:

■ Shareholders and Company Law
■ Issuing Shares – The Primary Market
■ Trading Shares – The Secondary Market
■ Settlement of Transactions
■ Major Overseas Exchanges and Indices
■ Dividends, Bonus Issues and Rights Issues
■ Company Accounts.

170pp paperback, ISBN: 1 84307 034 0, 2nd edition

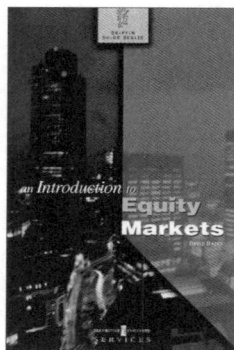

AN INTRODUCTION TO FUND MANAGEMENT

An Introduction to Fund Management introduces readers to the economic rationale for the existence of funds,
the different types available, investment strategies and
many other related issues from the perspective of the
investment manager. Topics include the features and
characteristics of funds, portfolio management and
administration, performance measurement and investment mathematics. Includes relevant formulae,
equations and examples.

- Features and characteristics of funds
- Portfolio management and administration
- Performance measurement
- Investment mathematics.

160pp paperback, ISBN: 1 84307 022 7, 2nd edition

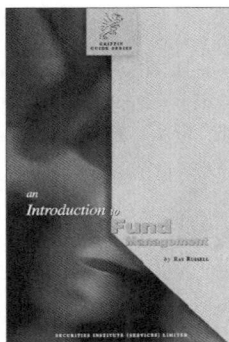

FUNDAMENTALS OF GLOBAL OPERATIONS MANAGEMENT

This book will help you to understand the role of
operations terms and what is happening in the industry
that impacts on operations. It is ideal for anyone new to or
aspiring to become a supervisor or manager.Contents
include:

- Operations management
- Markets
- Banking, broking and institutional clients
- Concepts of risk
- Clearing and settlement
- Custody
- Technology
- Regulation and compliance

272pp paperback, ISBN: 1 84307 014 6, 1st edition

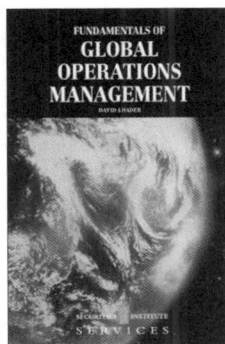

INTRODUCTION TO THE GILT STRIPS MARKET

Introduction to the Gilt Strips Market provides a thorough description and analysis of gilt strips. The contents describe and define strips as a financial instrument and examine the use and application of gilt strips within the context of the capital markets as a whole. Contents include:

- Zero–coupon bonds
- The yield curve
- Interest rate risk for strips
- Settlement, tax and regulatory issues
- Trading and strategy

192pp paperback, ISBN: 1 84307 006 5, 2nd edition

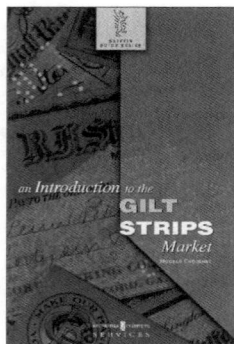

THE PREVENTION OF MONEY LAUNDERING

This quick guide looks at the scale of the problem and efforts taken to overcome it: an essential reference for all who are concerned to identify attempts at money laundering within their organisation.

- What is money laundering?
- Money laundering and the law
- How do you spot it in the process, and what to do.

48pp paperback, ISBN: 1 84307 005 7, 2nd edition

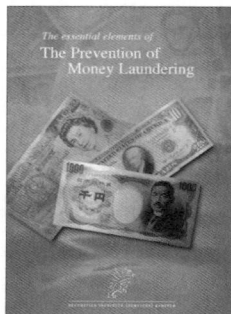

UNDERSTANDING REGULATION AND COMPLIANCE

Understanding Regulation & Compliance outlines the new regulatory structure in the post-N2 environment, introducing the areas regulated under the *Financial Services and Markets Act 2000*, the role of the *Financial Services Authority* and the rules imposed on firms. It also introduces other important regulatory areas such as *Insider Dealing and Money Laundering*. Topics include:

- Financial Services & Markets Act 2000
- Financial Services Authority
- FSA Handbook
- Control over individuals
- Conduct of business rules
- Client assets
- Improper dealings
- Money laundering

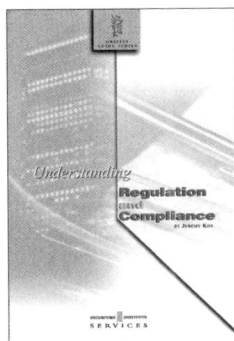

192pp paperback, ISBN: 1 84307 003 2, 2nd edition

INTRODUCTION TO REPO MARKETS

An Introduction to Repo Markets provides a comprehensive description and analysis of the repo markets. The text has been written to cater for those with little or no previous experience of the repo markets, though it also develops the subject matter to sufficient depth to be of use to more experienced practitioners. Contents include:

- Uses and economic functions of repo
- Accounting, Tax and Capital issues
- The UK gilt repo market
- The implied repo rate and basis trading
- Repo and the yield curve

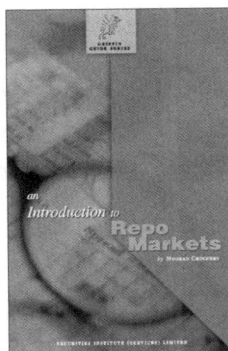

240pp paperback, ISBN: 1 900520 86 9, 2nd edition

AN INTRODUCTION TO SWAPS

An Introduction to Swaps gives a detailed overview of how the various categories of swap work, how they are traded and what they are used for. Topics include interest rate swaps, managing risk, asset swaps, currency swaps. The book is illustrated with over 50 diagrams and tables.

■ Managing risk with swaps
■ Asset swaps
■ Currency swaps.

160pp paperback, ISBN: 1 900520 21 4, 1st edition

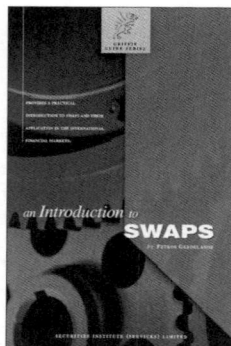

AN INTRODUCTION TO VALUE–AT–RISK

An Introduction to Value–at–Risk has been written for those with little or no previous understanding of or exposure to the concepts of risk management and Value–at–Risk. Topics include applications of VaR, instrument structures, stress testing, VaR for corporates, credit risk and legal/regulatory issues.

■ Risk and Risk management
■ VaR and Derivatives, Fixed Interest products.
■ VaR for Corporates

208pp paperback, ISBN: 1 84307 035 9, 3rd edition

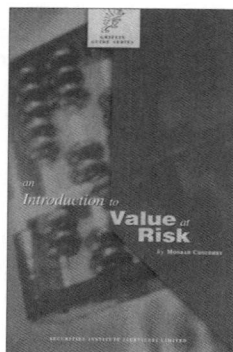

SECURITIES INSTITUTE PUBLISHING

For further details on these and other new titles, contact our Client Services Department on 020 7645 0680

Forthcoming titles

Retail Publications
- Advanced Operations Management
- Futures, Options and Other Derivatives Products
- Products, Trading and Operations
- Custody, Stock Lending and Derivatives Clearing
- Risk Management
- Clearing Settlement and Custody Operations
- Products and Trading from an Operations Perspective
- Mutual Funds

Securities Institute/Butterworth-Heinemann Global Capital Markets Series
- IPO and Equity Offerings
- Controls, Procedures and Risk
- Clearing, Settlement and Custody
- Managing Technology in the Operations Function
- Relationship and Resource Management in Operations
- Understanding the Markets
- Credit Risk

For further information on this series please call *01865 888180* or visit http://www.bh.com/finance/

We plan to introduce new titles into our retail range in the forthcoming year. All the titles listed are provisional and may be subject to alteration.